ALL·NEW X·MEN

GHOSTS OF CYCLOPS

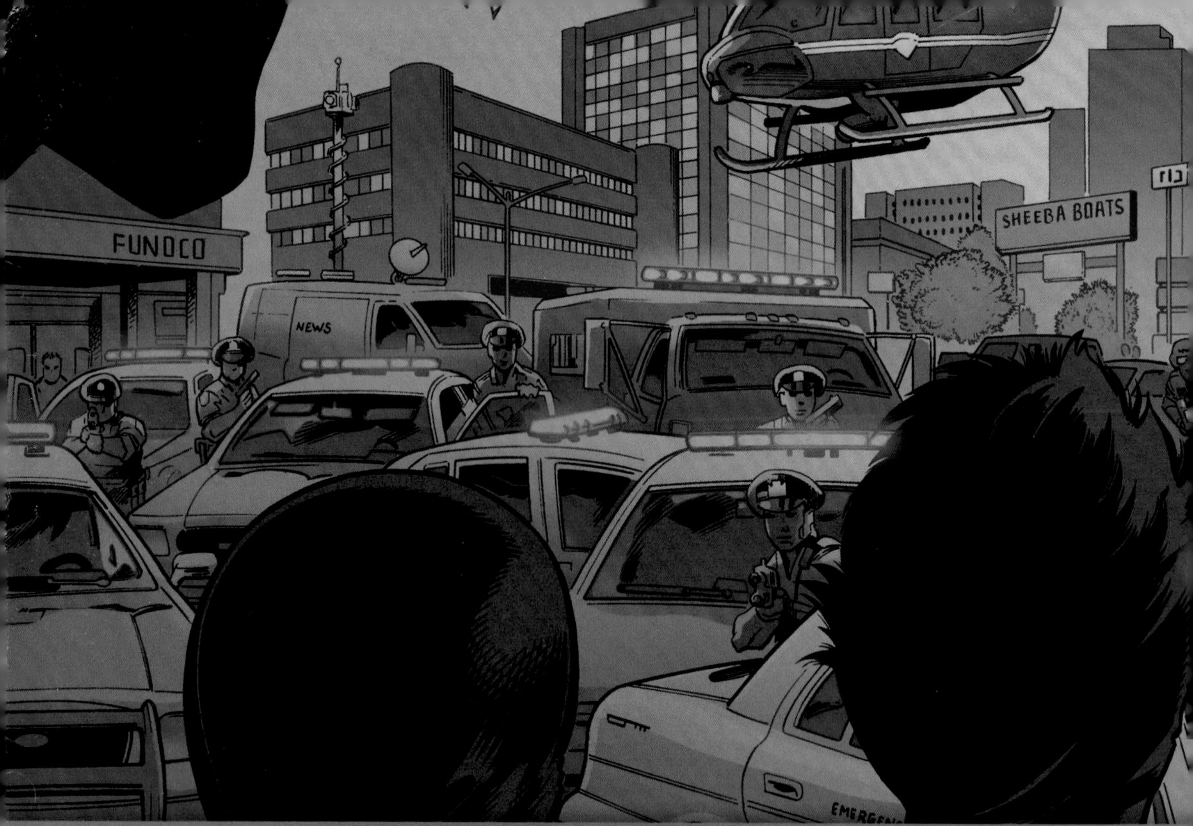
FUNDCO
NEWS
SHEEBA BOATS

THE ORIGINAL X-MEN—CYCLOPS, BEAST, ICEMAN AND ANGEL—WERE PLUCKED FROM THE PAST AND BROUGHT TO THE PRESENT IN HOPES OF REMINDING THEIR FUTURE SELVES OF THE OPTIMISM AND PROMISE THEY ONCE EMBODIED. BUT, TRAPPED IN THE PRESENT, THESE ALL-NEW X-MEN FOUND THEMSELVES IN A TIME WHEN MUTANTS ARE HATED AND FEARED MORE THAN EVER.

DETERMINED NOT TO LET THE WORLD GET THE BETTER OF THEM, THEY'VE TEAMED UP WITH THE ALL-NEW WOLVERINE, IDIE OKONKWO AND KID APOCALYPSE AND SET OUT ACROSS THE WORLD TO WRITE THEIR OWN FUTURES AND LEAVE BEHIND A LEGACY THEY CAN BE PROUD OF.

COLLECTION EDITOR: **JENNIFER GRÜNWALD**
ASSOCIATE EDITOR: **SARAH BRUNSTAD**
ASSOCIATE MANAGING EDITOR: **ALEX STARBUCK**
EDITOR, SPECIAL PROJECTS: **MARK D. BEAZLEY**
VP, PRODUCTION & SPECIAL PROJECTS: **JEFF YOUNGQUIST**
SVP PRINT, SALES & MARKETING: **DAVID GABRIEL**
BOOK DESIGNER: **JAY BOWEN**

EDITOR IN CHIEF: **AXEL ALONSO**
CHIEF CREATIVE OFFICER: **JOE QUESADA**
PUBLISHER: **DAN BUCKLEY**
EXECUTIVE PRODUCER: **ALAN FINE**

ALL-NEW X-MEN: INEVITABLE VOL. 1 — GHOSTS OF CYCLOPS. Contains material originally published in magazine form as ALL-NEW X-MEN #1-6. First printing 2016. ISBN# 978-0-7851-9630-3. Published by MARVEL WORLDWIDE, INC., a subsidiary of MARVEL ENTERTAINMENT, LLC. OFFICE OF PUBLICATION: 135 West 50th Street, New York, NY 10020. **Printed in Canada.** ALAN FINE, President, Marvel Entertainment; DAN BUCKLEY, President, TV, Publishing & Brand Management; JOE QUESADA, Chief Creative Officer; TOM BREVOORT, SVP of Publishing; DAVID BOGART, SVP of Business Affairs & Operations, Publishing & Partnership; C.B. CEBULSKI, VP of Brand Management & Development, Asia; DAVID GABRIEL, SVP of Sales & Marketing, Publishing; JEFF YOUNGQUIST, VP of Production & Special Projects; DAN CARR, Executive Director of Publishing Technology; ALEX MORALES, Director of Publishing Operations; SUSAN CRESPI, Production Manager; STAN LEE, Chairman Emeritus. For information regarding advertising in Marvel Comics or on Marvel.com, please contact Vit DeBellis, Integrated Sales Manager, at vdebellis@marvel.com. For Marvel subscription inquiries, please call 888-511-5480. **Manufactured between 3/11/2016 and 4/18/2016 by SOLISCO PRINTERS, SCOTT, QC, CANADA.**

10 9 8 7 6 5 4 3 2 1

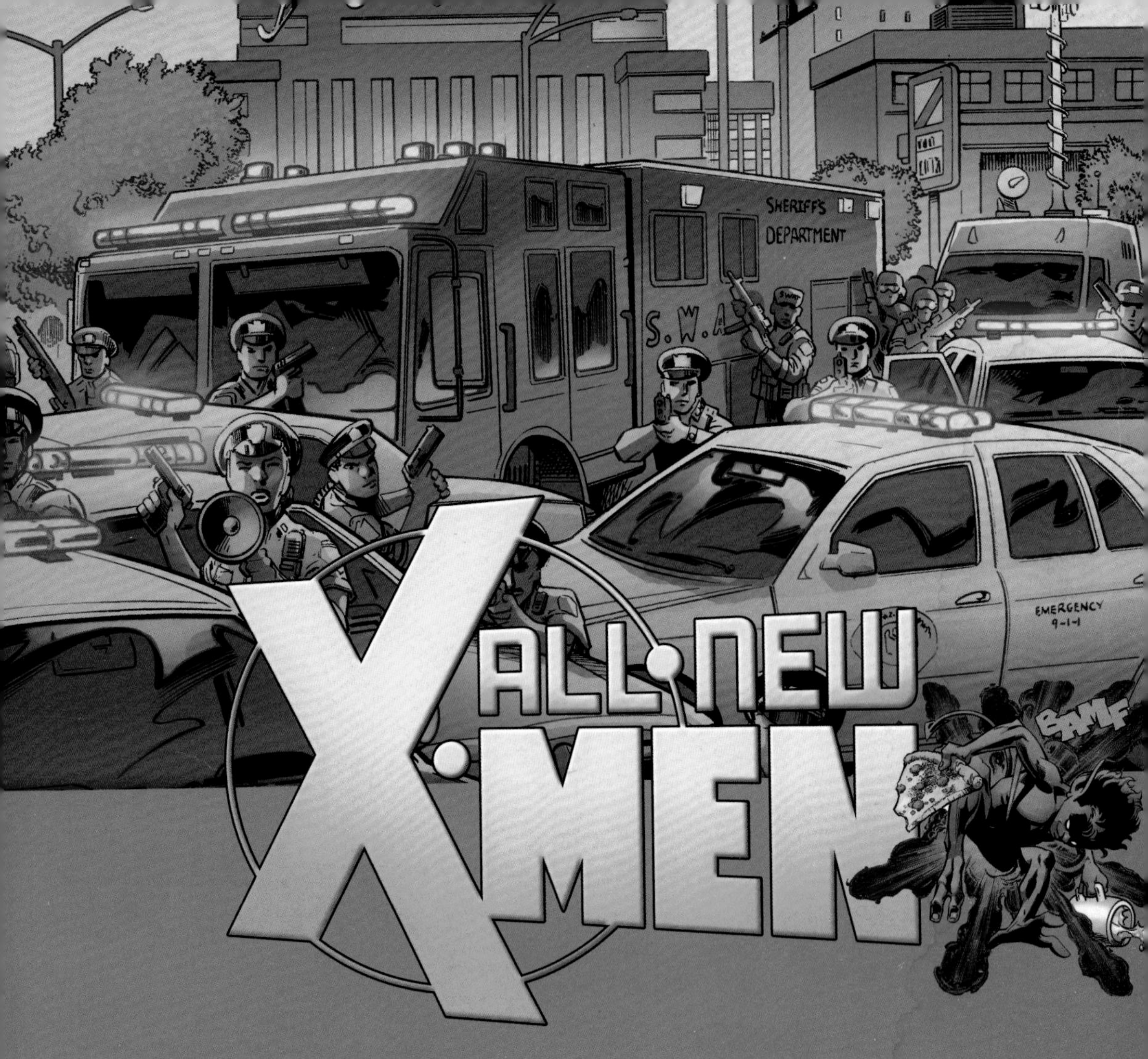
SHERIFF'S DEPARTMENT
S.W.A
EMERGENCY 9-1-1
BAMF

ALL-NEW X-MEN

GHOSTS OF CYCLOPS

DENNIS HOPELESS
WRITER

MARK BAGLEY
PENCILER

ANDREW HENNESSY
INKER

NOLAN WOODARD
COLORIST

VC'S CORY PETIT
LETTERER

COVER ART: MARK BAGLEY, ANDREW HENNESSY & NOLAN WOODARD

CHRISTINA HARRINGTON
ASSISTANT EDITOR

DANIEL KETCHUM
EDITOR

MARK PANICCIA
X-MEN GROUP EDITOR

X-MEN CREATED BY **STAN LEE** & **JACK KIRBY**

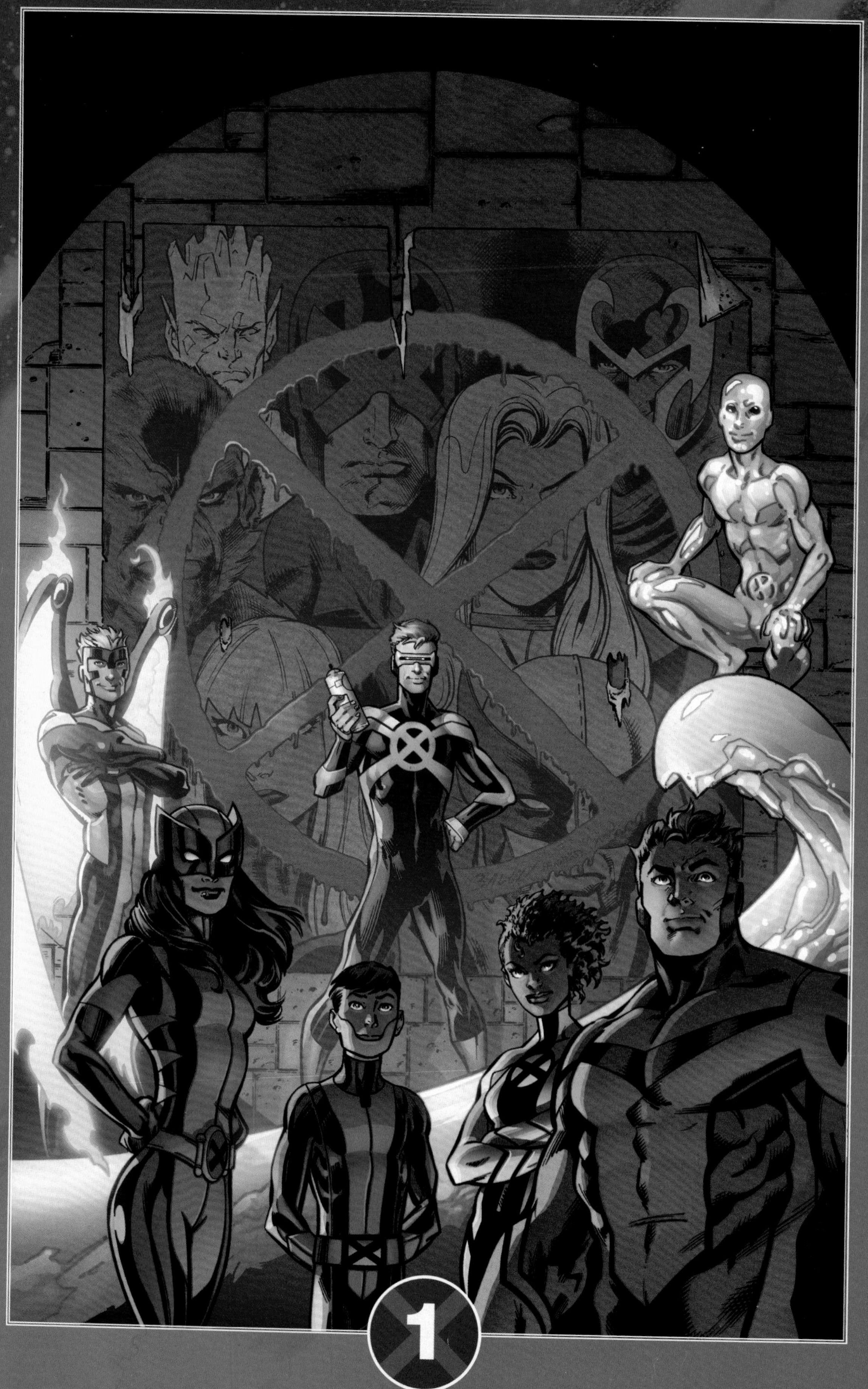
1

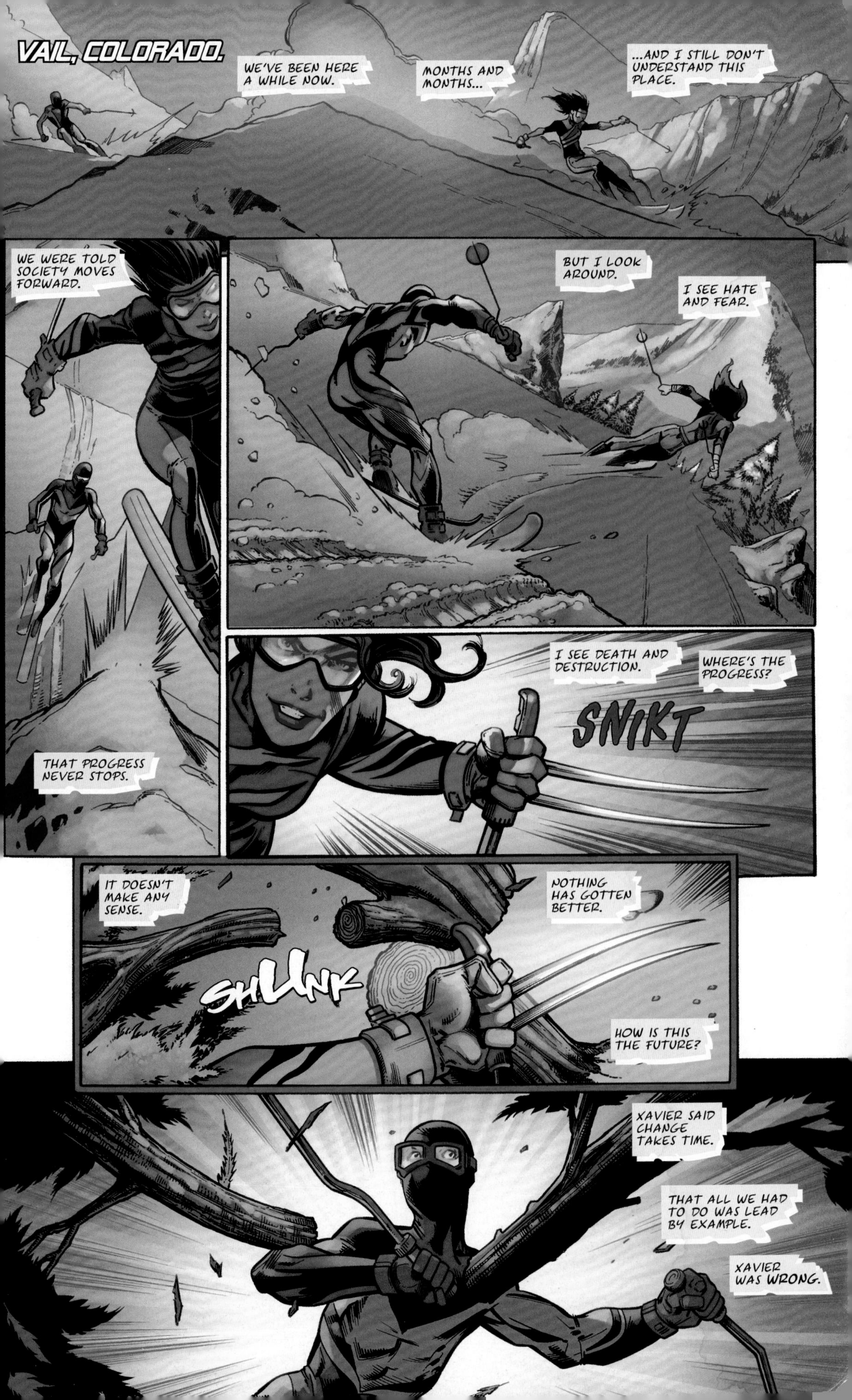
VAIL, COLORADO.
WE'VE BEEN HERE A WHILE NOW.
MONTHS AND MONTHS...
...AND I STILL DON'T UNDERSTAND THIS PLACE.
WE WERE TOLD SOCIETY MOVES FORWARD.
THAT PROGRESS NEVER STOPS.
BUT I LOOK AROUND.
I SEE HATE AND FEAR.
I SEE DEATH AND DESTRUCTION.
WHERE'S THE PROGRESS?
SNIKT
IT DOESN'T MAKE ANY SENSE.
NOTHING HAS GOTTEN BETTER.
SHUNK
HOW IS THIS THE FUTURE?
XAVIER SAID CHANGE TAKES TIME.
THAT ALL WE HAD TO DO WAS LEAD BY EXAMPLE.
XAVIER WAS WRONG.

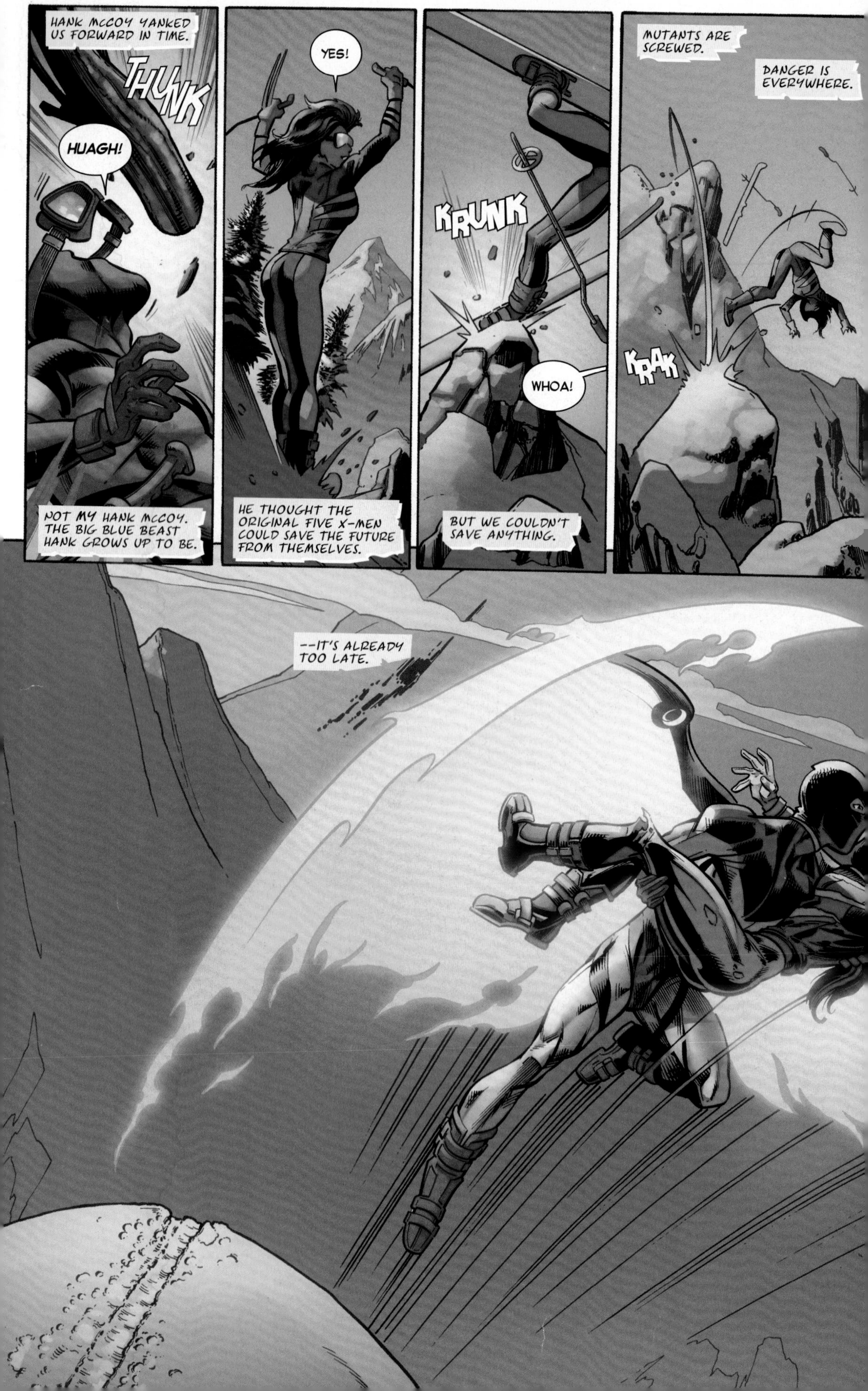
HANK McCOY YANKED US FORWARD IN TIME.
THUNK
HUAGH!
NOT MY HANK McCOY. THE BIG BLUE BEAST HANK GROWS UP TO BE.
YES!
HE THOUGHT THE ORIGINAL FIVE X-MEN COULD SAVE THE FUTURE FROM THEMSELVES.
KRUNK
WHOA!
BUT WE COULDN'T SAVE ANYTHING.
MUTANTS ARE SCREWED.
DANGER IS EVERYWHERE.
KRAK
--IT'S ALREADY TOO LATE.

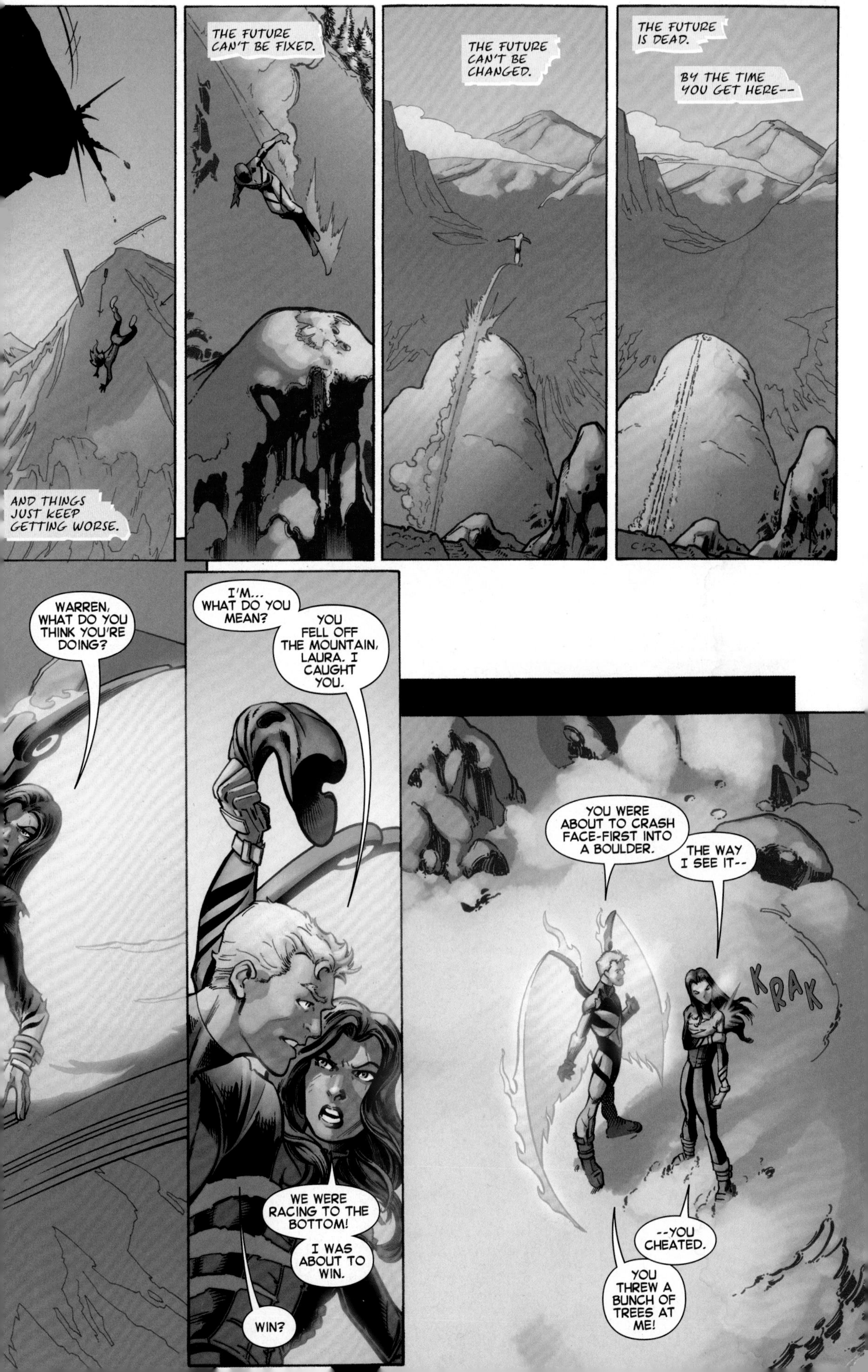
AND THINGS JUST KEEP GETTING WORSE.
THE FUTURE CAN'T BE FIXED.
THE FUTURE CAN'T BE CHANGED.
THE FUTURE IS DEAD.
BY THE TIME YOU GET HERE--
WARREN, WHAT DO YOU THINK YOU'RE DOING?
I'M... WHAT DO YOU MEAN?
YOU FELL OFF THE MOUNTAIN, LAURA. I CAUGHT YOU.
WE WERE RACING TO THE BOTTOM!
I WAS ABOUT TO WIN.
WIN?
YOU WERE ABOUT TO CRASH FACE-FIRST INTO A BOULDER.
THE WAY I SEE IT--
KRAK
--YOU CHEATED.
YOU THREW A BUNCH OF TREES AT ME!

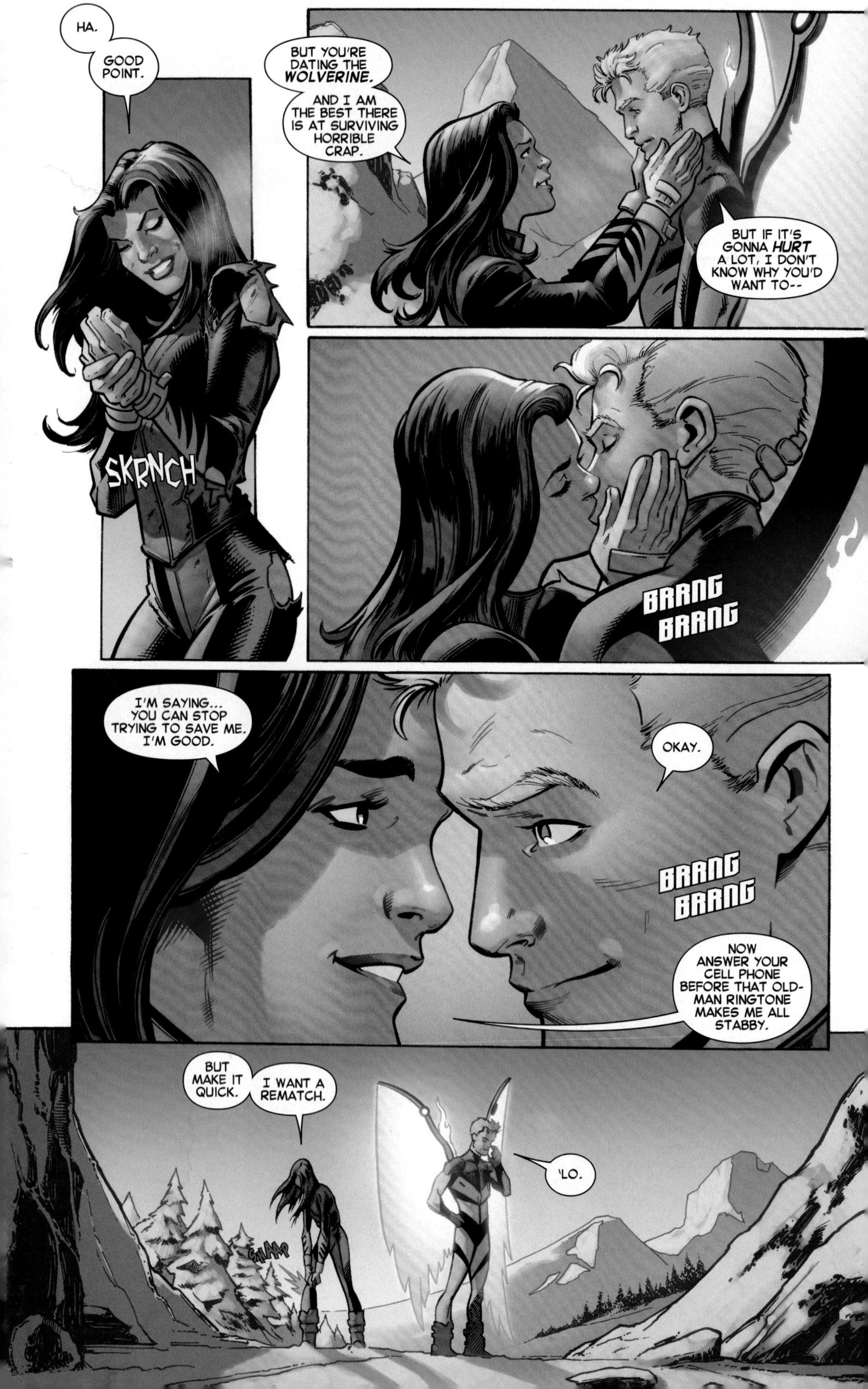
HA.
GOOD POINT.
BUT YOU'RE DATING THE WOLVERINE.
AND I AM THE BEST THERE IS AT SURVIVING HORRIBLE CRAP.
BUT IF IT'S GONNA HURT A LOT, I DON'T KNOW WHY YOU'D WANT TO--
SKRNCH
BRRNG BRRNG
I'M SAYING... YOU CAN STOP TRYING TO SAVE ME. I'M GOOD.
OKAY.
BRRNG BRRNG
NOW ANSWER YOUR CELL PHONE BEFORE THAT OLD-MAN RINGTONE MAKES ME ALL STABBY.
BUT MAKE IT QUICK.
I WANT A REMATCH.
'LO.

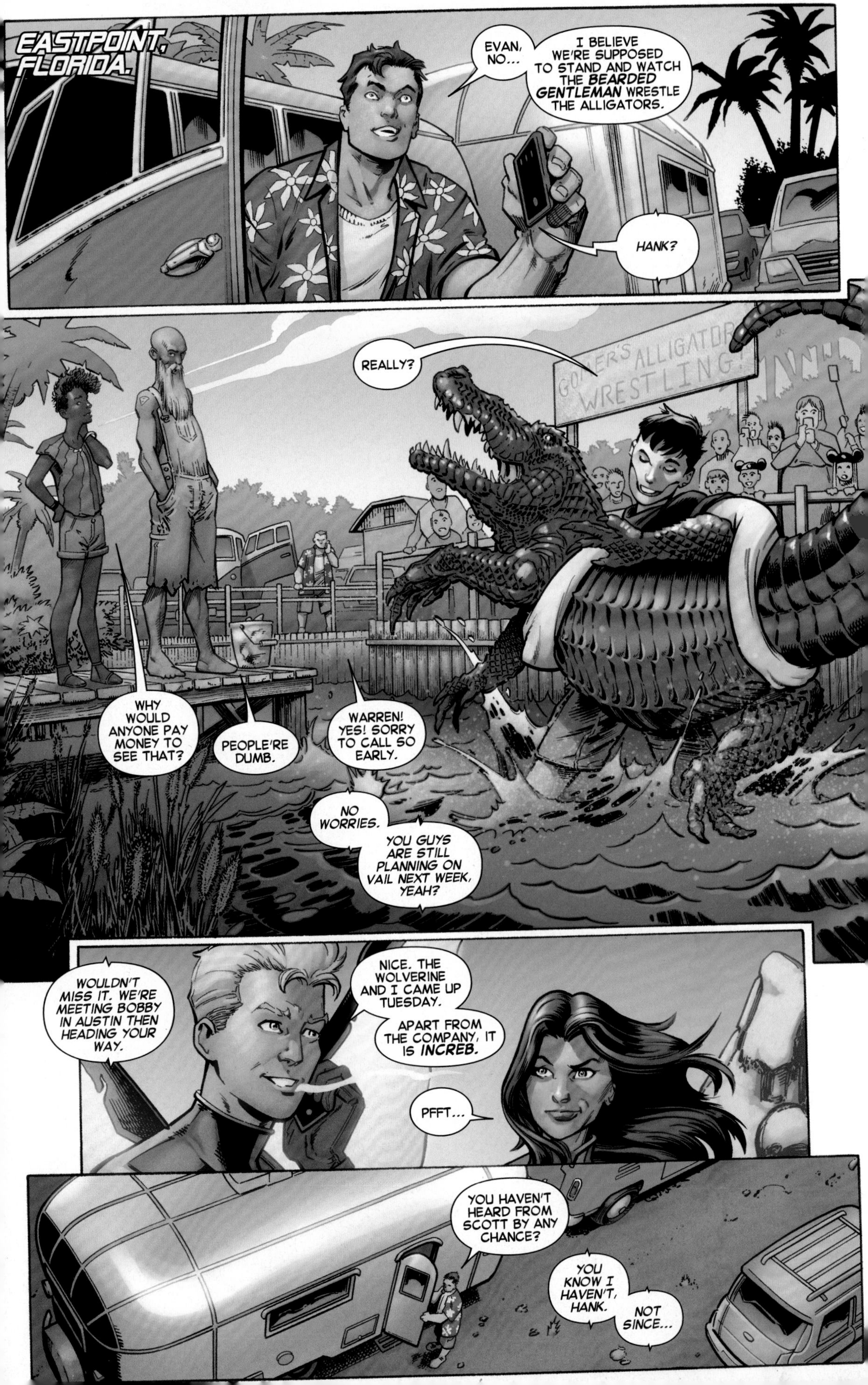

EASTPOINT, FLORIDA.
EVAN, NO...
I BELIEVE WE'RE SUPPOSED TO STAND AND WATCH THE BEARDED GENTLEMAN WRESTLE THE ALLIGATORS.
HANK?
REALLY?
GOMER'S ALLIGATOR WRESTLING!
WHY WOULD ANYONE PAY MONEY TO SEE THAT?
PEOPLE'RE DUMB.
WARREN! YES! SORRY TO CALL SO EARLY.
NO WORRIES.
YOU GUYS ARE STILL PLANNING ON VAIL NEXT WEEK, YEAH?
WOULDN'T MISS IT. WE'RE MEETING BOBBY IN AUSTIN THEN HEADING YOUR WAY.
NICE. THE WOLVERINE AND I CAME UP TUESDAY.
APART FROM THE COMPANY, IT IS INCREB.
PFFT...
YOU HAVEN'T HEARD FROM SCOTT BY ANY CHANCE?
YOU KNOW I HAVEN'T, HANK.
NOT SINCE...

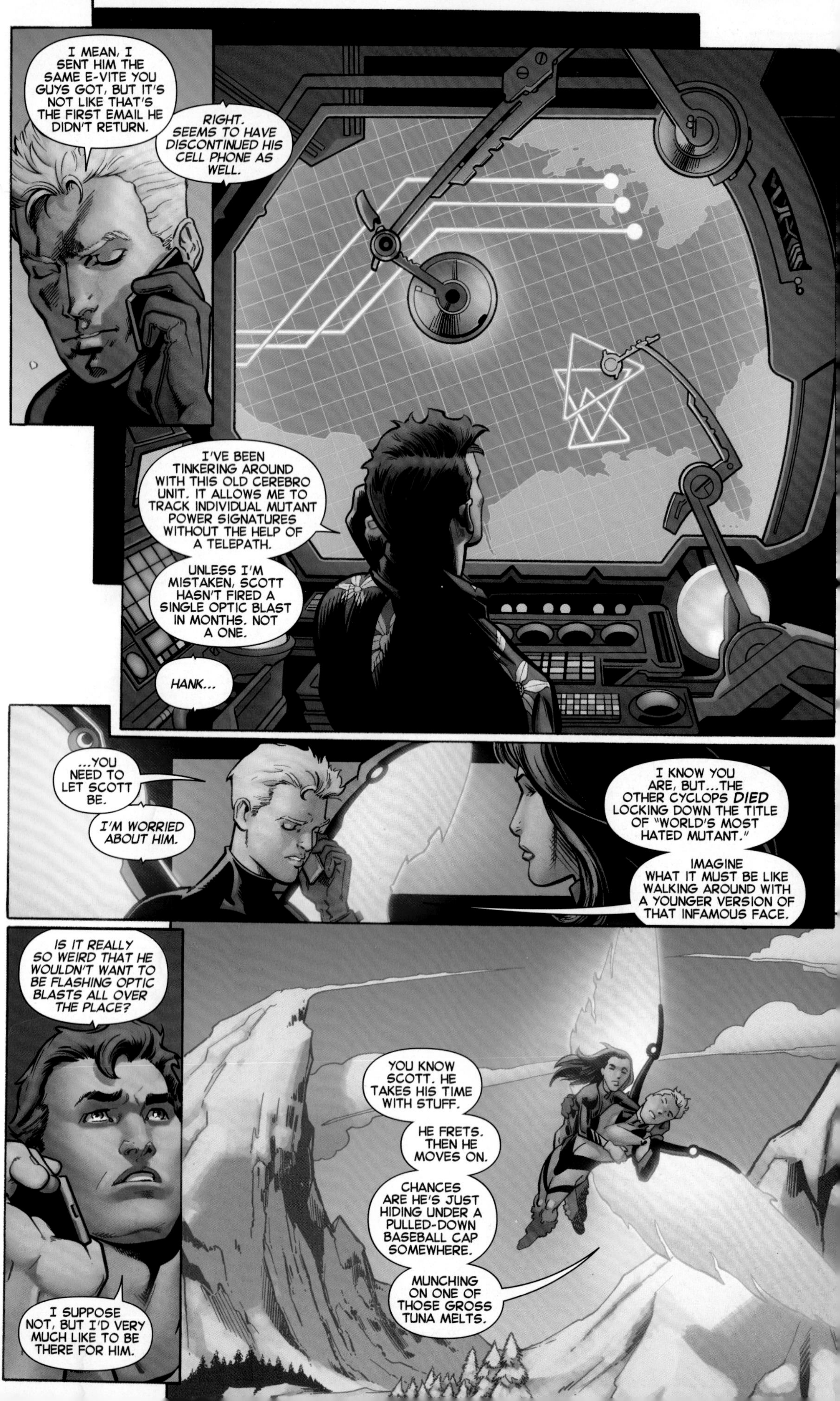
I MEAN, I SENT HIM THE SAME E-VITE YOU GUYS GOT, BUT IT'S NOT LIKE THAT'S THE FIRST EMAIL HE DIDN'T RETURN.
RIGHT. SEEMS TO HAVE DISCONTINUED HIS CELL PHONE AS WELL.
I'VE BEEN TINKERING AROUND WITH THIS OLD CEREBRO UNIT. IT ALLOWS ME TO TRACK INDIVIDUAL MUTANT POWER SIGNATURES WITHOUT THE HELP OF A TELEPATH.
UNLESS I'M MISTAKEN, SCOTT HASN'T FIRED A SINGLE OPTIC BLAST IN MONTHS. NOT A ONE.
HANK...
...YOU NEED TO LET SCOTT BE.
I'M WORRIED ABOUT HIM.
I KNOW YOU ARE, BUT...THE OTHER CYCLOPS DIED LOCKING DOWN THE TITLE OF "WORLD'S MOST HATED MUTANT."
IMAGINE WHAT IT MUST BE LIKE WALKING AROUND WITH A YOUNGER VERSION OF THAT INFAMOUS FACE.
IS IT REALLY SO WEIRD THAT HE WOULDN'T WANT TO BE FLASHING OPTIC BLASTS ALL OVER THE PLACE?
YOU KNOW SCOTT. HE TAKES HIS TIME WITH STUFF.
HE FRETS. THEN HE MOVES ON.
CHANCES ARE HE'S JUST HIDING UNDER A PULLED-DOWN BASEBALL CAP SOMEWHERE.
MUNCHING ON ONE OF THOSE GROSS TUNA MELTS.
I SUPPOSE NOT, BUT I'D VERY MUCH LIKE TO BE THERE FOR HIM.

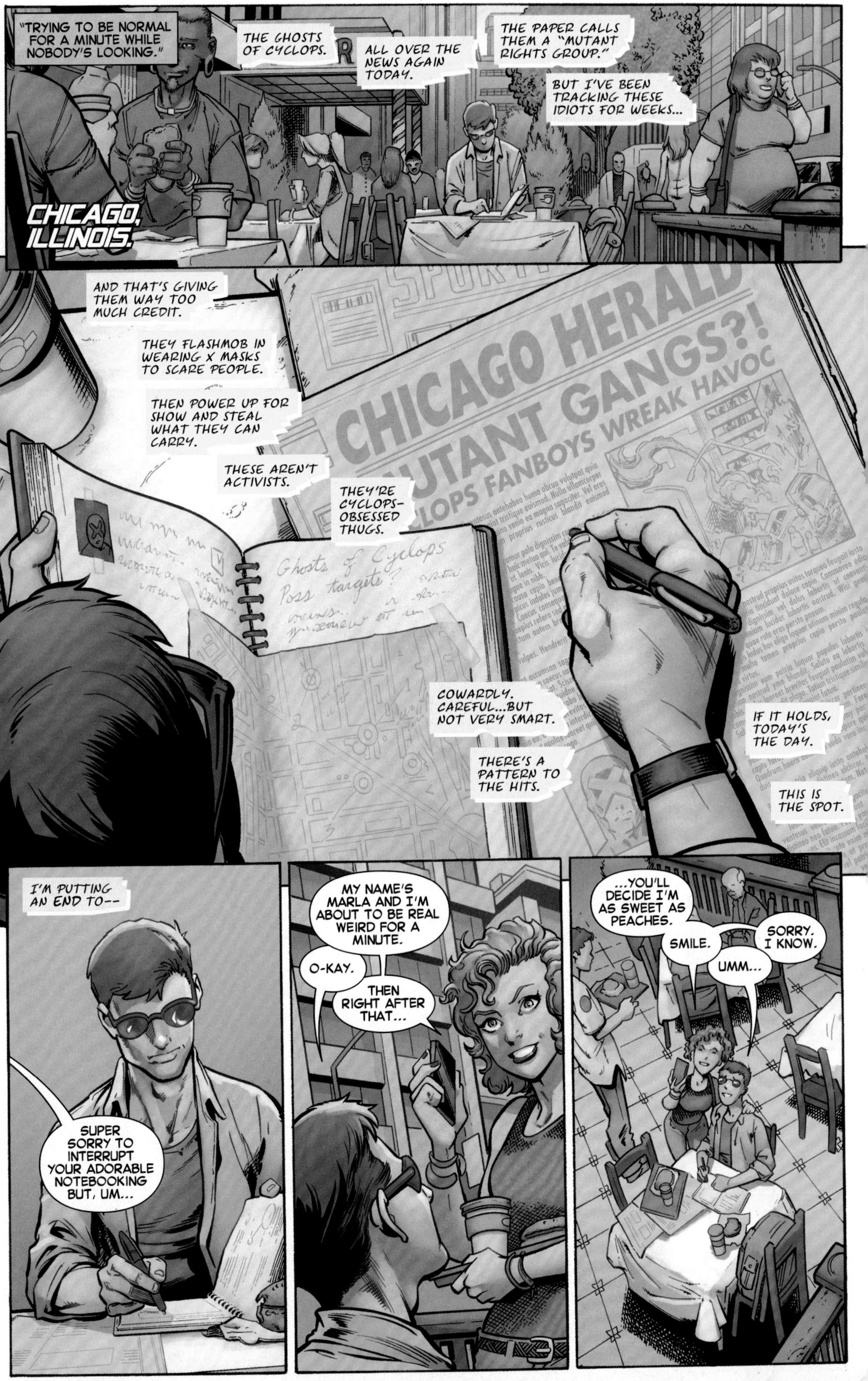
"TRYING TO BE NORMAL FOR A MINUTE WHILE NOBODY'S LOOKING."
THE GHOSTS OF CYCLOPS.
ALL OVER THE NEWS AGAIN TODAY.
THE PAPER CALLS THEM A "MUTANT RIGHTS GROUP."
BUT I'VE BEEN TRACKING THESE IDIOTS FOR WEEKS...
CHICAGO, ILLINOIS.
AND THAT'S GIVING THEM WAY TOO MUCH CREDIT.
THEY FLASHMOB IN WEARING X MASKS TO SCARE PEOPLE.
THEN POWER UP FOR SHOW AND STEAL WHAT THEY CAN CARRY.
THESE AREN'T ACTIVISTS.
THEY'RE CYCLOPS-OBSESSED THUGS.
CHICAGO HERALD
GANGS?!
WREAK HAVOC
Ghosts of Cyclops
Poss targets?
COWARDLY. CAREFUL...BUT NOT VERY SMART.
THERE'S A PATTERN TO THE HITS.
IF IT HOLDS, TODAY'S THE DAY.
THIS IS THE SPOT.
I'M PUTTING AN END TO--
SUPER SORRY TO INTERRUPT YOUR ADORABLE NOTEBOOKING BUT, UM...
MY NAME'S MARLA AND I'M ABOUT TO BE REAL WEIRD FOR A MINUTE.
O-KAY.
THEN RIGHT AFTER THAT...
...YOU'LL DECIDE I'M AS SWEET AS PEACHES.
SMILE.
SORRY. I KNOW.
UMM...

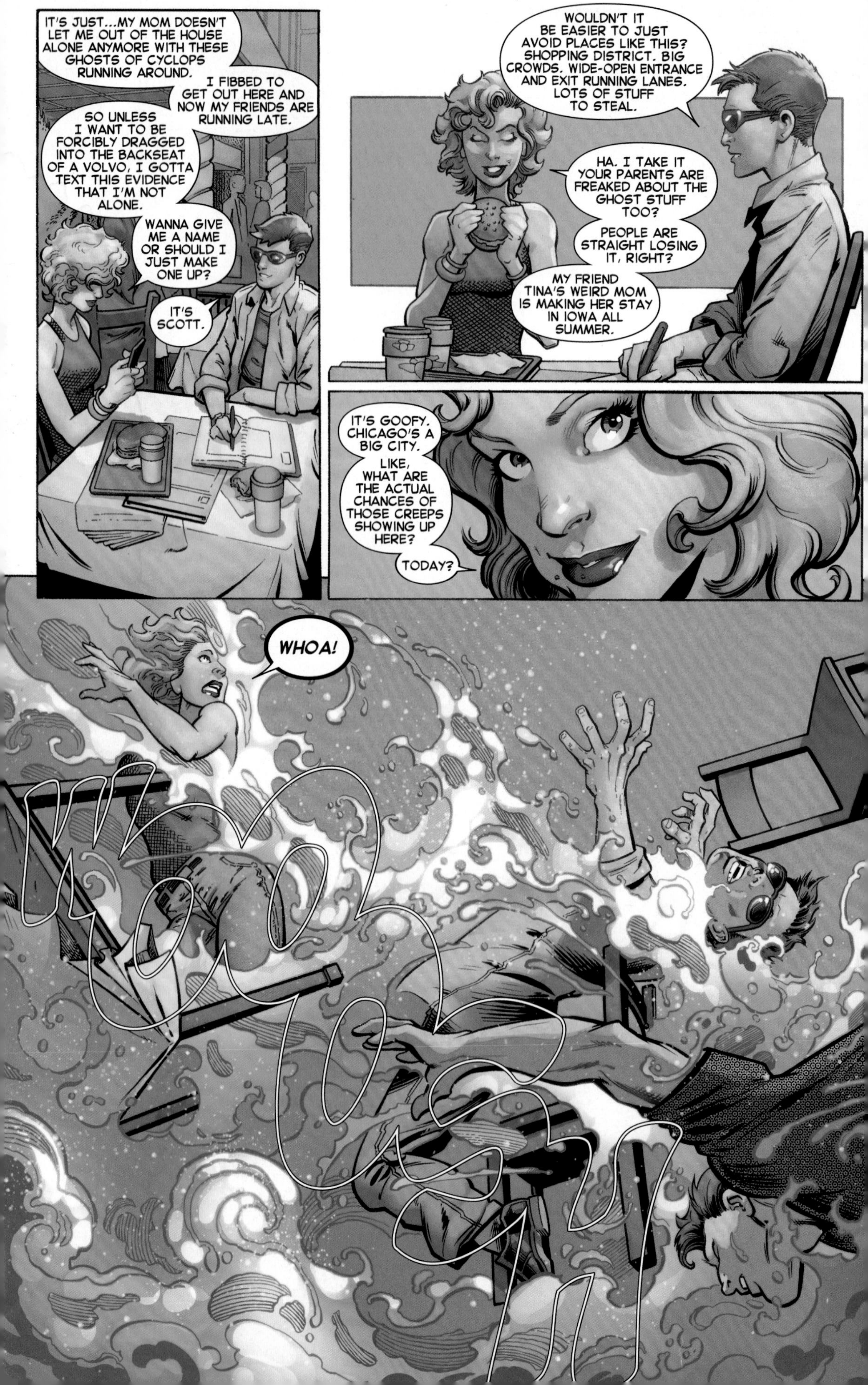

IT'S JUST...MY MOM DOESN'T LET ME OUT OF THE HOUSE ALONE ANYMORE WITH THESE GHOSTS OF CYCLOPS RUNNING AROUND.
I FIBBED TO GET OUT HERE AND NOW MY FRIENDS ARE RUNNING LATE.
SO UNLESS I WANT TO BE FORCIBLY DRAGGED INTO THE BACKSEAT OF A VOLVO, I GOTTA TEXT THIS EVIDENCE THAT I'M NOT ALONE.
WANNA GIVE ME A NAME OR SHOULD I JUST MAKE ONE UP?
IT'S SCOTT.
WOULDN'T IT BE EASIER TO JUST AVOID PLACES LIKE THIS? SHOPPING DISTRICT. BIG CROWDS. WIDE-OPEN ENTRANCE AND EXIT RUNNING LANES. LOTS OF STUFF TO STEAL.
HA. I TAKE IT YOUR PARENTS ARE FREAKED ABOUT THE GHOST STUFF TOO?
PEOPLE ARE STRAIGHT LOSING IT, RIGHT?
MY FRIEND TINA'S WEIRD MOM IS MAKING HER STAY IN IOWA ALL SUMMER.
IT'S GOOFY. CHICAGO'S A BIG CITY.
LIKE, WHAT ARE THE ACTUAL CHANCES OF THOSE CREEPS SHOWING UP HERE?
TODAY?
WHOA!

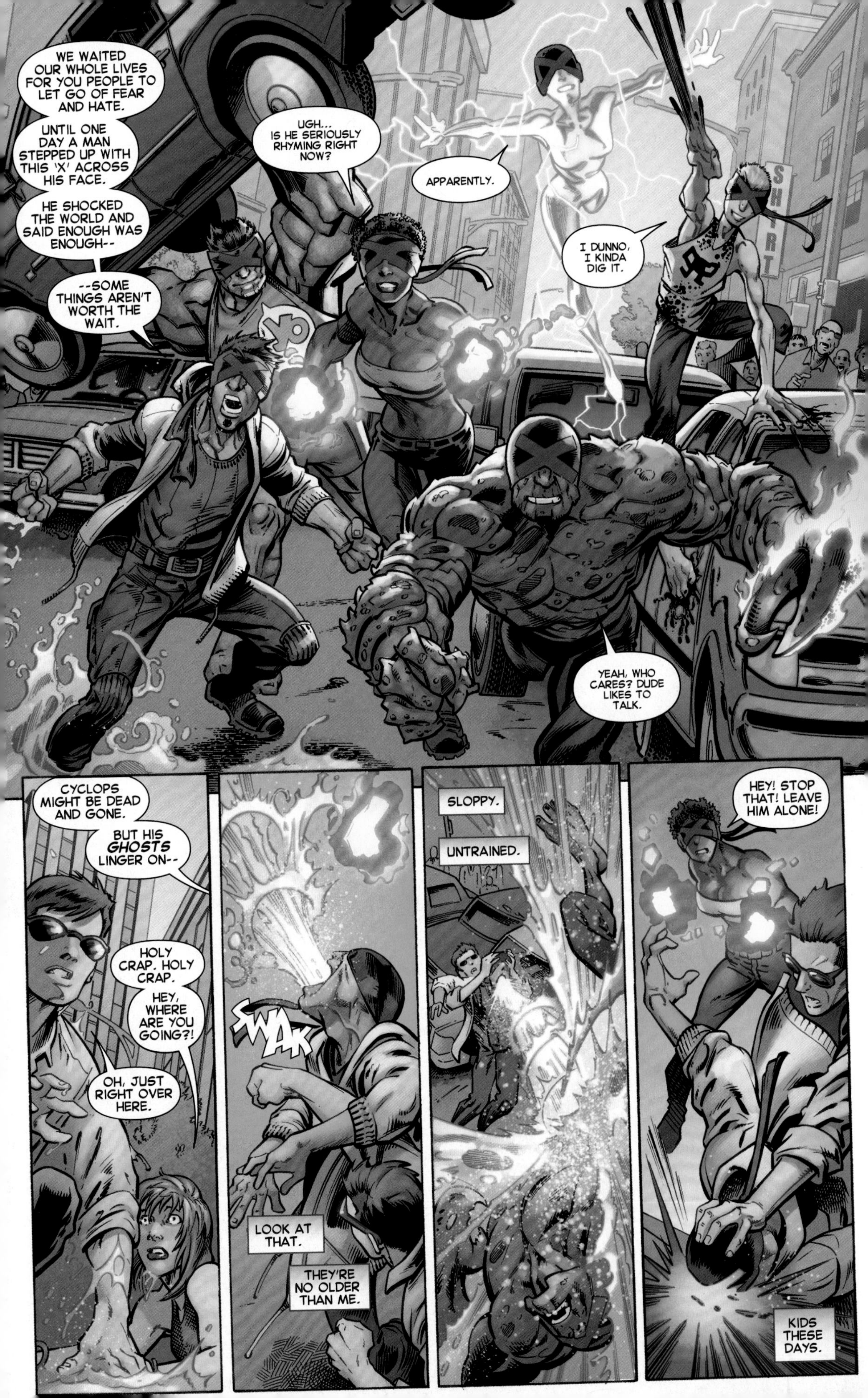
WE WAITED OUR WHOLE LIVES FOR YOU PEOPLE TO LET GO OF FEAR AND HATE.
UNTIL ONE DAY A MAN STEPPED UP WITH THIS 'X' ACROSS HIS FACE.
HE SHOCKED THE WORLD AND SAID ENOUGH WAS ENOUGH--
--SOME THINGS AREN'T WORTH THE WAIT.
UGH... IS HE SERIOUSLY RHYMING RIGHT NOW?
APPARENTLY.
I DUNNO, I KINDA DIG IT.
YEAH, WHO CARES? DUDE LIKES TO TALK.
CYCLOPS MIGHT BE DEAD AND GONE.
BUT HIS GHOSTS LINGER ON--
HOLY CRAP. HOLY CRAP.
HEY, WHERE ARE YOU GOING?!
OH, JUST RIGHT OVER HERE.
SWAK
LOOK AT THAT.
THEY'RE NO OLDER THAN ME.
SLOPPY.
UNTRAINED.
HEY! STOP THAT! LEAVE HIM ALONE!
KIDS THESE DAYS.

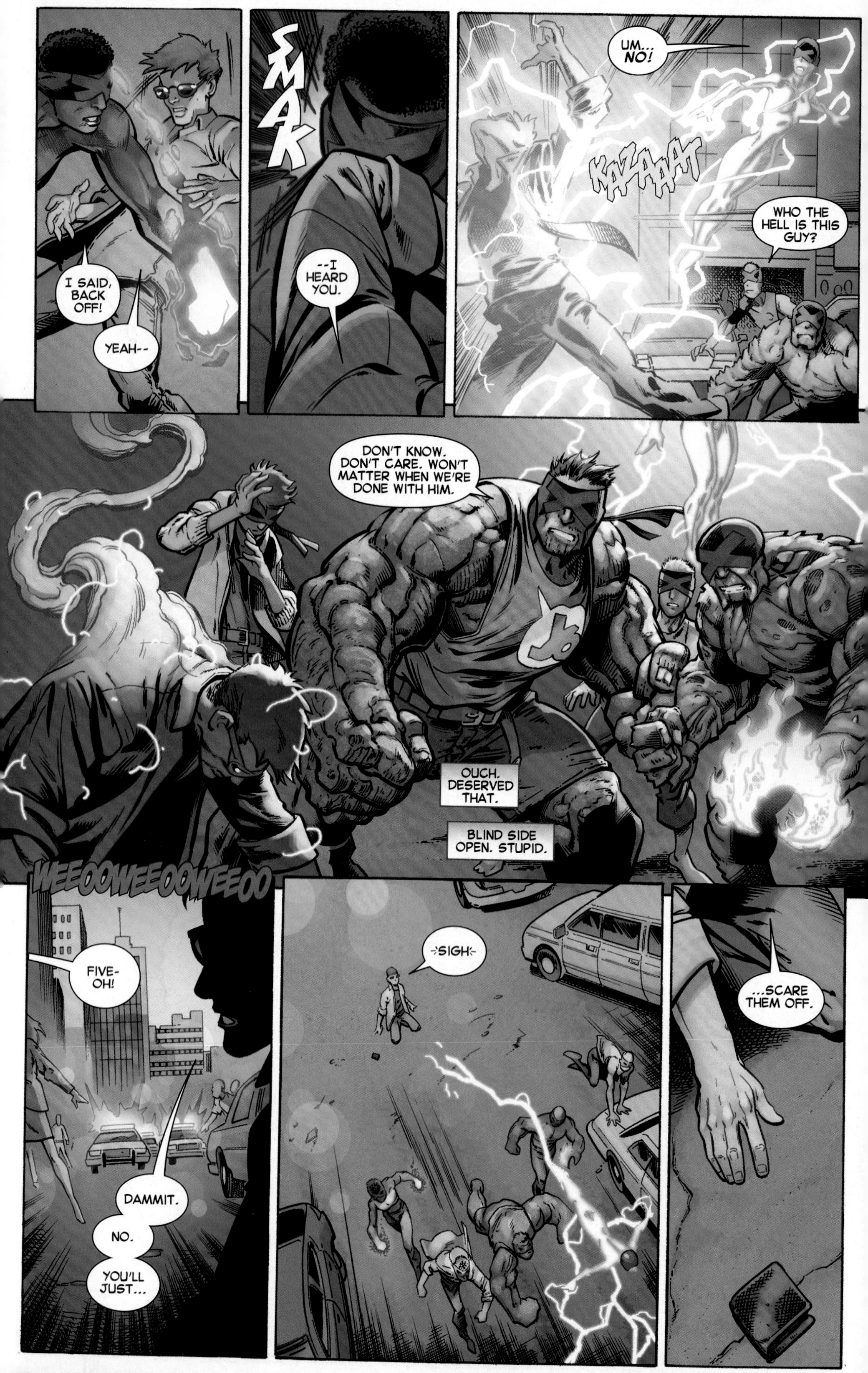
I SAID, BACK OFF!
YEAH--
SMAK
--I HEARD YOU.
UM... NO!
KAZAAAT
WHO THE HELL IS THIS GUY?
DON'T KNOW. DON'T CARE. WON'T MATTER WHEN WE'RE DONE WITH HIM.
OUCH. DESERVED THAT.
BLIND SIDE OPEN. STUPID.
WEEOOWEEOOWEEOO
FIVE-OH!
DAMMIT.
NO.
YOU'LL JUST...
-SIGH-
...SCARE THEM OFF.

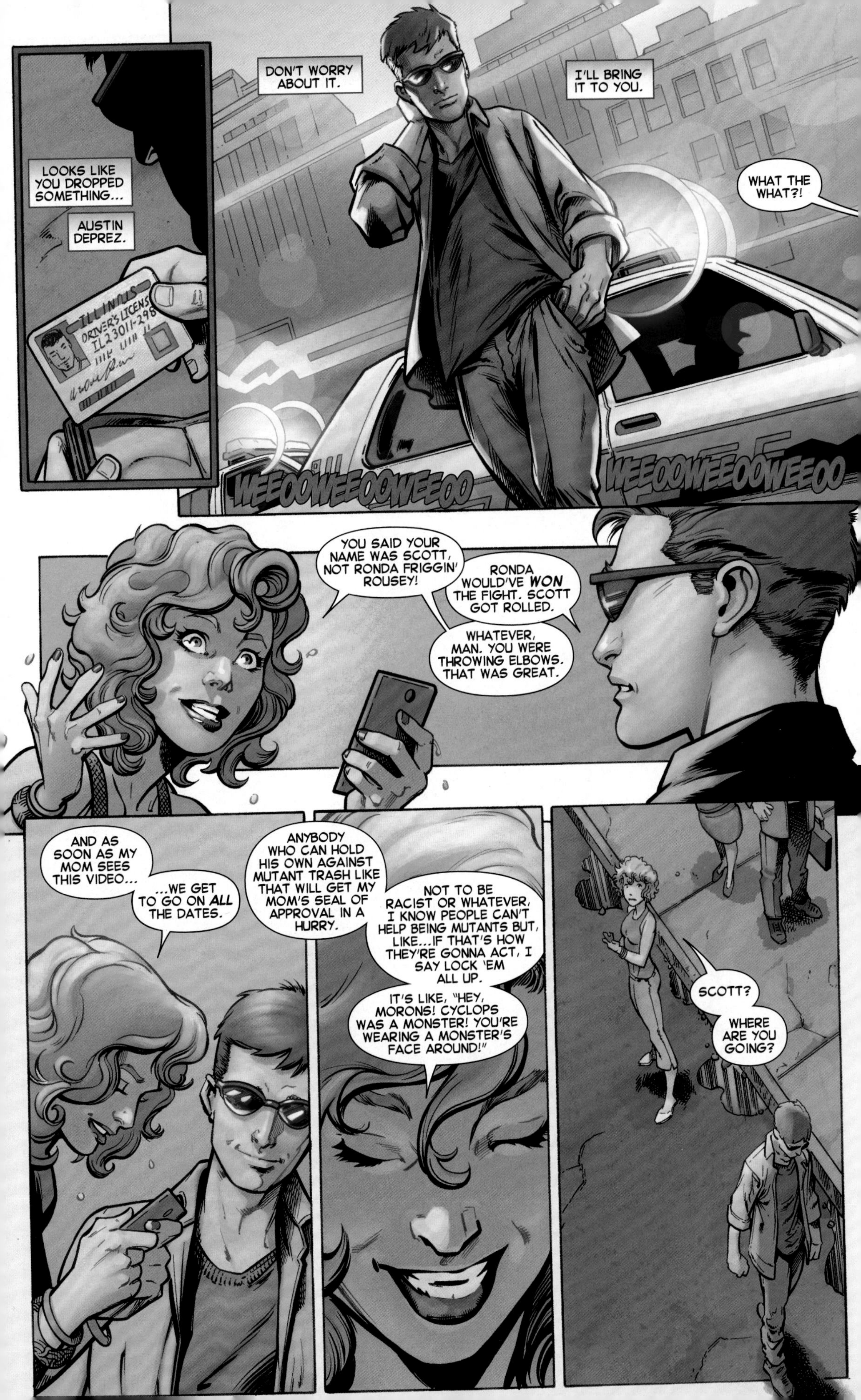
LOOKS LIKE YOU DROPPED SOMETHING...
AUSTIN DEPREZ.
ILLINOIS
DRIVER'S LICENSE
DON'T WORRY ABOUT IT.
I'LL BRING IT TO YOU.
WHAT THE WHAT?!
WEEOOWEEOOWEEOO
WEEOOWEEOOWEEOO
YOU SAID YOUR NAME WAS SCOTT, NOT RONDA FRIGGIN' ROUSEY!
RONDA WOULD'VE WON THE FIGHT. SCOTT GOT ROLLED.
WHATEVER, MAN. YOU WERE THROWING ELBOWS. THAT WAS GREAT.
AND AS SOON AS MY MOM SEES THIS VIDEO...
...WE GET TO GO ON ALL THE DATES.
ANYBODY WHO CAN HOLD HIS OWN AGAINST MUTANT TRASH LIKE THAT WILL GET MY MOM'S SEAL OF APPROVAL IN A HURRY.
NOT TO BE RACIST OR WHATEVER, I KNOW PEOPLE CAN'T HELP BEING MUTANTS BUT, LIKE...IF THAT'S HOW THEY'RE GONNA ACT, I SAY LOCK 'EM ALL UP.
IT'S LIKE, "HEY, MORONS! CYCLOPS WAS A MONSTER! YOU'RE WEARING A MONSTER'S FACE AROUND!"
SCOTT?
WHERE ARE YOU GOING?

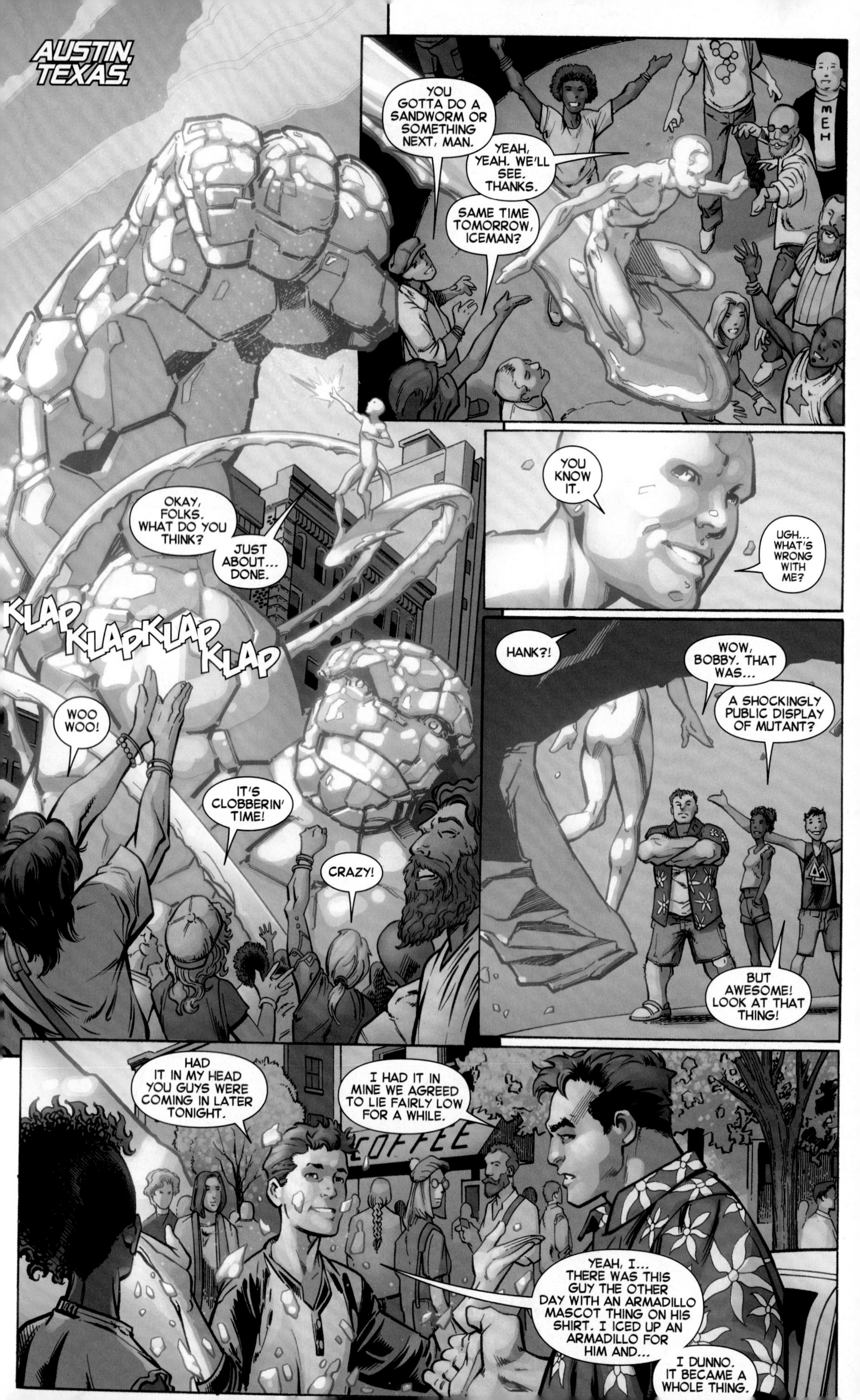
AUSTIN, TEXAS.
YOU GOTTA DO A SANDWORM OR SOMETHING NEXT, MAN.
YEAH, YEAH. WE'LL SEE. THANKS.
SAME TIME TOMORROW, ICEMAN?
MEH
OKAY, FOLKS. WHAT DO YOU THINK?
JUST ABOUT... DONE.
KLAP KLAPKLAP KLAP KLAP
WOO WOO!
IT'S CLOBBERIN' TIME!
CRAZY!
YOU KNOW IT.
UGH... WHAT'S WRONG WITH ME?
HANK?!
WOW, BOBBY. THAT WAS...
A SHOCKINGLY PUBLIC DISPLAY OF MUTANT?
BUT AWESOME! LOOK AT THAT THING!
HAD IT IN MY HEAD YOU GUYS WERE COMING IN LATER TONIGHT.
I HAD IT IN MINE WE AGREED TO LIE FAIRLY LOW FOR A WHILE.
COFFEE
YEAH, I... THERE WAS THIS GUY THE OTHER DAY WITH AN ARMADILLO MASCOT THING ON HIS SHIRT. I ICED UP AN ARMADILLO FOR HIM AND...
I DUNNO. IT BECAME A WHOLE THING.

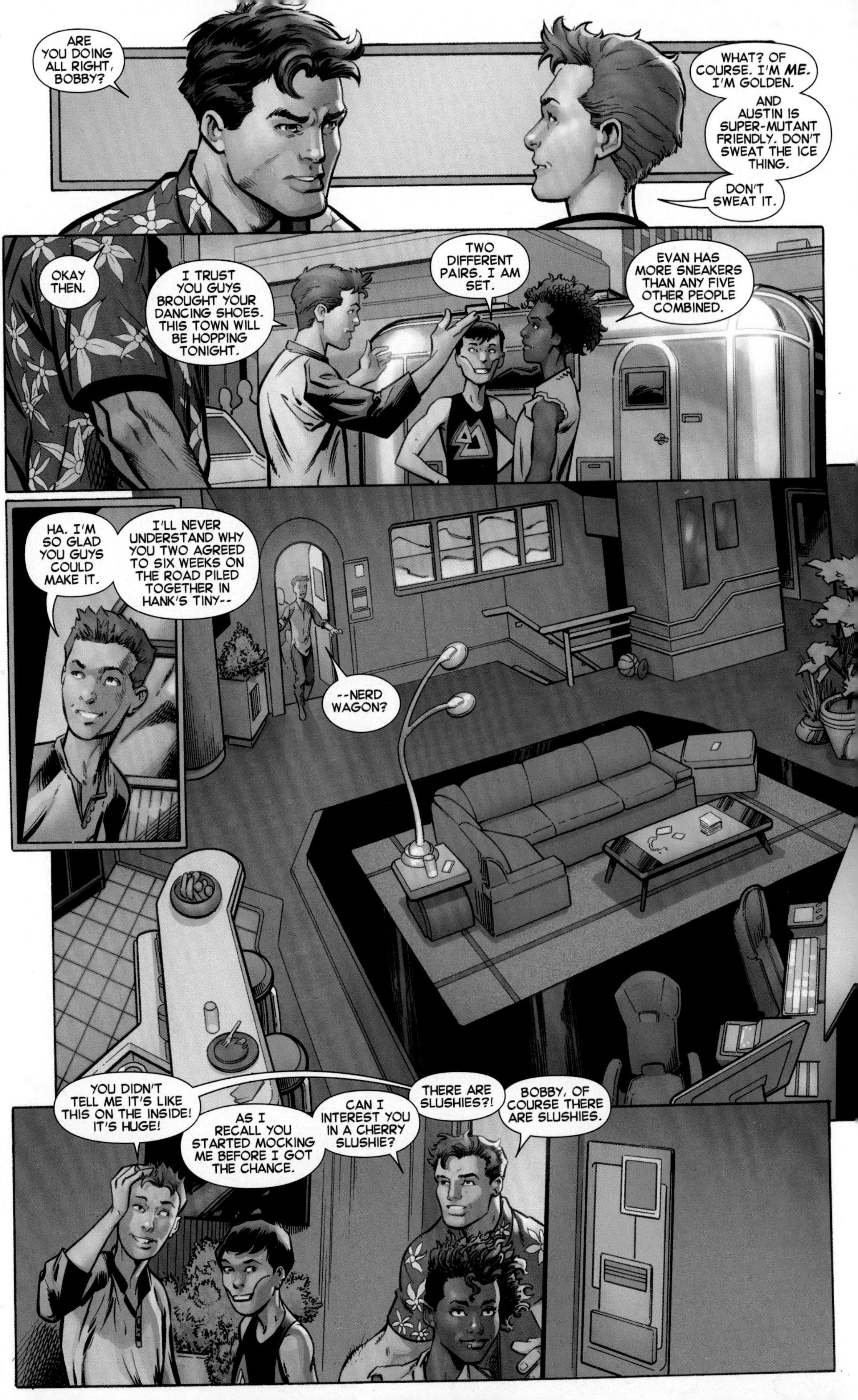
ARE YOU DOING ALL RIGHT, BOBBY?
WHAT? OF COURSE. I'M *ME.* I'M GOLDEN.
AND AUSTIN IS SUPER-MUTANT FRIENDLY. DON'T SWEAT THE ICE THING.
DON'T SWEAT IT.
OKAY THEN.
I TRUST YOU GUYS BROUGHT YOUR DANCING SHOES. THIS TOWN WILL BE HOPPING TONIGHT.
TWO DIFFERENT PAIRS. I AM SET.
EVAN HAS MORE SNEAKERS THAN ANY FIVE OTHER PEOPLE COMBINED.
HA. I'M SO GLAD YOU GUYS COULD MAKE IT.
I'LL NEVER UNDERSTAND WHY YOU TWO AGREED TO SIX WEEKS ON THE ROAD PILED TOGETHER IN HANK'S TINY--
--NERD WAGON?
YOU DIDN'T TELL ME IT'S LIKE THIS ON THE INSIDE! IT'S HUGE!
AS I RECALL YOU STARTED MOCKING ME BEFORE I GOT THE CHANCE.
CAN I INTEREST YOU IN A CHERRY SLUSHIE?
THERE ARE SLUSHIES?!
BOBBY, OF COURSE THERE ARE SLUSHIES.

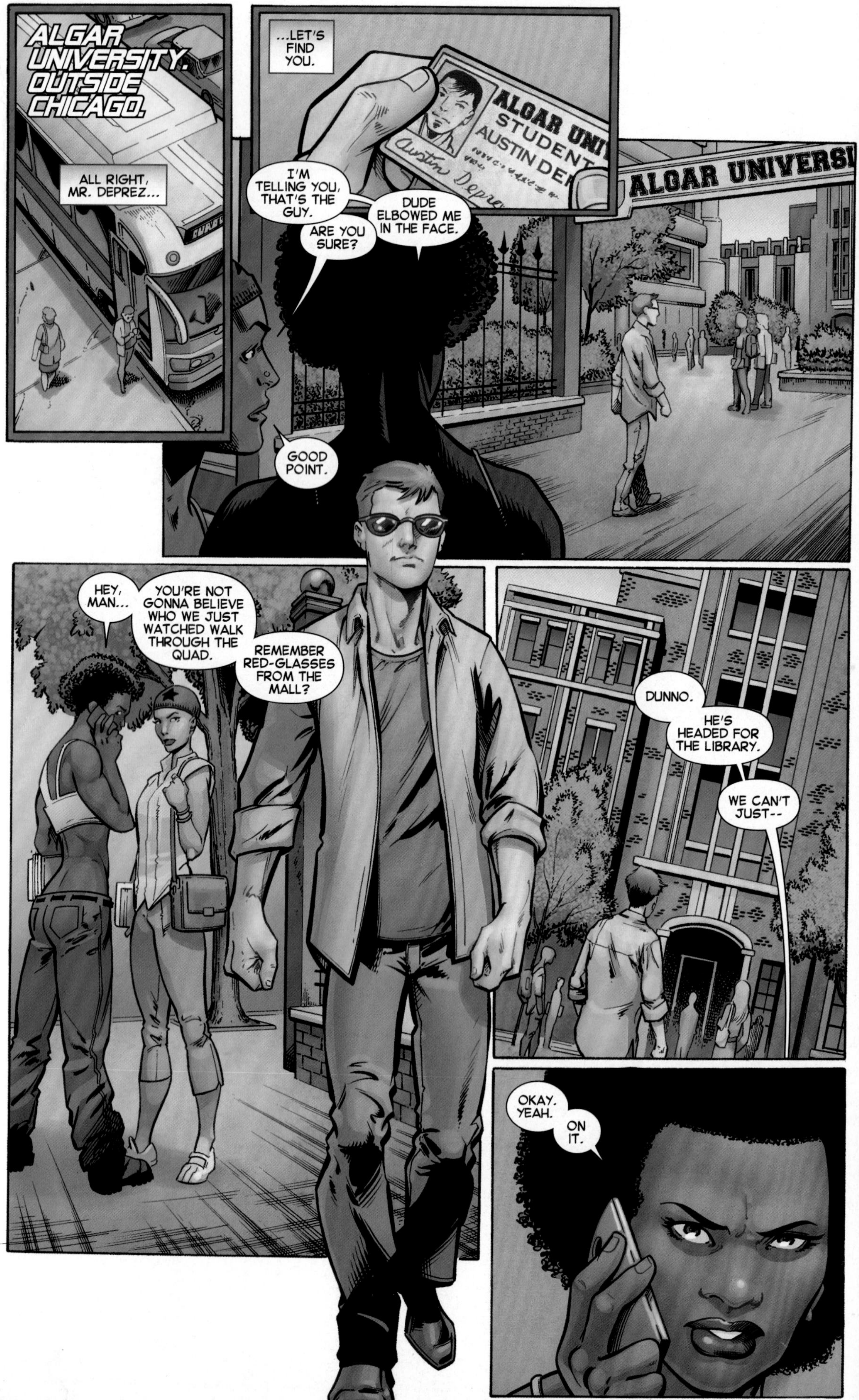
ALGAR UNIVERSITY. OUTSIDE CHICAGO.
ALL RIGHT, MR. DEPREZ...
...LET'S FIND YOU.
STUDENT
I'M TELLING YOU, THAT'S THE GUY.
ARE YOU SURE?
DUDE ELBOWED ME IN THE FACE.
GOOD POINT.
HEY, MAN...
YOU'RE NOT GONNA BELIEVE WHO WE JUST WATCHED WALK THROUGH THE QUAD.
REMEMBER RED-GLASSES FROM THE MALL?
DUNNO.
HE'S HEADED FOR THE LIBRARY.
WE CAN'T JUST--
OKAY. YEAH.
ON IT.

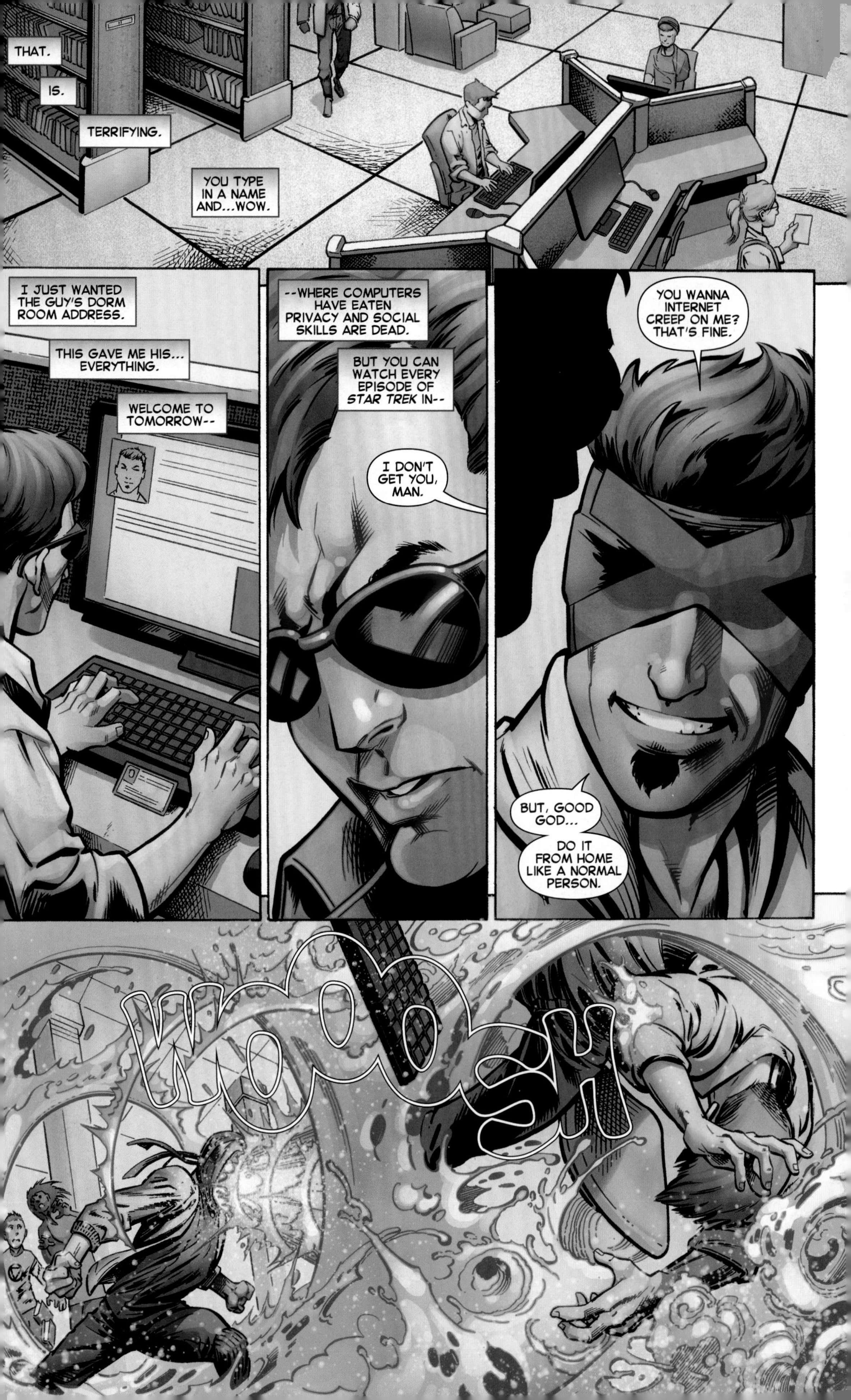
THAT.
IS.
TERRIFYING.
YOU TYPE IN A NAME AND...WOW.
I JUST WANTED THE GUY'S DORM ROOM ADDRESS.
THIS GAVE ME HIS... EVERYTHING.
WELCOME TO TOMORROW--
--WHERE COMPUTERS HAVE EATEN PRIVACY AND SOCIAL SKILLS ARE DEAD.
BUT YOU CAN WATCH EVERY EPISODE OF *STAR TREK* IN--
I DON'T GET YOU, MAN.
YOU WANNA INTERNET CREEP ON ME? THAT'S FINE.
BUT, GOOD GOD...
DO IT FROM HOME LIKE A NORMAL PERSON.
WHOOSH

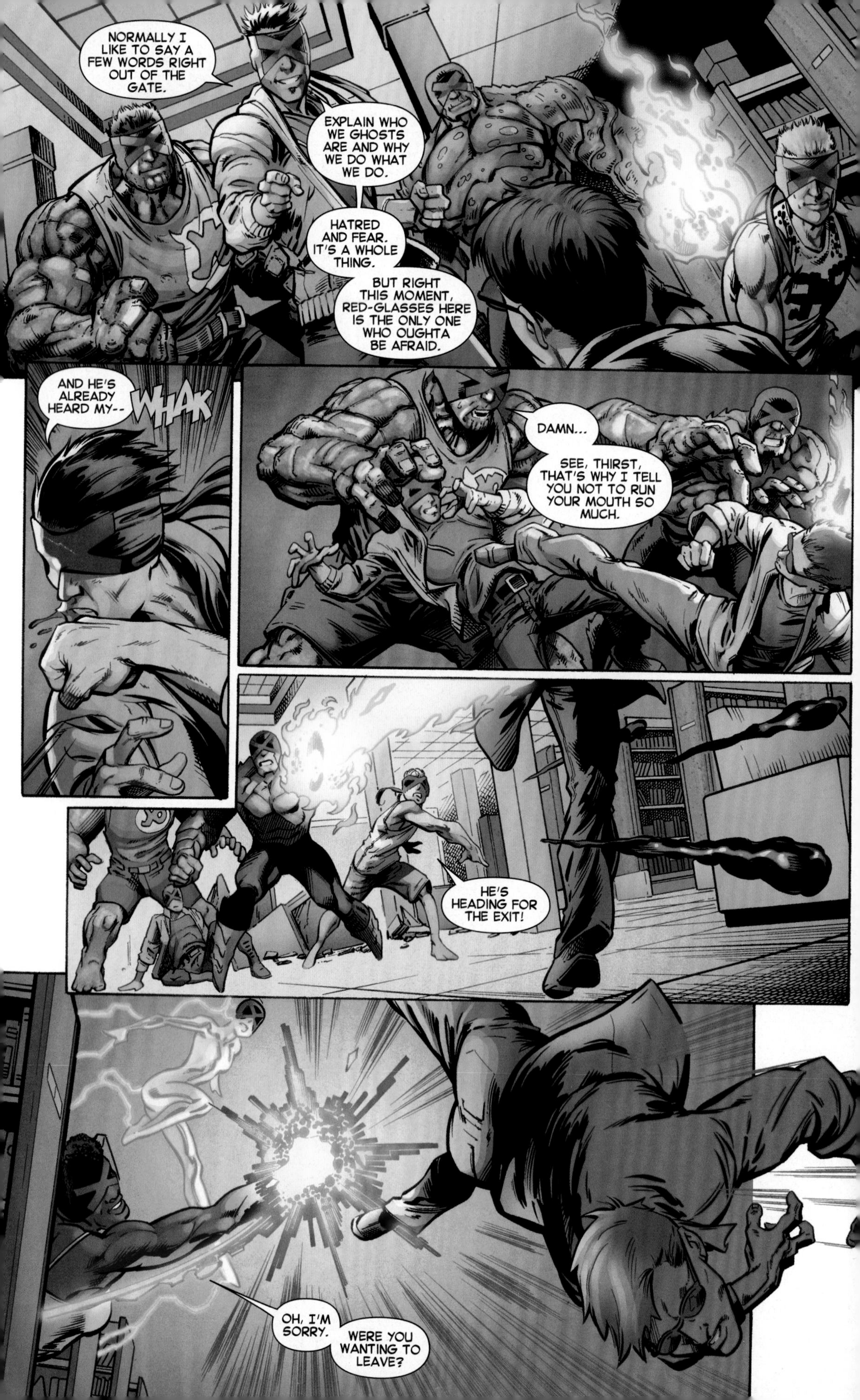
NORMALLY I LIKE TO SAY A FEW WORDS RIGHT OUT OF THE GATE.
EXPLAIN WHO WE GHOSTS ARE AND WHY WE DO WHAT WE DO.
HATRED AND FEAR. IT'S A WHOLE THING.
BUT RIGHT THIS MOMENT, RED-GLASSES HERE IS THE ONLY ONE WHO OUGHTA BE AFRAID.
AND HE'S ALREADY HEARD MY--
WHAK
DAMN...
SEE, THIRST, THAT'S WHY I TELL YOU NOT TO RUN YOUR MOUTH SO MUCH.
HE'S HEADING FOR THE EXIT!
OH, I'M SORRY.
WERE YOU WANTING TO LEAVE?

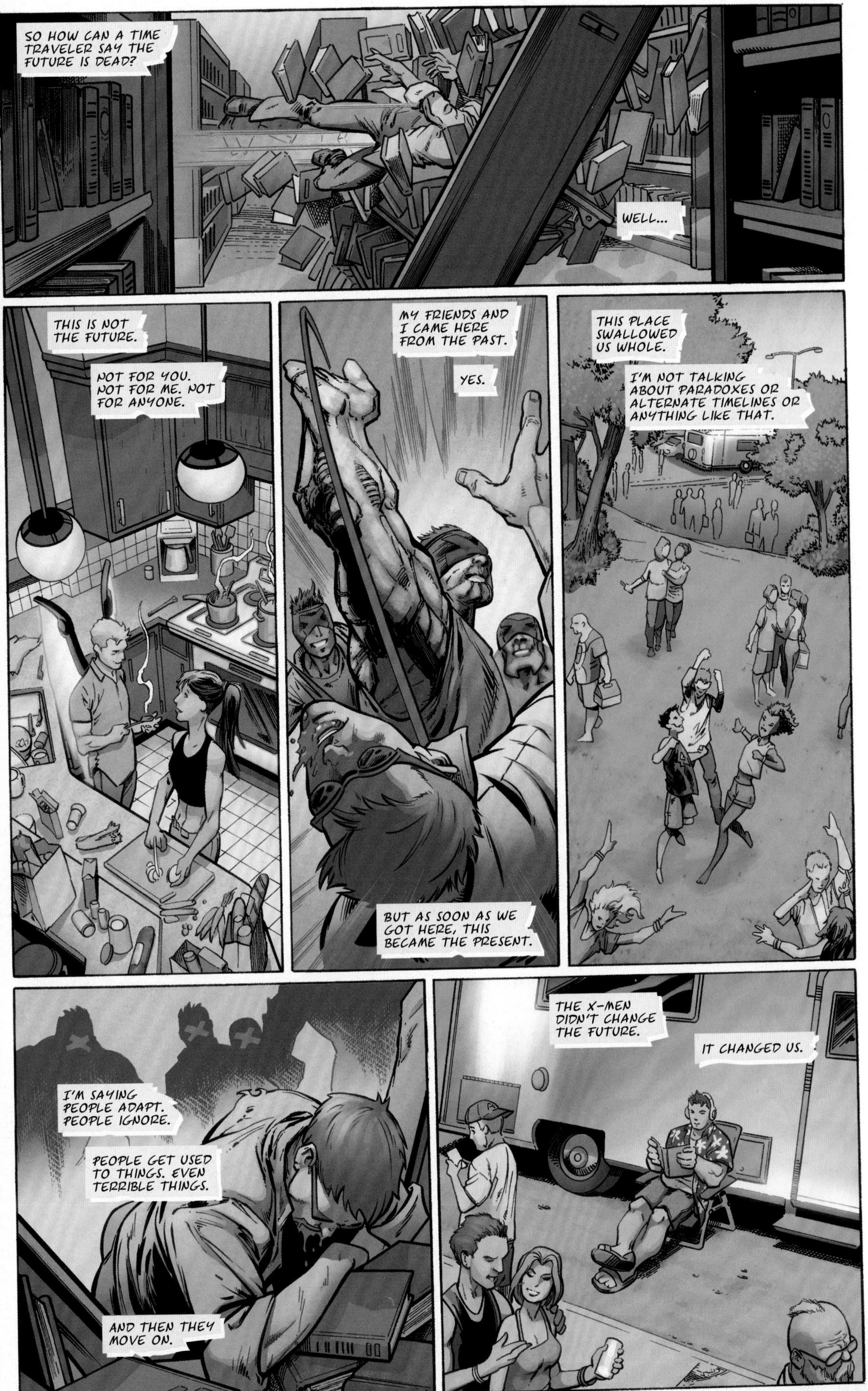
SO HOW CAN A TIME TRAVELER SAY THE FUTURE IS DEAD?
WELL...
THIS IS NOT THE FUTURE.
NOT FOR YOU. NOT FOR ME. NOT FOR ANYONE.
MY FRIENDS AND I CAME HERE FROM THE PAST.
YES.
BUT AS SOON AS WE GOT HERE, THIS BECAME THE PRESENT.
THIS PLACE SWALLOWED US WHOLE.
I'M NOT TALKING ABOUT PARADOXES OR ALTERNATE TIMELINES OR ANYTHING LIKE THAT.
I'M SAYING PEOPLE ADAPT. PEOPLE IGNORE.
PEOPLE GET USED TO THINGS. EVEN TERRIBLE THINGS.
AND THEN THEY MOVE ON.
THE X-MEN DIDN'T CHANGE THE FUTURE.
IT CHANGED US.

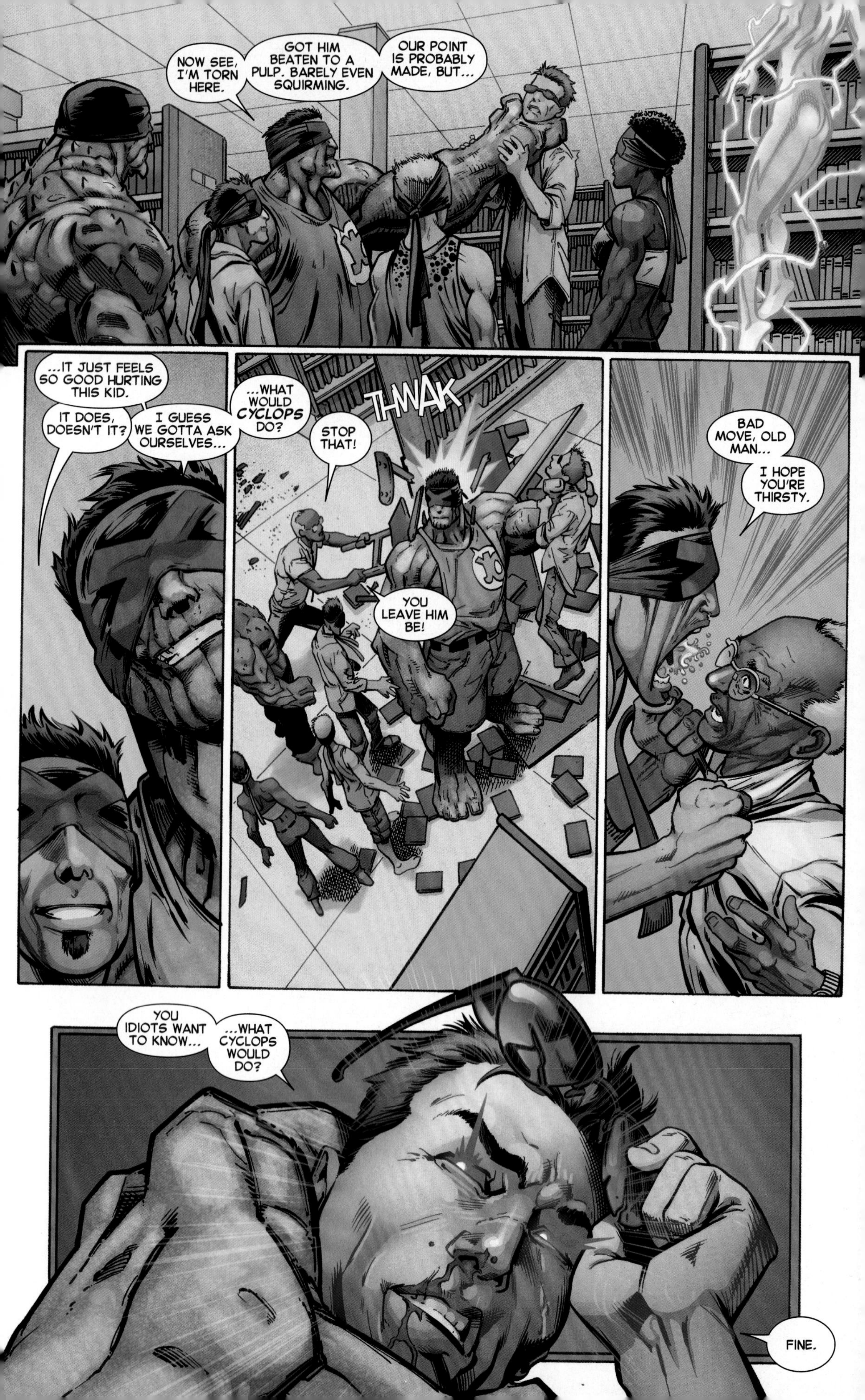
NOW SEE, I'M TORN HERE.
GOT HIM BEATEN TO A PULP. BARELY EVEN SQUIRMING.
OUR POINT IS PROBABLY MADE, BUT...
...IT JUST FEELS SO GOOD HURTING THIS KID.
IT DOES, DOESN'T IT?
I GUESS WE GOTTA ASK OURSELVES...
...WHAT WOULD CYCLOPS DO?
THWAK
STOP THAT!
YOU LEAVE HIM BE!
BAD MOVE, OLD MAN...
I HOPE YOU'RE THIRSTY.
YOU IDIOTS WANT TO KNOW...
...WHAT CYCLOPS WOULD DO?
FINE.

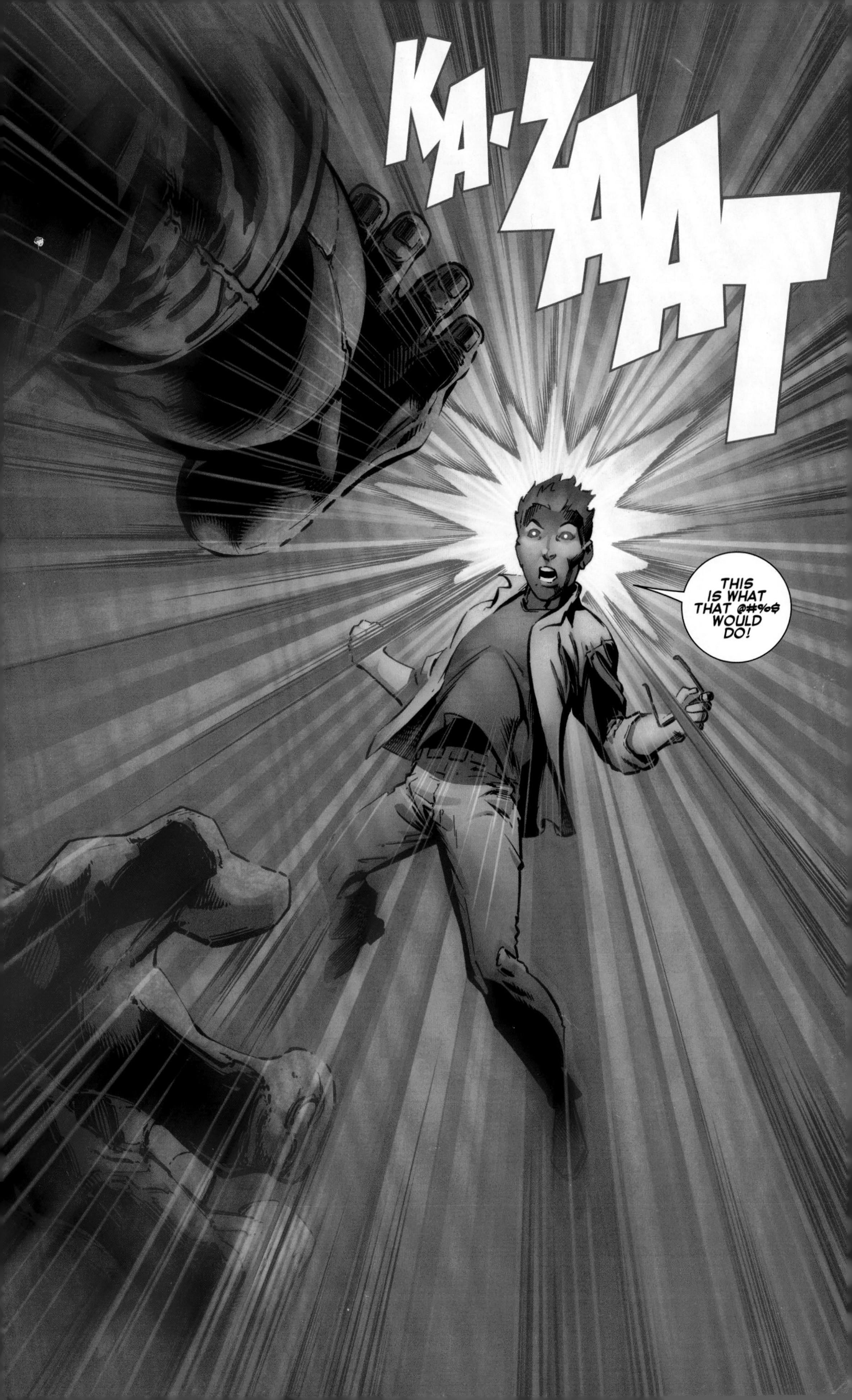
KA-ZAAAT
THIS IS WHAT THAT @#%$ WOULD DO!

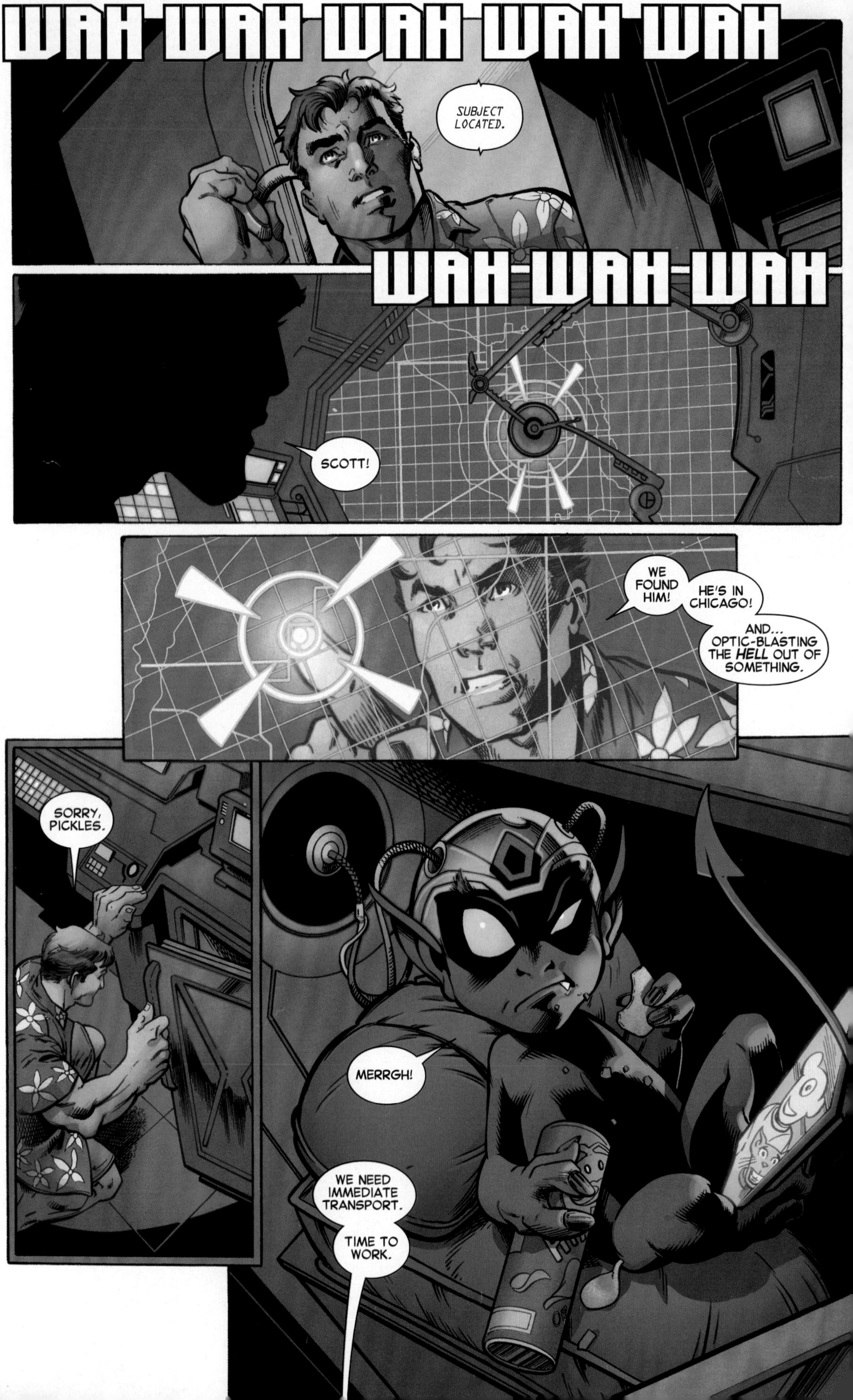
WAH WAH WAH WAH WAH
SUBJECT LOCATED.
WAH WAH WAH
SCOTT!
WE FOUND HIM!
HE'S IN CHICAGO!
AND... OPTIC-BLASTING THE HELL OUT OF SOMETHING.
SORRY, PICKLES.
MERRGH!
WE NEED IMMEDIATE TRANSPORT.
TIME TO WORK.

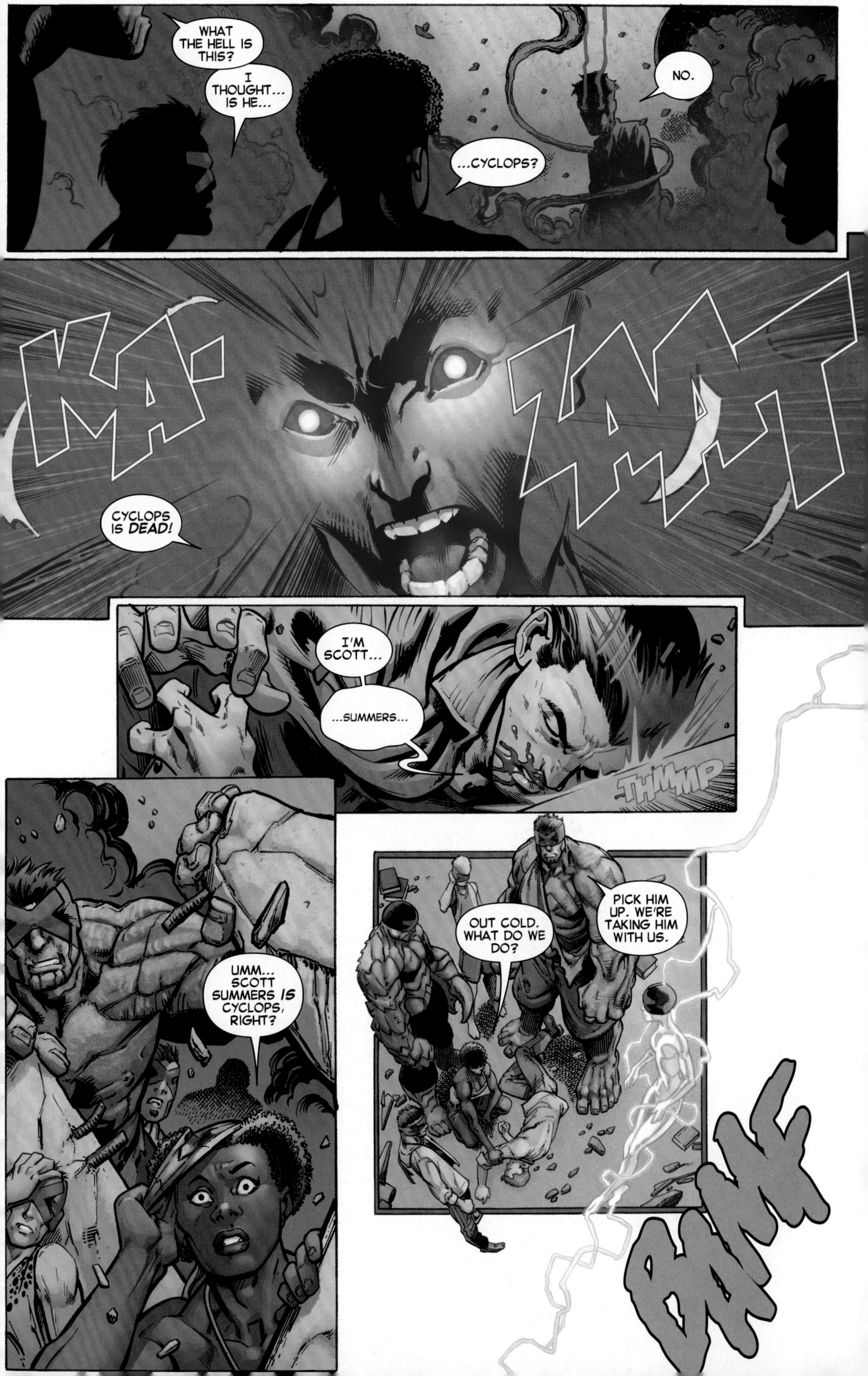
WHAT THE HELL IS THIS?
I THOUGHT... IS HE...
...CYCLOPS?
NO.
KA-ZAAT
CYCLOPS IS DEAD!
I'M SCOTT...
...SUMMERS...
THMMP
UMM... SCOTT SUMMERS IS CYCLOPS, RIGHT?
OUT COLD. WHAT DO WE DO?
PICK HIM UP. WE'RE TAKING HIM WITH US.
BAMF

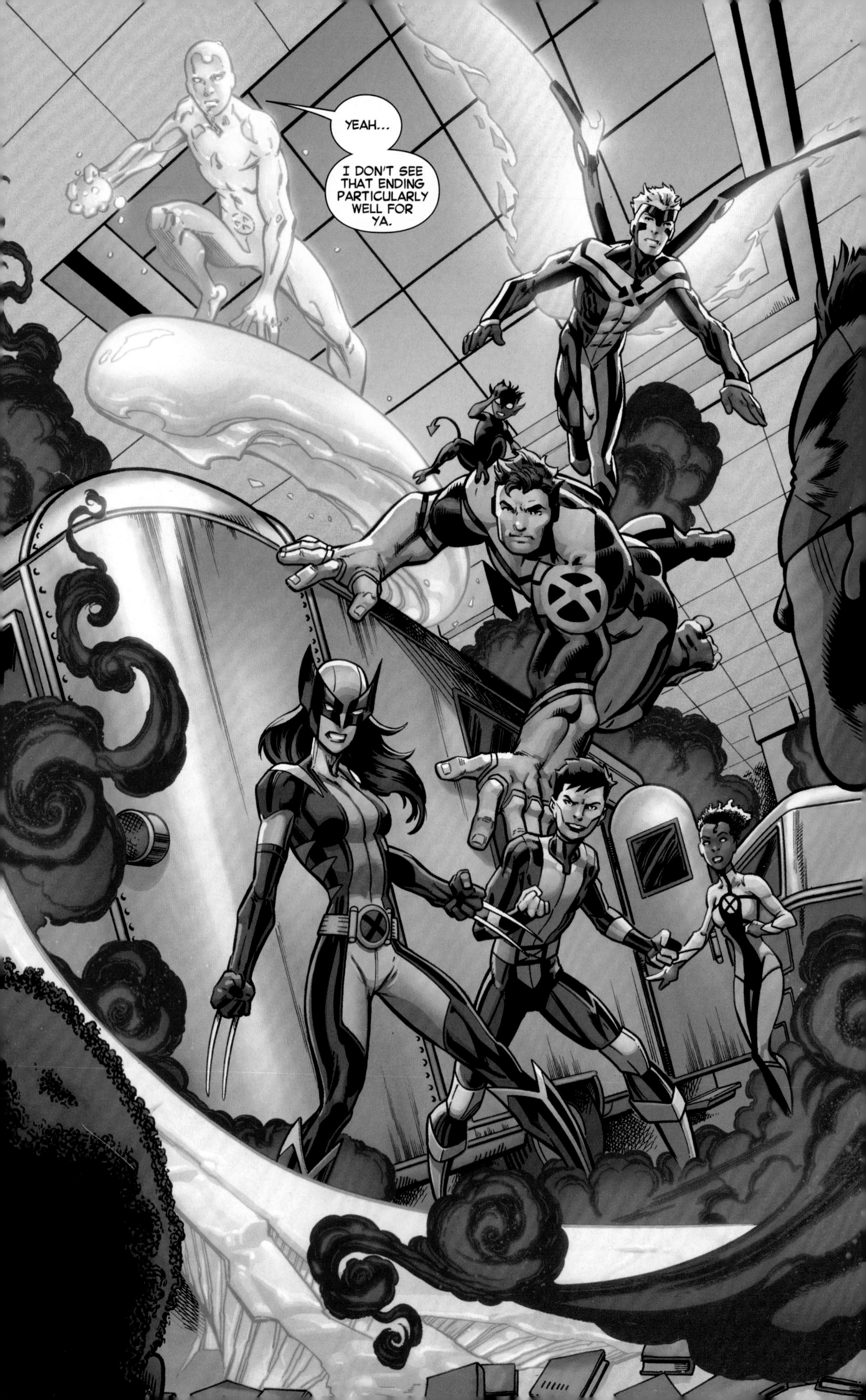
YEAH...
I DON'T SEE THAT ENDING PARTICULARLY WELL FOR YA.

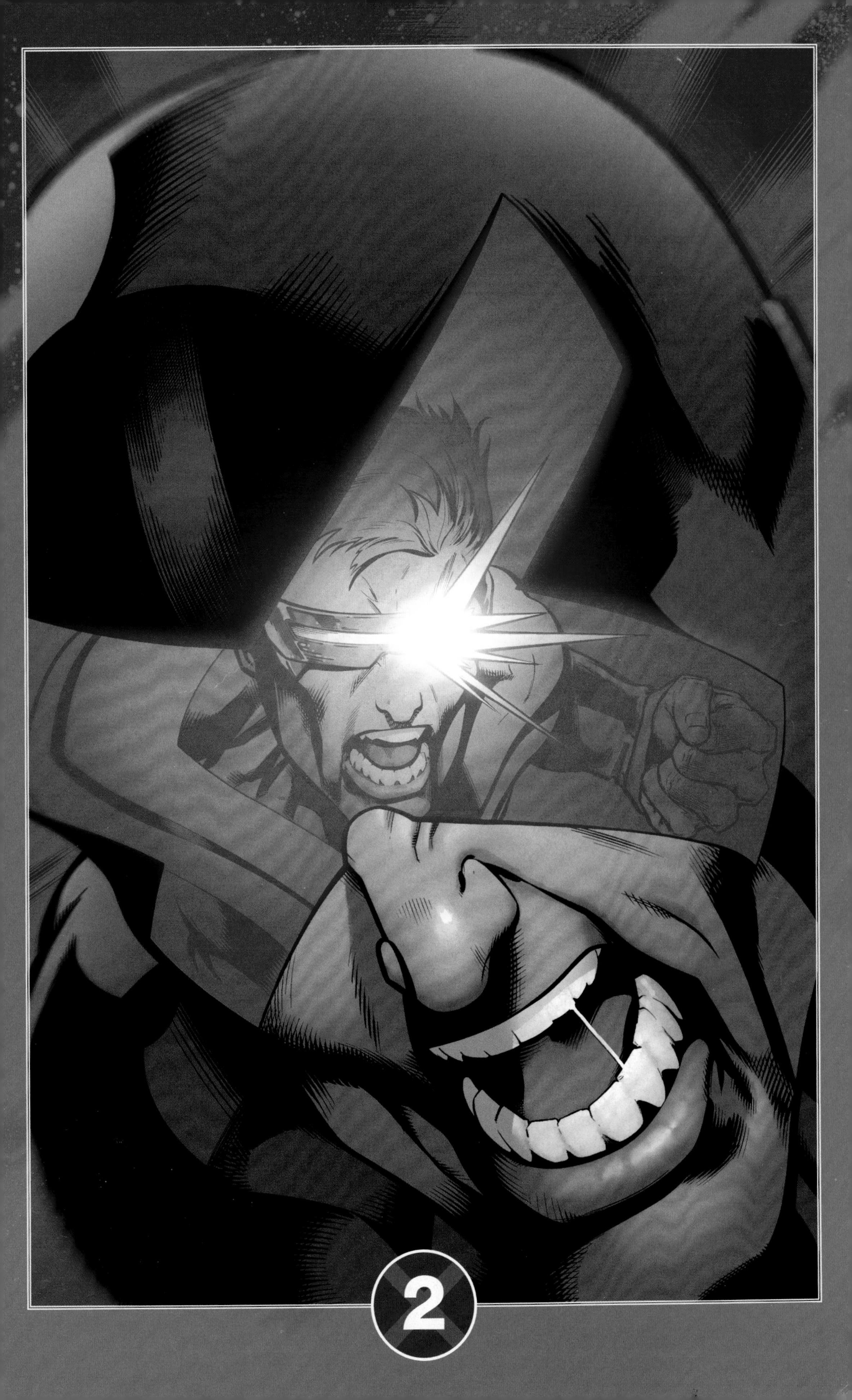
2

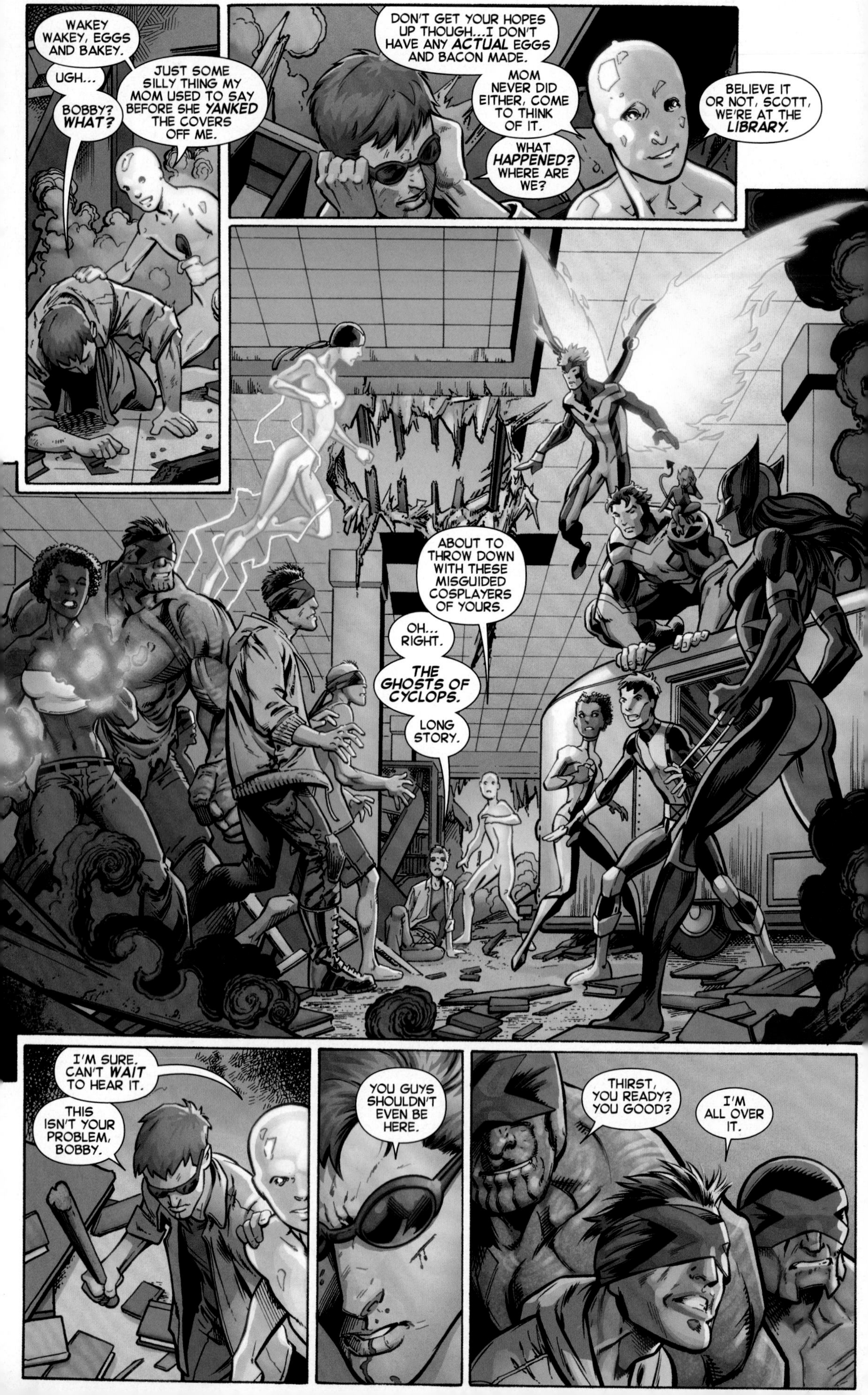

WAKEY WAKEY, EGGS AND BAKEY.
UGH...
BOBBY? WHAT?
JUST SOME SILLY THING MY MOM USED TO SAY BEFORE SHE YANKED THE COVERS OFF ME.
DON'T GET YOUR HOPES UP THOUGH...I DON'T HAVE ANY ACTUAL EGGS AND BACON MADE.
MOM NEVER DID EITHER, COME TO THINK OF IT.
WHAT HAPPENED? WHERE ARE WE?
BELIEVE IT OR NOT, SCOTT, WE'RE AT THE LIBRARY.
ABOUT TO THROW DOWN WITH THESE MISGUIDED COSPLAYERS OF YOURS.
OH... RIGHT.
THE GHOSTS OF CYCLOPS.
LONG STORY.
I'M SURE. CAN'T WAIT TO HEAR IT.
THIS ISN'T YOUR PROBLEM, BOBBY.
YOU GUYS SHOULDN'T EVEN BE HERE.
THIRST, YOU READY? YOU GOOD?
I'M ALL OVER IT.

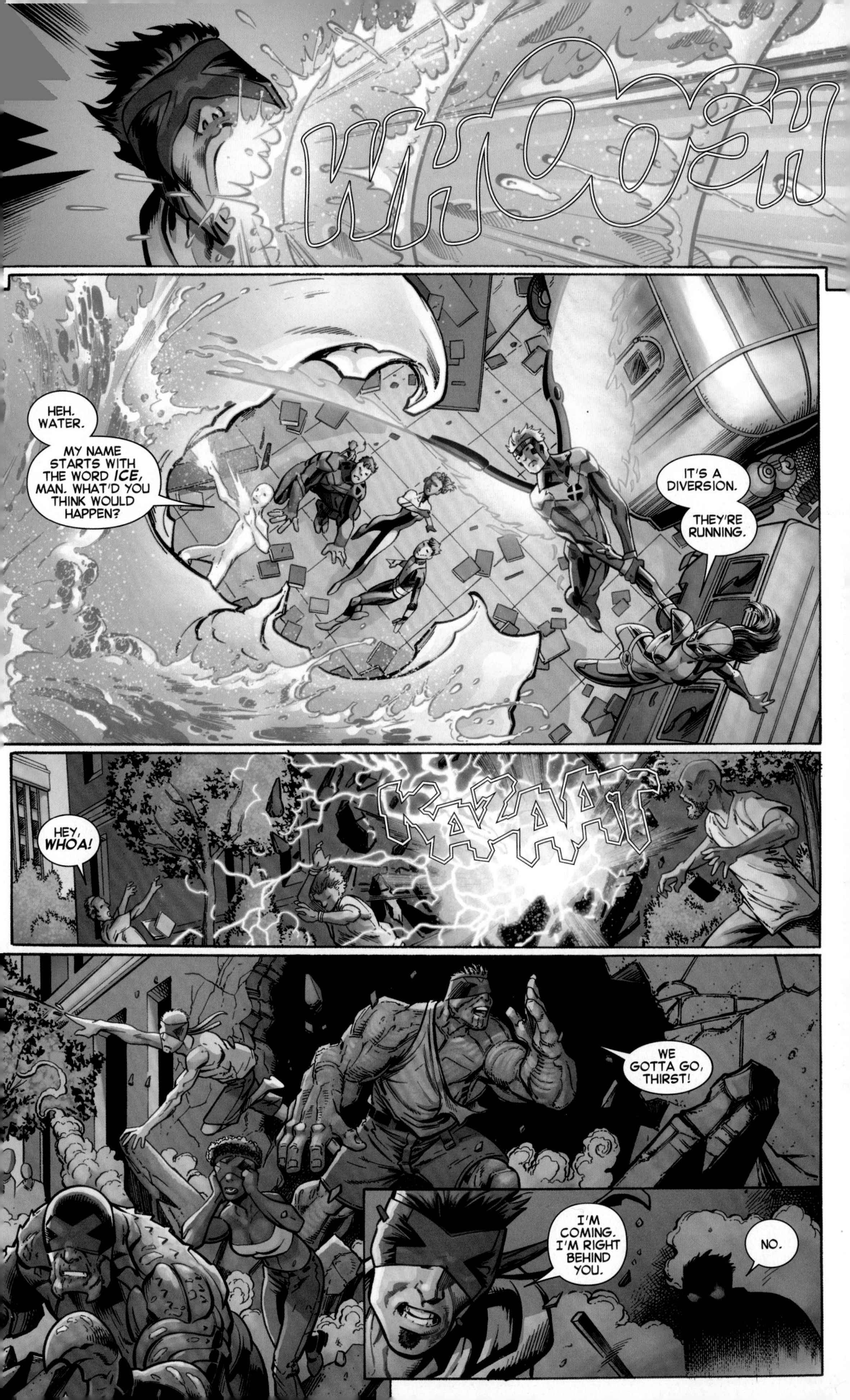
WHOOSH
HEH. WATER.
MY NAME STARTS WITH THE WORD ICE, MAN. WHAT'D YOU THINK WOULD HAPPEN?
IT'S A DIVERSION.
THEY'RE RUNNING.
HEY, WHOA!
KRAAT
WE GOTTA GO, THIRST!
I'M COMING. I'M RIGHT BEHIND YOU.
NO.

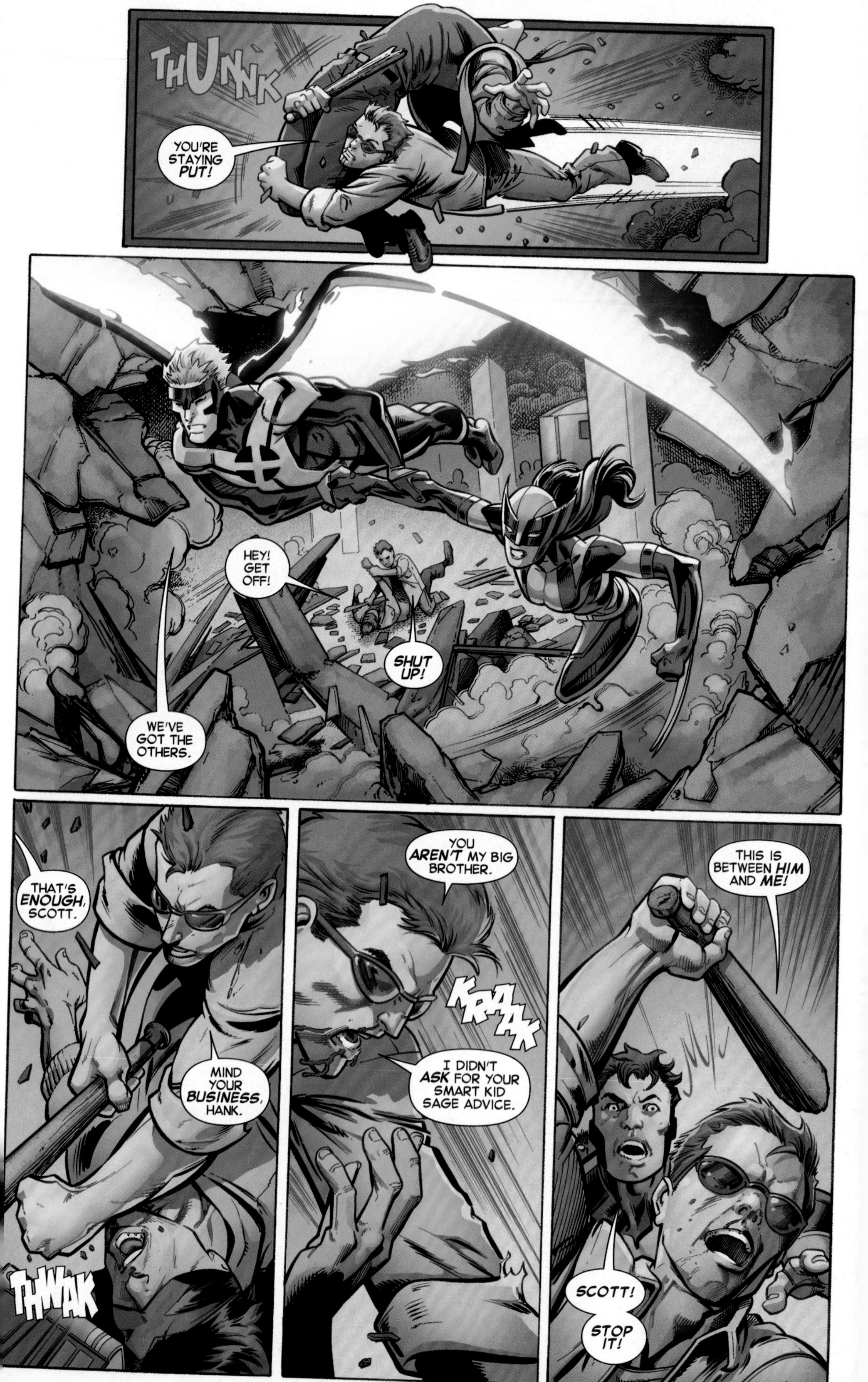
THUNNNK
YOU'RE STAYING PUT!
HEY! GET OFF!
SHUT UP!
WE'VE GOT THE OTHERS.
THAT'S ENOUGH, SCOTT.
MIND YOUR BUSINESS, HANK.
THWAK
YOU AREN'T MY BIG BROTHER.
KRAAAK
I DIDN'T ASK FOR YOUR SMART KID SAGE ADVICE.
THIS IS BETWEEN HIM AND ME!
SCOTT!
STOP IT!

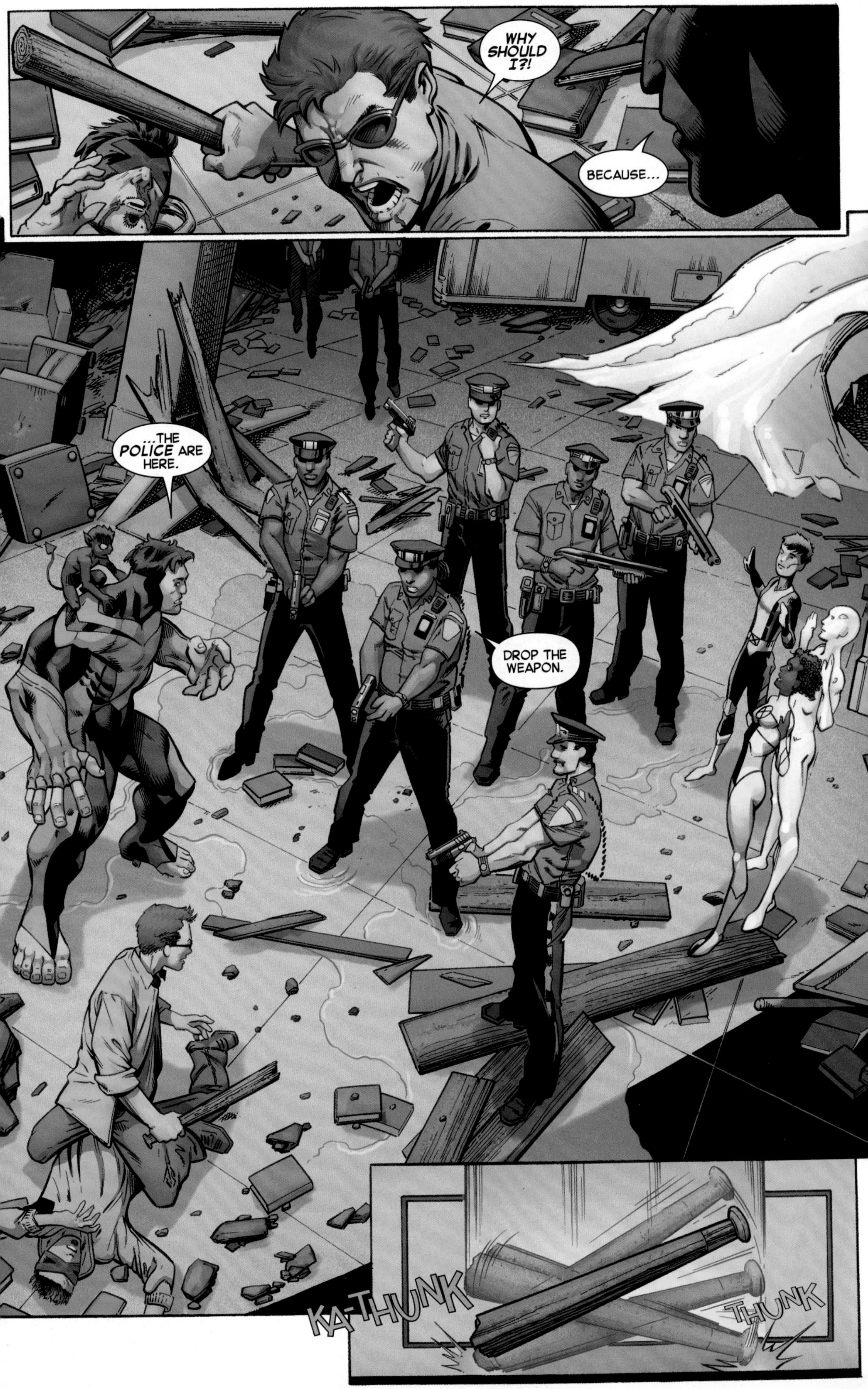
WHY SHOULD I?!
BECAUSE...
...THE POLICE ARE HERE.
DROP THE WEAPON.
KA-THUNK
THUNK

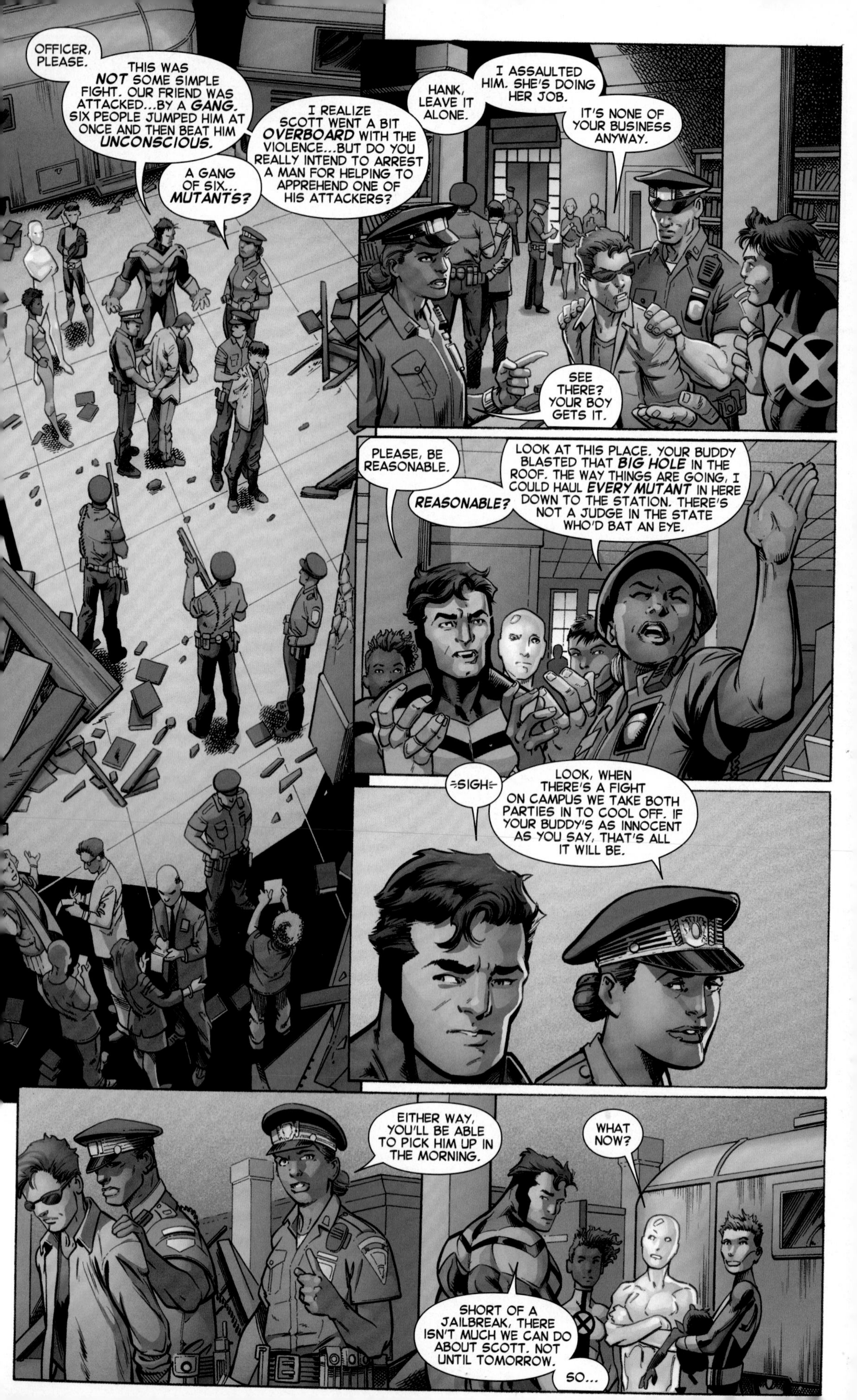

OFFICER, PLEASE.
THIS WAS NOT SOME SIMPLE FIGHT. OUR FRIEND WAS ATTACKED...BY A GANG. SIX PEOPLE JUMPED HIM AT ONCE AND THEN BEAT HIM UNCONSCIOUS.
A GANG OF SIX... MUTANTS?
I REALIZE SCOTT WENT A BIT OVERBOARD WITH THE VIOLENCE...BUT DO YOU REALLY INTEND TO ARREST A MAN FOR HELPING TO APPREHEND ONE OF HIS ATTACKERS?
HANK, LEAVE IT ALONE.
I ASSAULTED HIM. SHE'S DOING HER JOB.
IT'S NONE OF YOUR BUSINESS ANYWAY.
SEE THERE? YOUR BOY GETS IT.
PLEASE, BE REASONABLE.
REASONABLE?
LOOK AT THIS PLACE. YOUR BUDDY BLASTED THAT BIG HOLE IN THE ROOF. THE WAY THINGS ARE GOING, I COULD HAUL EVERY MUTANT IN HERE DOWN TO THE STATION. THERE'S NOT A JUDGE IN THE STATE WHO'D BAT AN EYE.
=SIGH=
LOOK, WHEN THERE'S A FIGHT ON CAMPUS WE TAKE BOTH PARTIES IN TO COOL OFF. IF YOUR BUDDY'S AS INNOCENT AS YOU SAY, THAT'S ALL IT WILL BE.
EITHER WAY, YOU'LL BE ABLE TO PICK HIM UP IN THE MORNING.
WHAT NOW?
SHORT OF A JAILBREAK, THERE ISN'T MUCH WE CAN DO ABOUT SCOTT. NOT UNTIL TOMORROW.
SO...

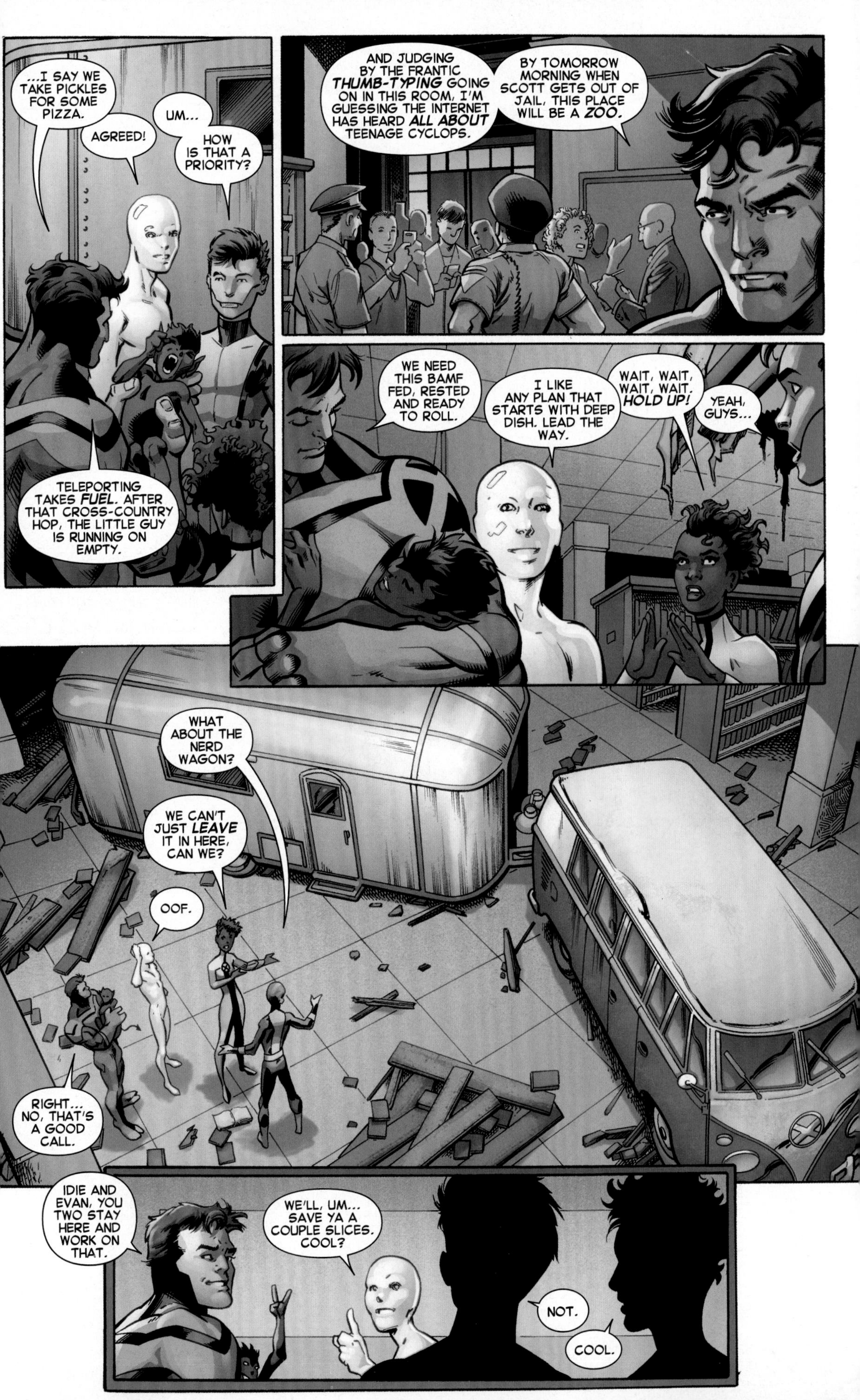
...I SAY WE TAKE PICKLES FOR SOME PIZZA.
AGREED!
UM...
HOW IS THAT A PRIORITY?
TELEPORTING TAKES FUEL. AFTER THAT CROSS-COUNTRY HOP, THE LITTLE GUY IS RUNNING ON EMPTY.
AND JUDGING BY THE FRANTIC THUMB-TYPING GOING ON IN THIS ROOM, I'M GUESSING THE INTERNET HAS HEARD ALL ABOUT TEENAGE CYCLOPS.
BY TOMORROW MORNING WHEN SCOTT GETS OUT OF JAIL, THIS PLACE WILL BE A ZOO.
WE NEED THIS BAMF FED, RESTED AND READY TO ROLL.
I LIKE ANY PLAN THAT STARTS WITH DEEP DISH. LEAD THE WAY.
WAIT, WAIT, WAIT, WAIT. HOLD UP!
YEAH, GUYS...
WHAT ABOUT THE NERD WAGON?
WE CAN'T JUST LEAVE IT IN HERE, CAN WE?
OOF.
RIGHT... NO, THAT'S A GOOD CALL.
IDIE AND EVAN, YOU TWO STAY HERE AND WORK ON THAT.
WE'LL, UM... SAVE YA A COUPLE SLICES. COOL?
NOT.
COOL.

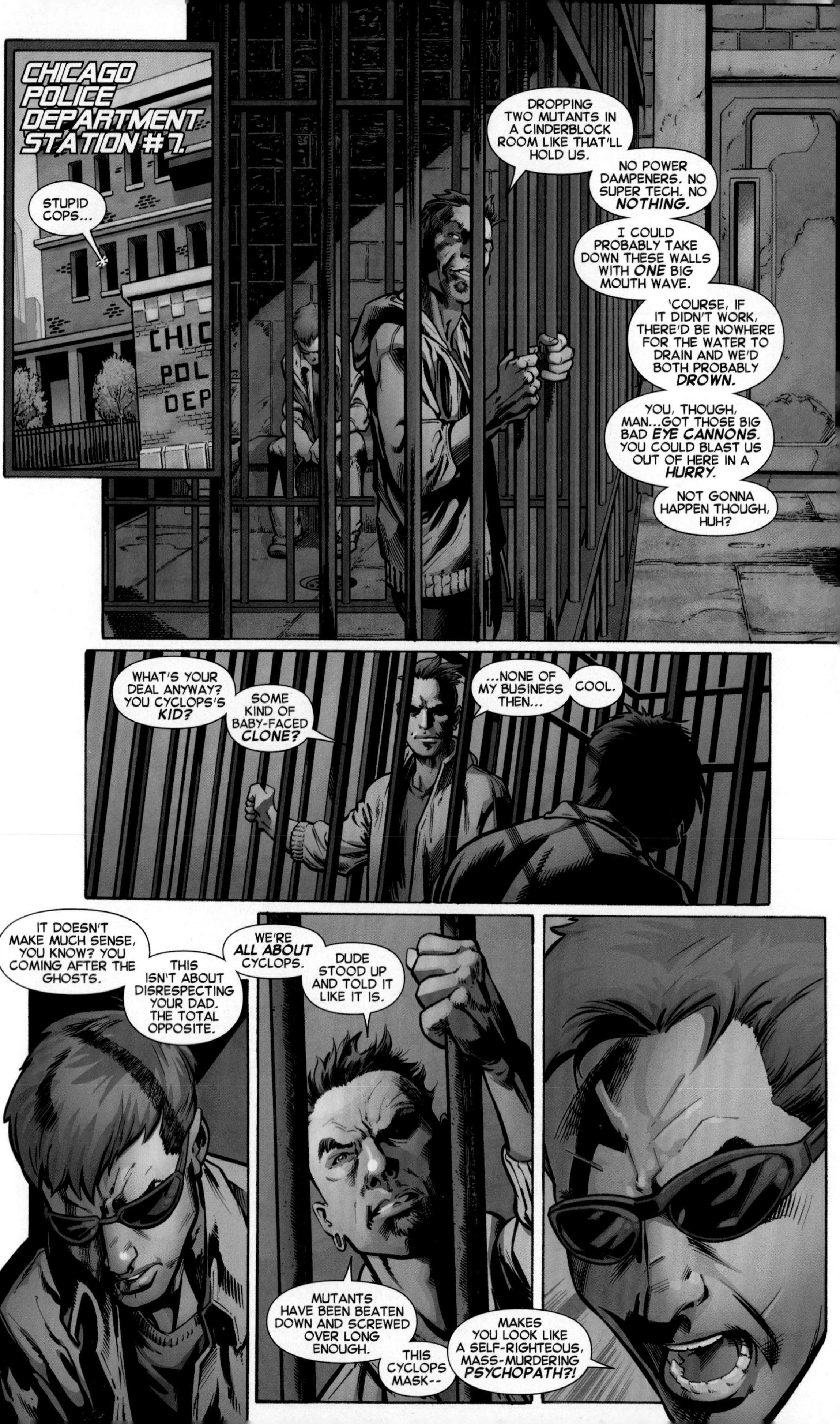
CHICAGO POLICE DEPARTMENT STATION #7.
STUPID COPS...
CHIC POL DEP
DROPPING TWO MUTANTS IN A CINDERBLOCK ROOM LIKE THAT'LL HOLD US.
NO POWER DAMPENERS. NO SUPER TECH. NO NOTHING.
I COULD PROBABLY TAKE DOWN THESE WALLS WITH ONE BIG MOUTH WAVE.
'COURSE, IF IT DIDN'T WORK, THERE'D BE NOWHERE FOR THE WATER TO DRAIN AND WE'D BOTH PROBABLY DROWN.
YOU, THOUGH, MAN...GOT THOSE BIG BAD EYE CANNONS. YOU COULD BLAST US OUT OF HERE IN A HURRY.
NOT GONNA HAPPEN THOUGH, HUH?
WHAT'S YOUR DEAL ANYWAY? YOU CYCLOPS'S KID?
SOME KIND OF BABY-FACED CLONE?
...NONE OF MY BUSINESS THEN...
COOL.
IT DOESN'T MAKE MUCH SENSE, YOU KNOW? YOU COMING AFTER THE GHOSTS.
THIS ISN'T ABOUT DISRESPECTING YOUR DAD. THE TOTAL OPPOSITE.
WE'RE ALL ABOUT CYCLOPS.
DUDE STOOD UP AND TOLD IT LIKE IT IS.
MUTANTS HAVE BEEN BEATEN DOWN AND SCREWED OVER LONG ENOUGH.
THIS CYCLOPS MASK--
MAKES YOU LOOK LIKE A SELF-RIGHTEOUS, MASS-MURDERING PSYCHOPATH?!

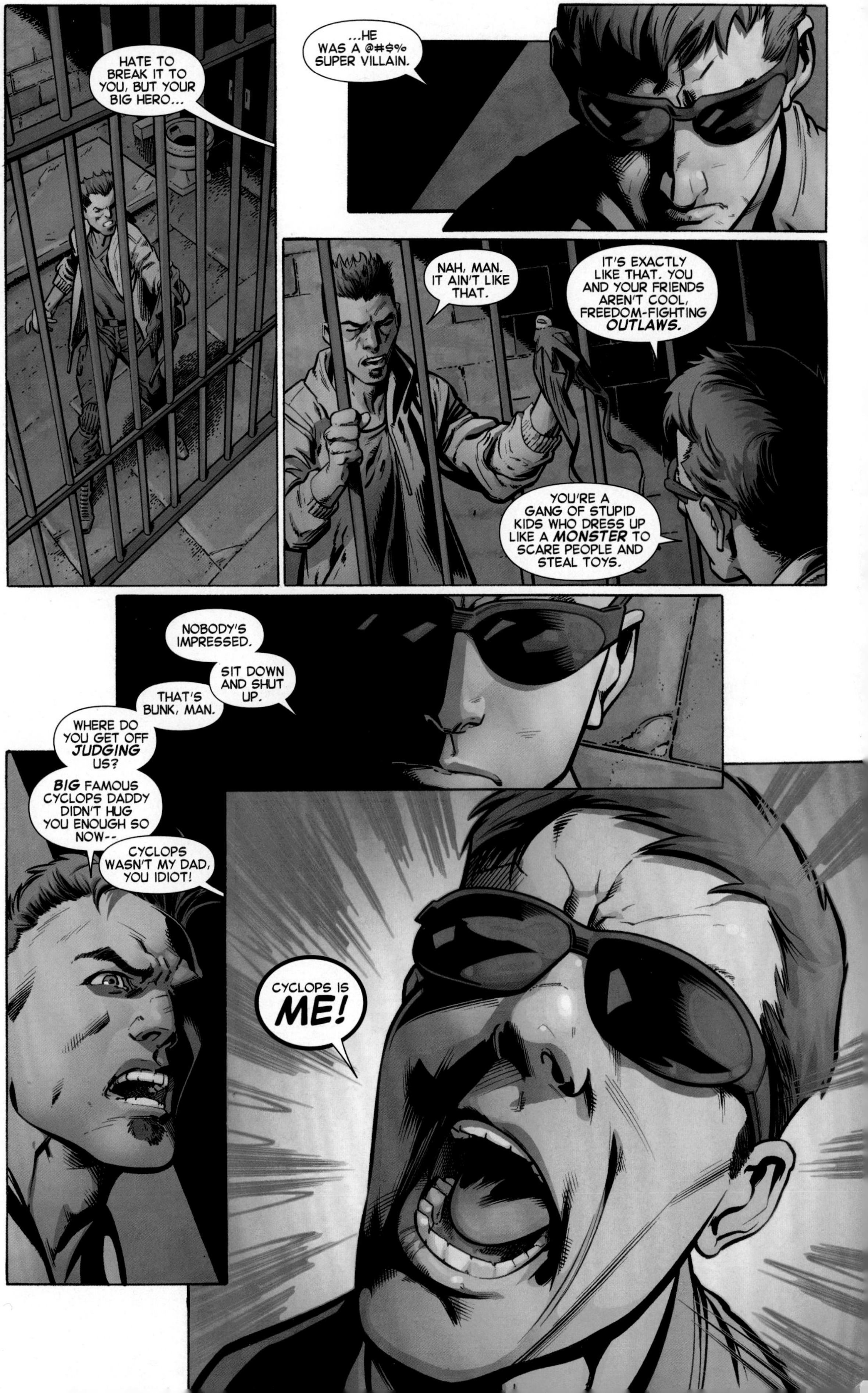
HATE TO BREAK IT TO YOU, BUT YOUR BIG HERO...
...HE WAS A @#$% SUPER VILLAIN.
NAH, MAN. IT AIN'T LIKE THAT.
IT'S EXACTLY LIKE THAT. YOU AND YOUR FRIENDS AREN'T COOL, FREEDOM-FIGHTING OUTLAWS.
YOU'RE A GANG OF STUPID KIDS WHO DRESS UP LIKE A MONSTER TO SCARE PEOPLE AND STEAL TOYS.
NOBODY'S IMPRESSED.
SIT DOWN AND SHUT UP.
THAT'S BUNK, MAN.
WHERE DO YOU GET OFF JUDGING US?
BIG FAMOUS CYCLOPS DADDY DIDN'T HUG YOU ENOUGH SO NOW--
CYCLOPS WASN'T MY DAD, YOU IDIOT!
CYCLOPS IS ME!

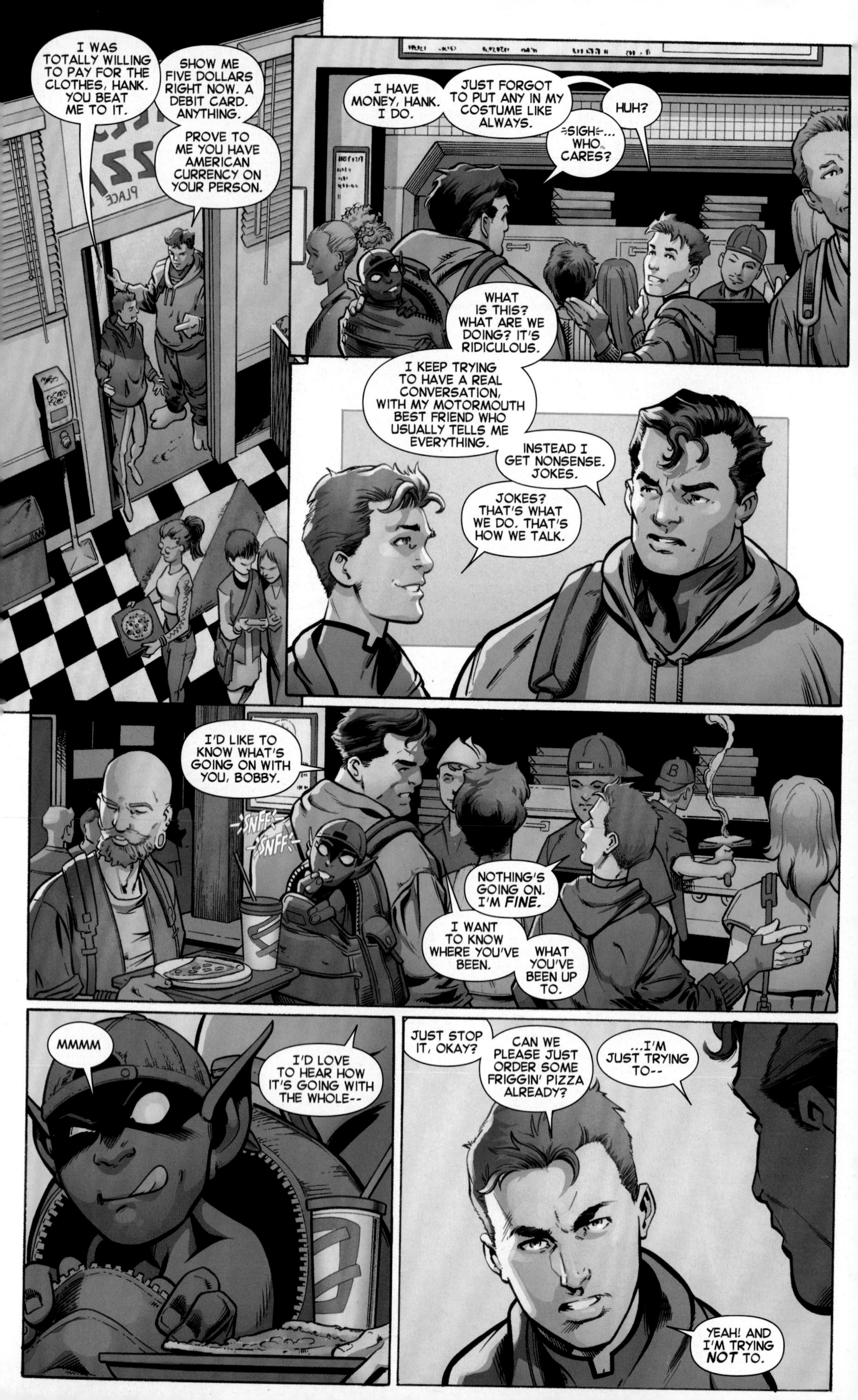
I WAS TOTALLY WILLING TO PAY FOR THE CLOTHES, HANK. YOU BEAT ME TO IT.
SHOW ME FIVE DOLLARS RIGHT NOW. A DEBIT CARD. ANYTHING.
PROVE TO ME YOU HAVE AMERICAN CURRENCY ON YOUR PERSON.
I HAVE MONEY, HANK. I DO.
JUST FORGOT TO PUT ANY IN MY COSTUME LIKE ALWAYS.
HUH?
=SIGH=... WHO CARES?
WHAT IS THIS? WHAT ARE WE DOING? IT'S RIDICULOUS.
I KEEP TRYING TO HAVE A REAL CONVERSATION, WITH MY MOTORMOUTH BEST FRIEND WHO USUALLY TELLS ME EVERYTHING.
INSTEAD I GET NONSENSE. JOKES.
JOKES? THAT'S WHAT WE DO. THAT'S HOW WE TALK.
I'D LIKE TO KNOW WHAT'S GOING ON WITH YOU, BOBBY.
SNFF
SNFF
NOTHING'S GOING ON. I'M *FINE.*
I WANT TO KNOW WHERE YOU'VE BEEN.
WHAT YOU'VE BEEN UP TO.
MMMM
I'D LOVE TO HEAR HOW IT'S GOING WITH THE WHOLE--
JUST STOP IT, OKAY?
CAN WE PLEASE JUST ORDER SOME FRIGGIN' PIZZA ALREADY?
...I'M JUST TRYING TO--
YEAH! AND I'M TRYING *NOT* TO.

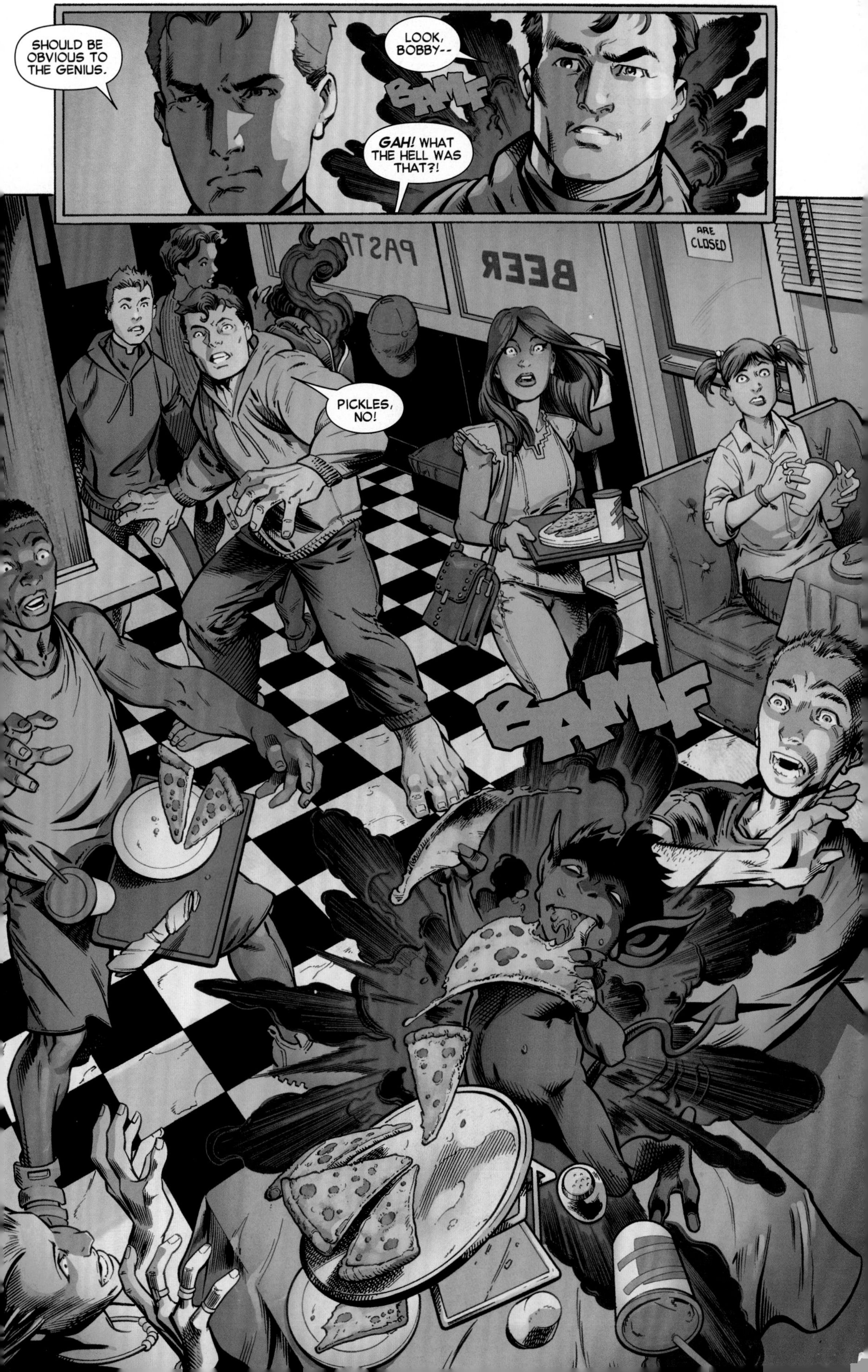
SHOULD BE OBVIOUS TO THE GENIUS.
LOOK, BOBBY--
BAMF
GAH! WHAT THE HELL WAS THAT?!
PASTA
BEER
ARE CLOSED
PICKLES, NO!
BAMF

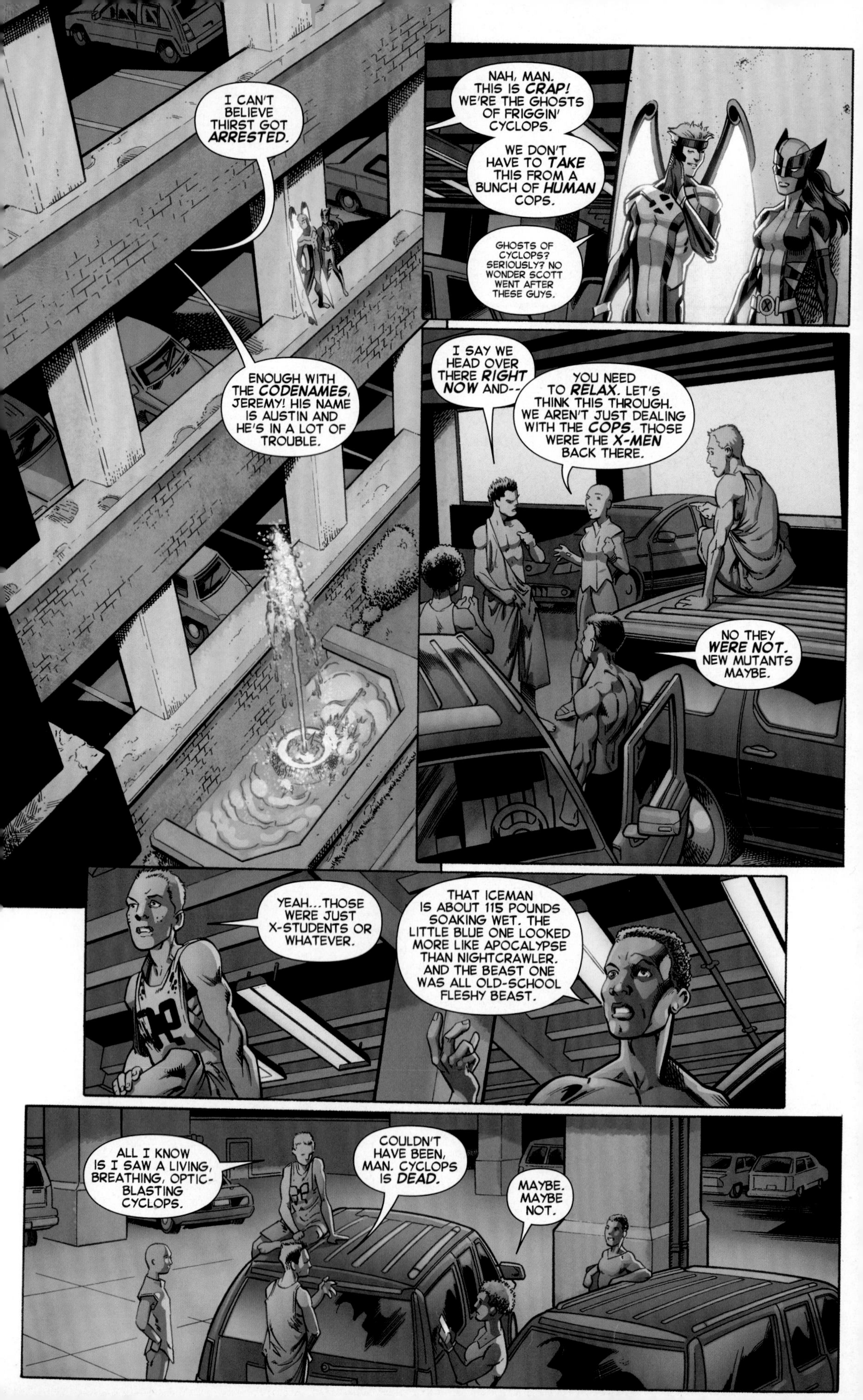
I CAN'T BELIEVE THIRST GOT ARRESTED.
NAH, MAN. THIS IS CRAP! WE'RE THE GHOSTS OF FRIGGIN' CYCLOPS.
WE DON'T HAVE TO TAKE THIS FROM A BUNCH OF HUMAN COPS.
GHOSTS OF CYCLOPS? SERIOUSLY? NO WONDER SCOTT WENT AFTER THESE GUYS.
ENOUGH WITH THE CODENAMES, JEREMY! HIS NAME IS AUSTIN AND HE'S IN A LOT OF TROUBLE.
I SAY WE HEAD OVER THERE RIGHT NOW AND--
YOU NEED TO RELAX. LET'S THINK THIS THROUGH. WE AREN'T JUST DEALING WITH THE COPS. THOSE WERE THE X-MEN BACK THERE.
NO THEY WERE NOT. NEW MUTANTS MAYBE.
YEAH...THOSE WERE JUST X-STUDENTS OR WHATEVER.
THAT ICEMAN IS ABOUT 115 POUNDS SOAKING WET. THE LITTLE BLUE ONE LOOKED MORE LIKE APOCALYPSE THAN NIGHTCRAWLER. AND THE BEAST ONE WAS ALL OLD-SCHOOL FLESHY BEAST.
ALL I KNOW IS I SAW A LIVING, BREATHING, OPTIC-BLASTING CYCLOPS.
COULDN'T HAVE BEEN, MAN. CYCLOPS IS DEAD.
MAYBE. MAYBE NOT.

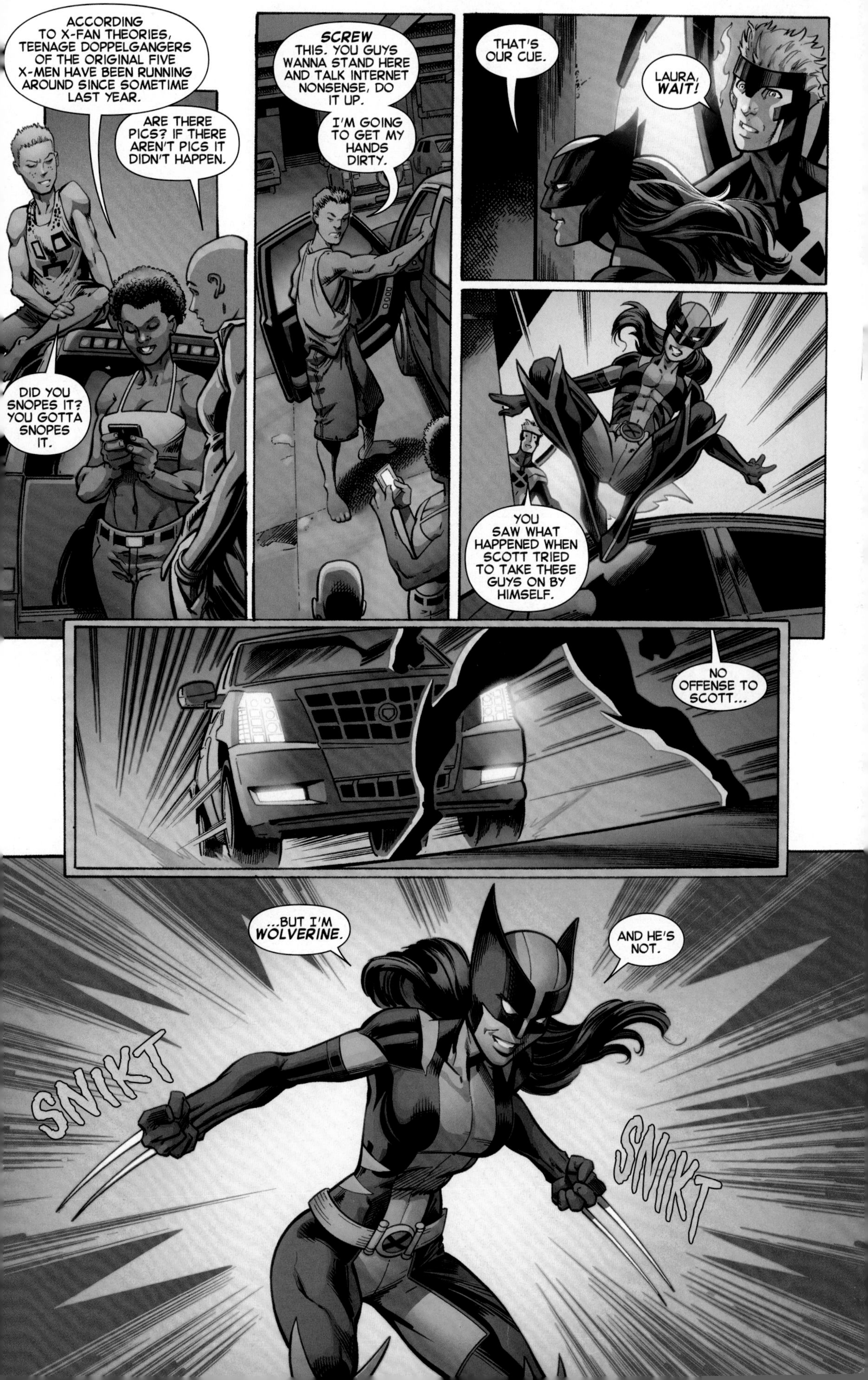
ACCORDING TO X-FAN THEORIES, TEENAGE DOPPELGANGERS OF THE ORIGINAL FIVE X-MEN HAVE BEEN RUNNING AROUND SINCE SOMETIME LAST YEAR.
ARE THERE PICS? IF THERE AREN'T PICS IT DIDN'T HAPPEN.
DID YOU SNOPES IT? YOU GOTTA SNOPES IT.
SCREW THIS. YOU GUYS WANNA STAND HERE AND TALK INTERNET NONSENSE, DO IT UP.
I'M GOING TO GET MY HANDS DIRTY.
THAT'S OUR CUE.
LAURA, WAIT!
YOU SAW WHAT HAPPENED WHEN SCOTT TRIED TO TAKE THESE GUYS ON BY HIMSELF.
NO OFFENSE TO SCOTT...
...BUT I'M WOLVERINE.
AND HE'S NOT.
SNIKT
SNIKT

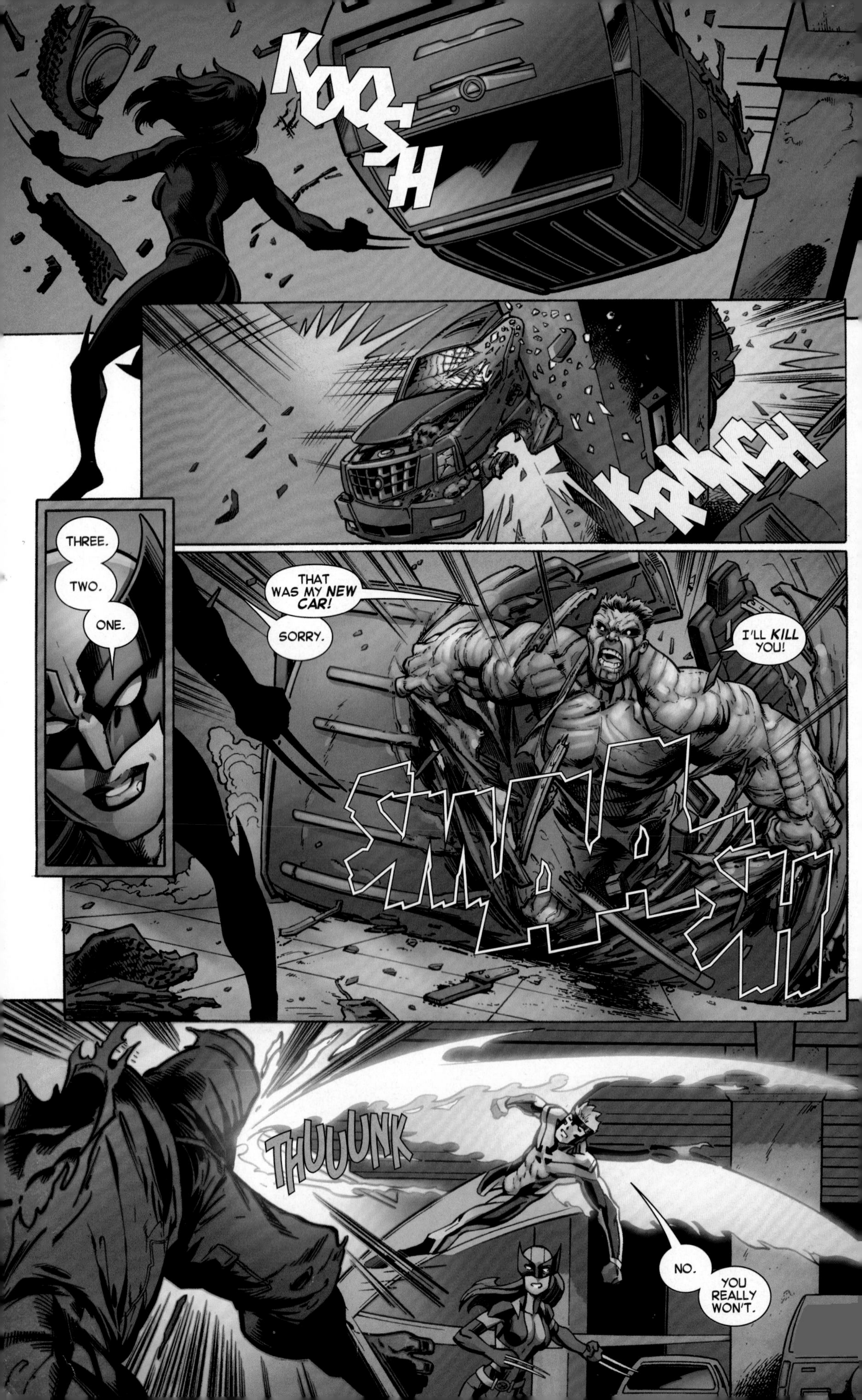
KOOSH
KRNCH
THREE.
TWO.
ONE.
THAT WAS MY NEW CAR!
SORRY.
I'LL KILL YOU!
SMASH
THUUUNK
NO.
YOU REALLY WON'T.

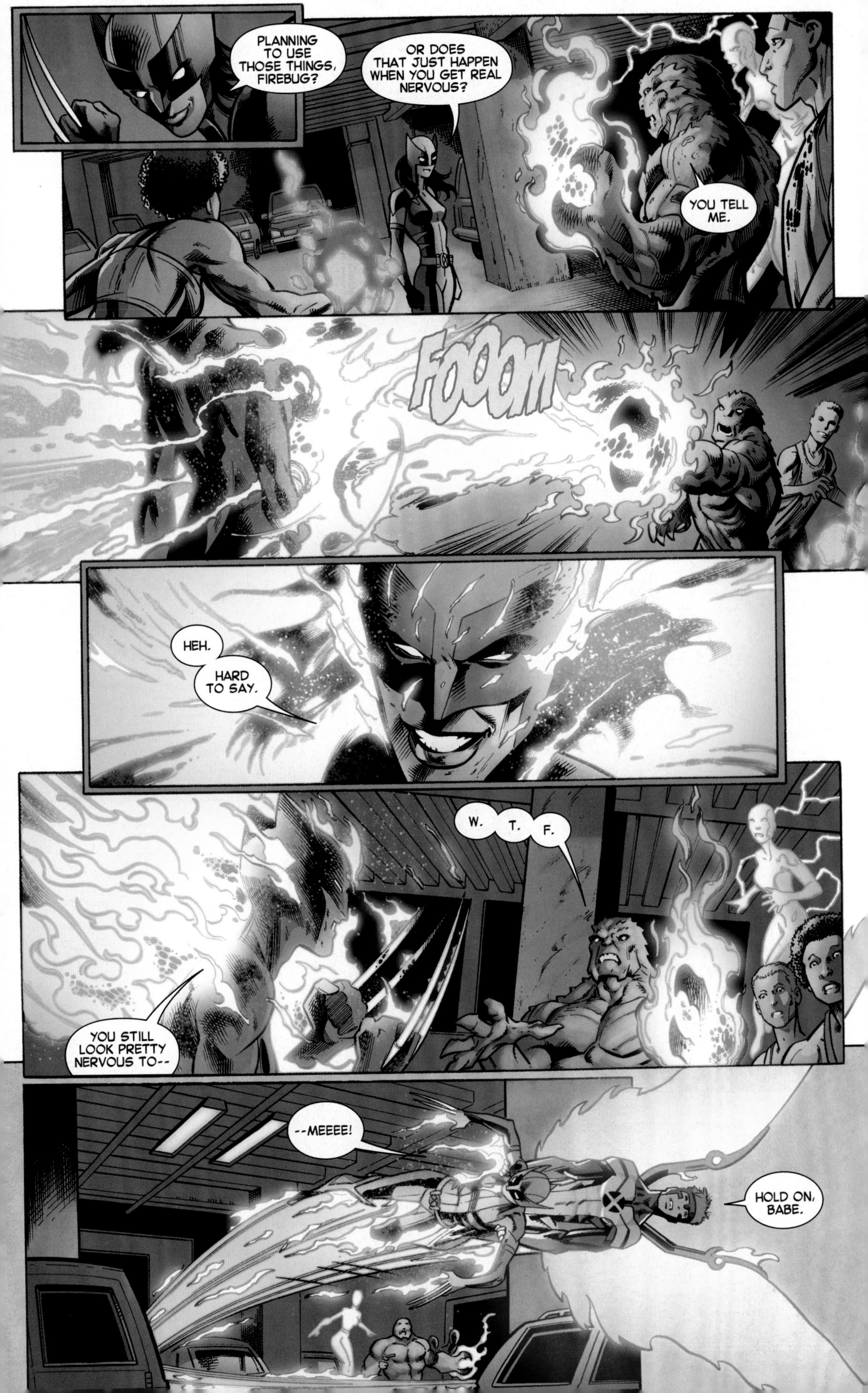
PLANNING TO USE THOSE THINGS, FIREBUG?
OR DOES THAT JUST HAPPEN WHEN YOU GET REAL NERVOUS?
YOU TELL ME.
FOOOM
HEH.
HARD TO SAY.
W.
T.
F.
YOU STILL LOOK PRETTY NERVOUS TO--
--MEEEE!
HOLD ON, BABE.

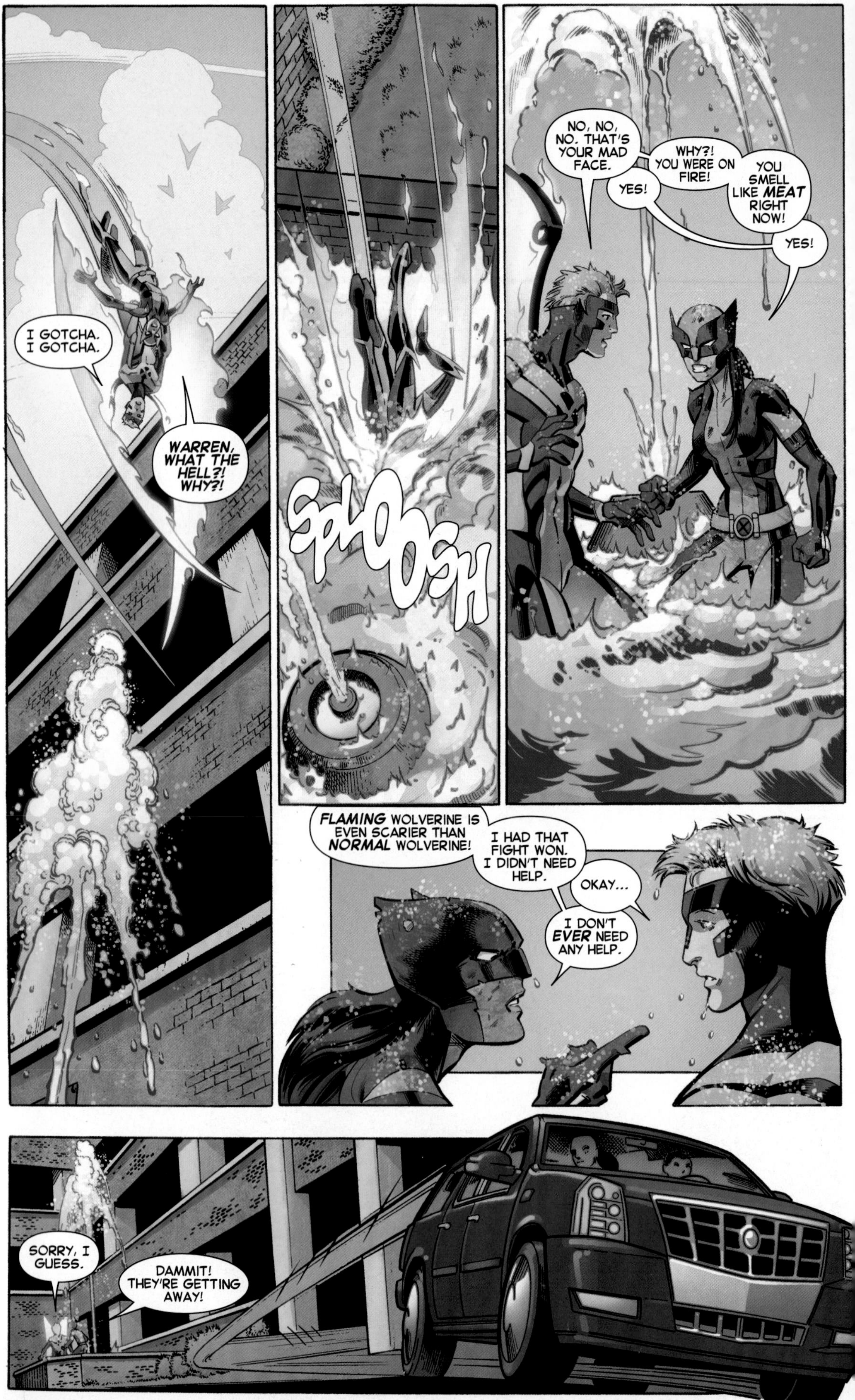
I GOTCHA. I GOTCHA.
WARREN, WHAT THE HELL?! WHY?!
SPLOOSH
NO, NO, NO. THAT'S YOUR MAD FACE.
YES!
WHY?! YOU WERE ON FIRE!
YOU SMELL LIKE MEAT RIGHT NOW!
YES!
FLAMING WOLVERINE IS EVEN SCARIER THAN NORMAL WOLVERINE!
I HAD THAT FIGHT WON. I DIDN'T NEED HELP.
OKAY...
I DON'T EVER NEED ANY HELP.
SORRY, I GUESS.
DAMMIT! THEY'RE GETTING AWAY!

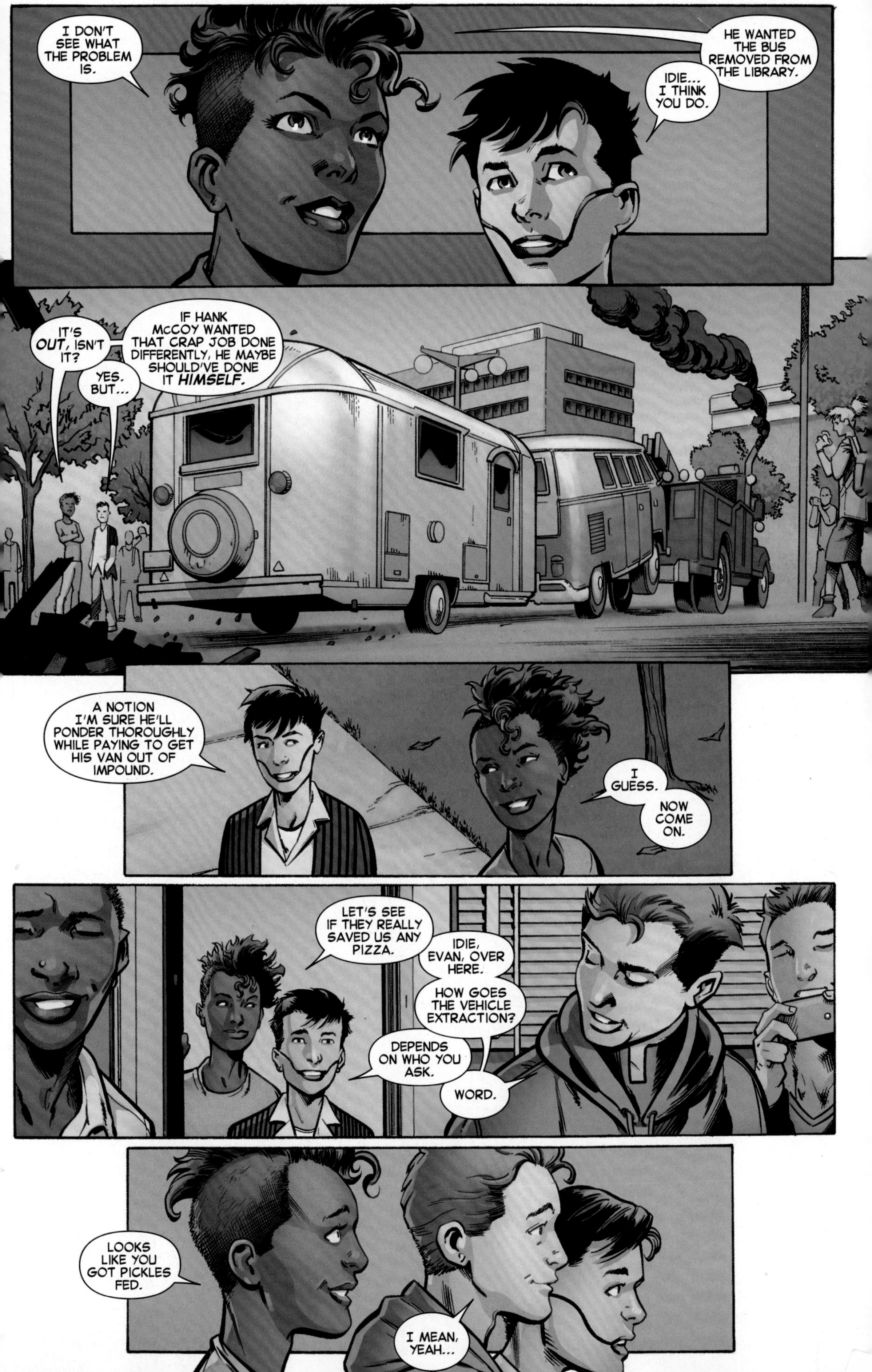

I DON'T SEE WHAT THE PROBLEM IS.
HE WANTED THE BUS REMOVED FROM THE LIBRARY.
IDIE... I THINK YOU DO.
IT'S OUT, ISN'T IT?
YES. BUT...
IF HANK McCOY WANTED THAT CRAP JOB DONE DIFFERENTLY, HE MAYBE SHOULD'VE DONE IT HIMSELF.
A NOTION I'M SURE HE'LL PONDER THOROUGHLY WHILE PAYING TO GET HIS VAN OUT OF IMPOUND.
I GUESS.
NOW COME ON.
LET'S SEE IF THEY REALLY SAVED US ANY PIZZA.
IDIE, EVAN, OVER HERE.
HOW GOES THE VEHICLE EXTRACTION?
DEPENDS ON WHO YOU ASK.
WORD.
LOOKS LIKE YOU GOT PICKLES FED.
I MEAN, YEAH...

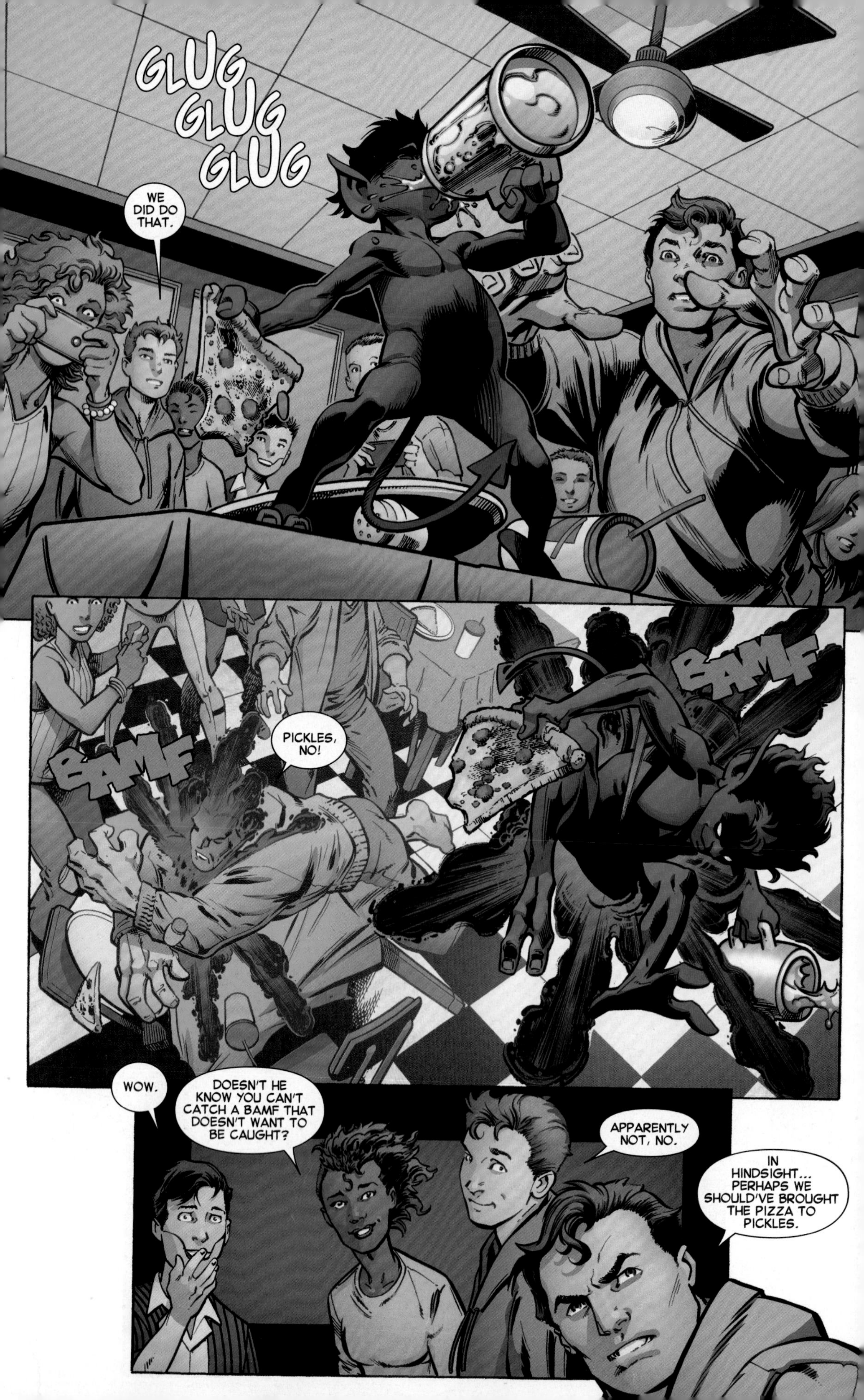
GLUG GLUG GLUG
WE DID DO THAT.
PICKLES, NO!
BAMF
BAMF
WOW.
DOESN'T HE KNOW YOU CAN'T CATCH A BAMF THAT DOESN'T WANT TO BE CAUGHT?
APPARENTLY NOT, NO.
IN HINDSIGHT... PERHAPS WE SHOULD'VE BROUGHT THE PIZZA TO PICKLES.

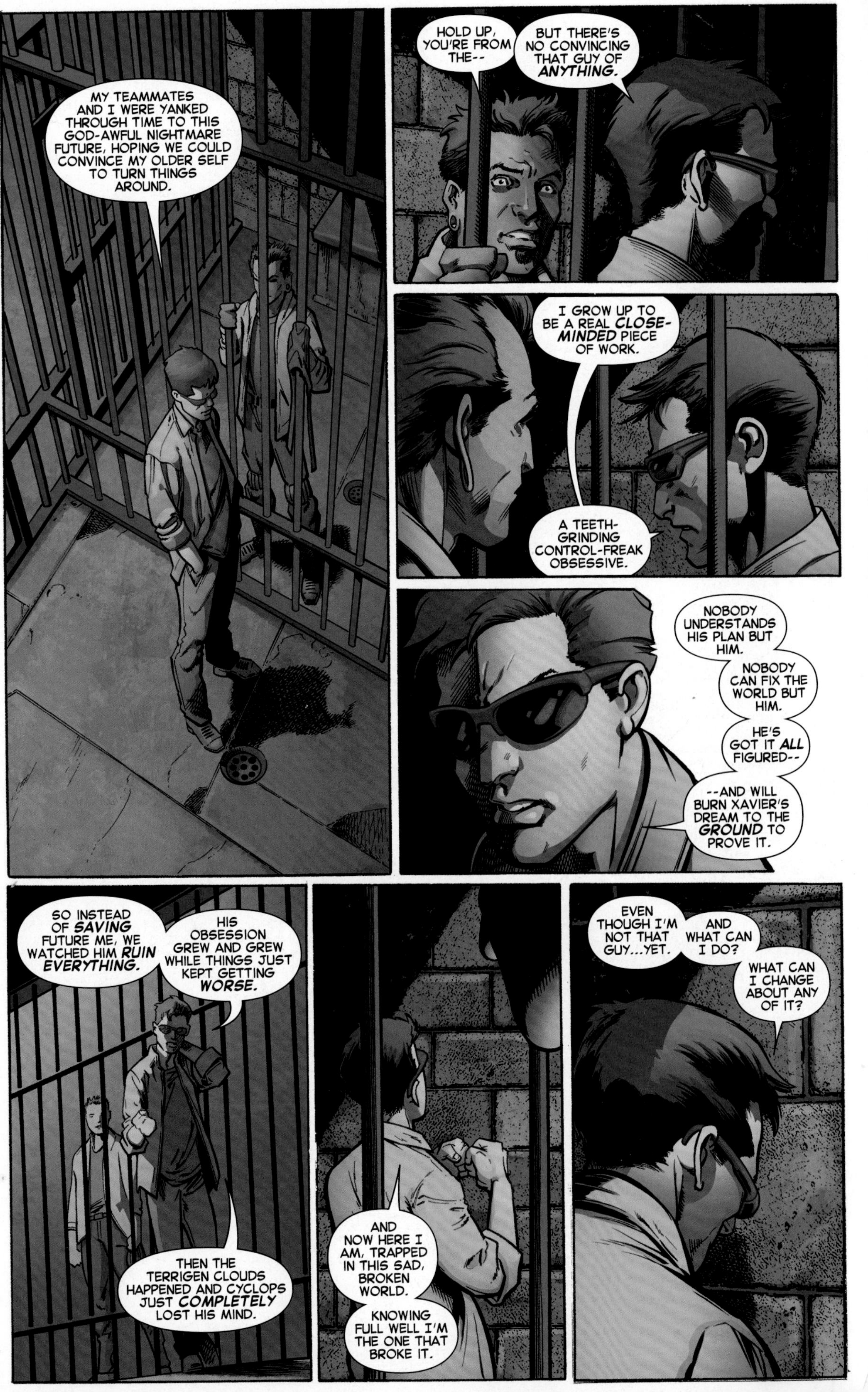
MY TEAMMATES AND I WERE YANKED THROUGH TIME TO THIS GOD-AWFUL NIGHTMARE FUTURE, HOPING WE COULD CONVINCE MY OLDER SELF TO TURN THINGS AROUND.
HOLD UP, YOU'RE FROM THE--
BUT THERE'S NO CONVINCING THAT GUY OF ANYTHING.
I GROW UP TO BE A REAL CLOSE-MINDED PIECE OF WORK.
A TEETH-GRINDING CONTROL-FREAK OBSESSIVE.
NOBODY UNDERSTANDS HIS PLAN BUT HIM.
NOBODY CAN FIX THE WORLD BUT HIM.
HE'S GOT IT ALL FIGURED--
--AND WILL BURN XAVIER'S DREAM TO THE GROUND TO PROVE IT.
SO INSTEAD OF SAVING FUTURE ME, WE WATCHED HIM RUIN EVERYTHING.
HIS OBSESSION GREW AND GREW WHILE THINGS JUST KEPT GETTING WORSE.
THEN THE TERRIGEN CLOUDS HAPPENED AND CYCLOPS JUST COMPLETELY LOST HIS MIND.
AND NOW HERE I AM, TRAPPED IN THIS SAD, BROKEN WORLD.
KNOWING FULL WELL I'M THE ONE THAT BROKE IT.
EVEN THOUGH I'M NOT THAT GUY...YET.
AND WHAT CAN I DO?
WHAT CAN I CHANGE ABOUT ANY OF IT?

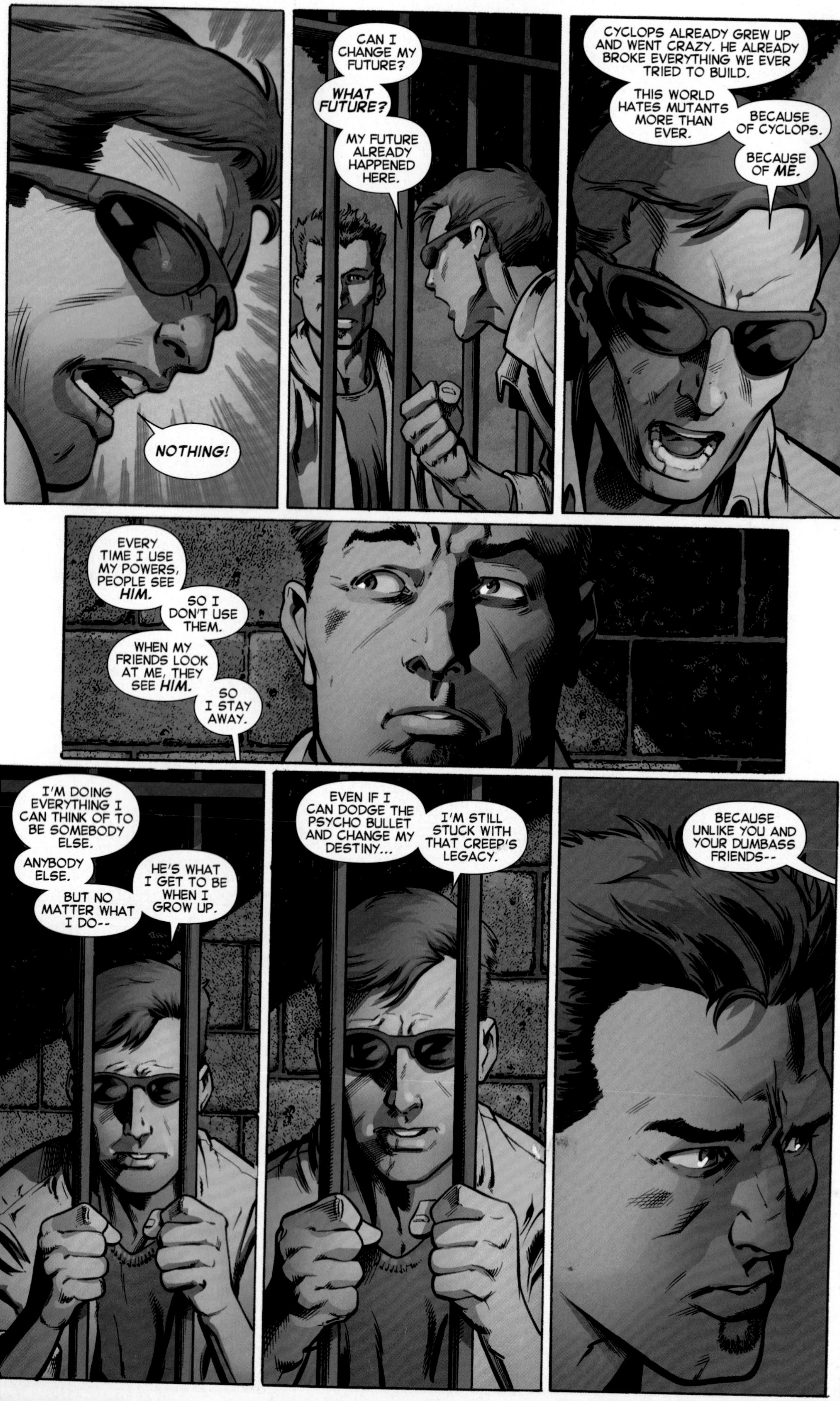
NOTHING!
CAN I CHANGE MY FUTURE?
WHAT FUTURE?
MY FUTURE ALREADY HAPPENED HERE.
CYCLOPS ALREADY GREW UP AND WENT CRAZY. HE ALREADY BROKE EVERYTHING WE EVER TRIED TO BUILD.
THIS WORLD HATES MUTANTS MORE THAN EVER.
BECAUSE OF CYCLOPS.
BECAUSE OF ME.
EVERY TIME I USE MY POWERS, PEOPLE SEE HIM.
SO I DON'T USE THEM.
WHEN MY FRIENDS LOOK AT ME, THEY SEE HIM.
SO I STAY AWAY.
I'M DOING EVERYTHING I CAN THINK OF TO BE SOMEBODY ELSE.
ANYBODY ELSE.
BUT NO MATTER WHAT I DO--
HE'S WHAT I GET TO BE WHEN I GROW UP.
EVEN IF I CAN DODGE THE PSYCHO BULLET AND CHANGE MY DESTINY...
I'M STILL STUCK WITH THAT CREEP'S LEGACY.
BECAUSE UNLIKE YOU AND YOUR DUMBASS FRIENDS--

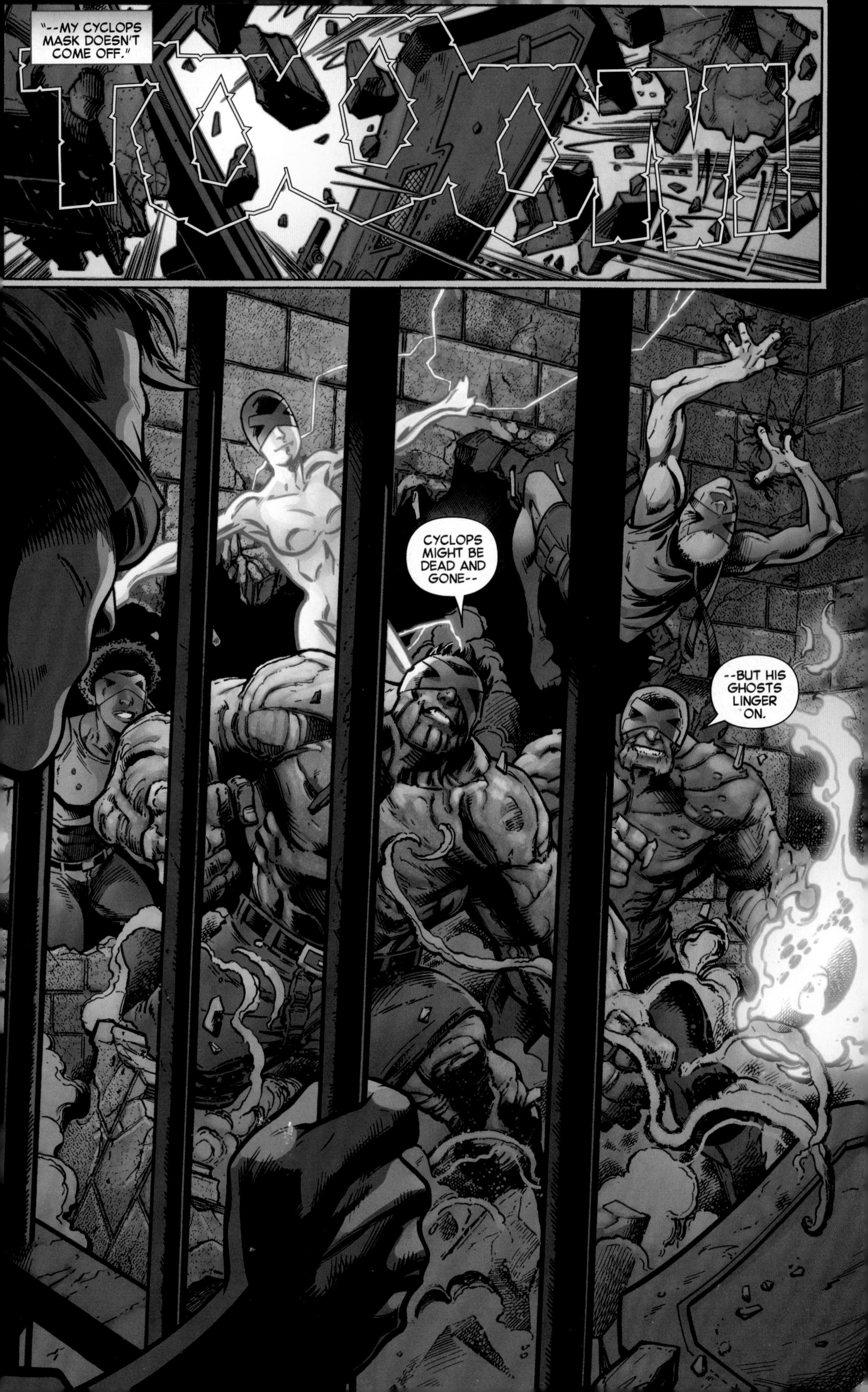
"--MY CYCLOPS MASK DOESN'T COME OFF."
CYCLOPS MIGHT BE DEAD AND GONE--
--BUT HIS GHOSTS LINGER ON.

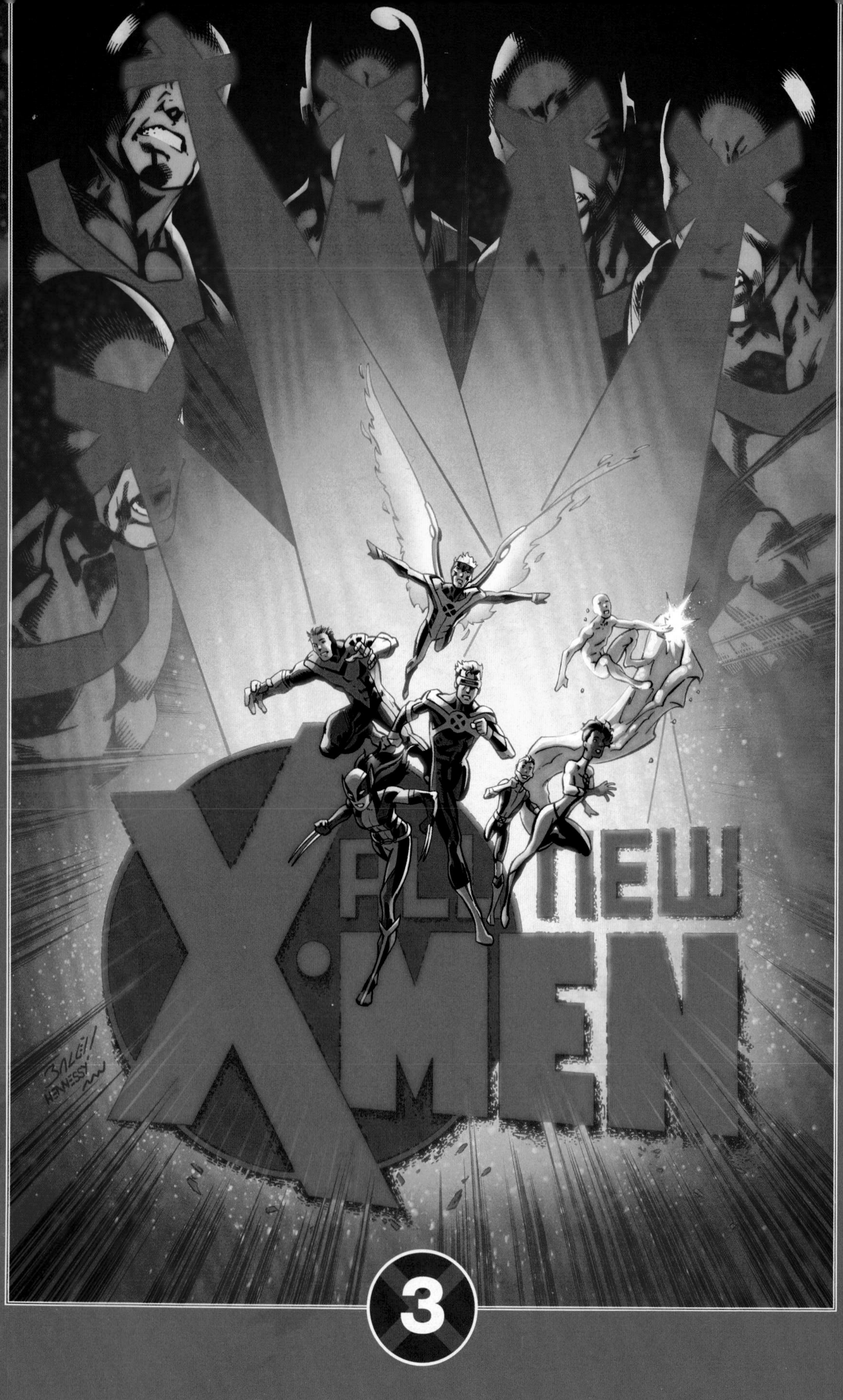
NEW
X·MEN
HENNESSY
3

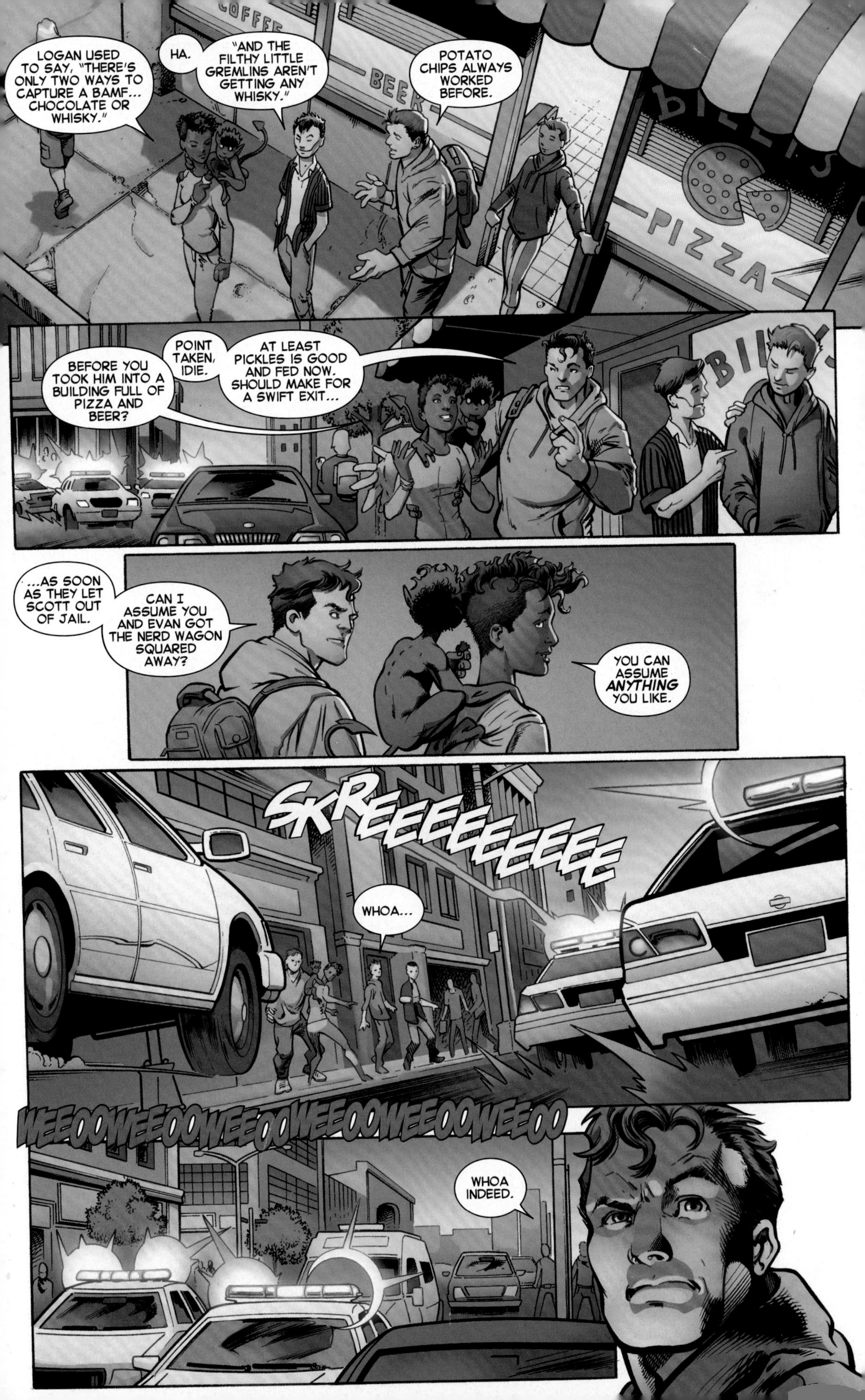
COFFEE
BEER
PIZZA
LOGAN USED TO SAY, "THERE'S ONLY TWO WAYS TO CAPTURE A BAMF... CHOCOLATE OR WHISKY."
HA.
"AND THE FILTHY LITTLE GREMLINS AREN'T GETTING ANY WHISKY."
POTATO CHIPS ALWAYS WORKED BEFORE.
BEFORE YOU TOOK HIM INTO A BUILDING FULL OF PIZZA AND BEER?
POINT TAKEN, IDIE.
AT LEAST PICKLES IS GOOD AND FED NOW. SHOULD MAKE FOR A SWIFT EXIT...
...AS SOON AS THEY LET SCOTT OUT OF JAIL.
CAN I ASSUME YOU AND EVAN GOT THE NERD WAGON SQUARED AWAY?
YOU CAN ASSUME ANYTHING YOU LIKE.
SKREEEEEEEEEEE
WHOA...
WEEOOWEEOOWEEOOWEEOOWEEOOWEEOO
WHOA INDEED.

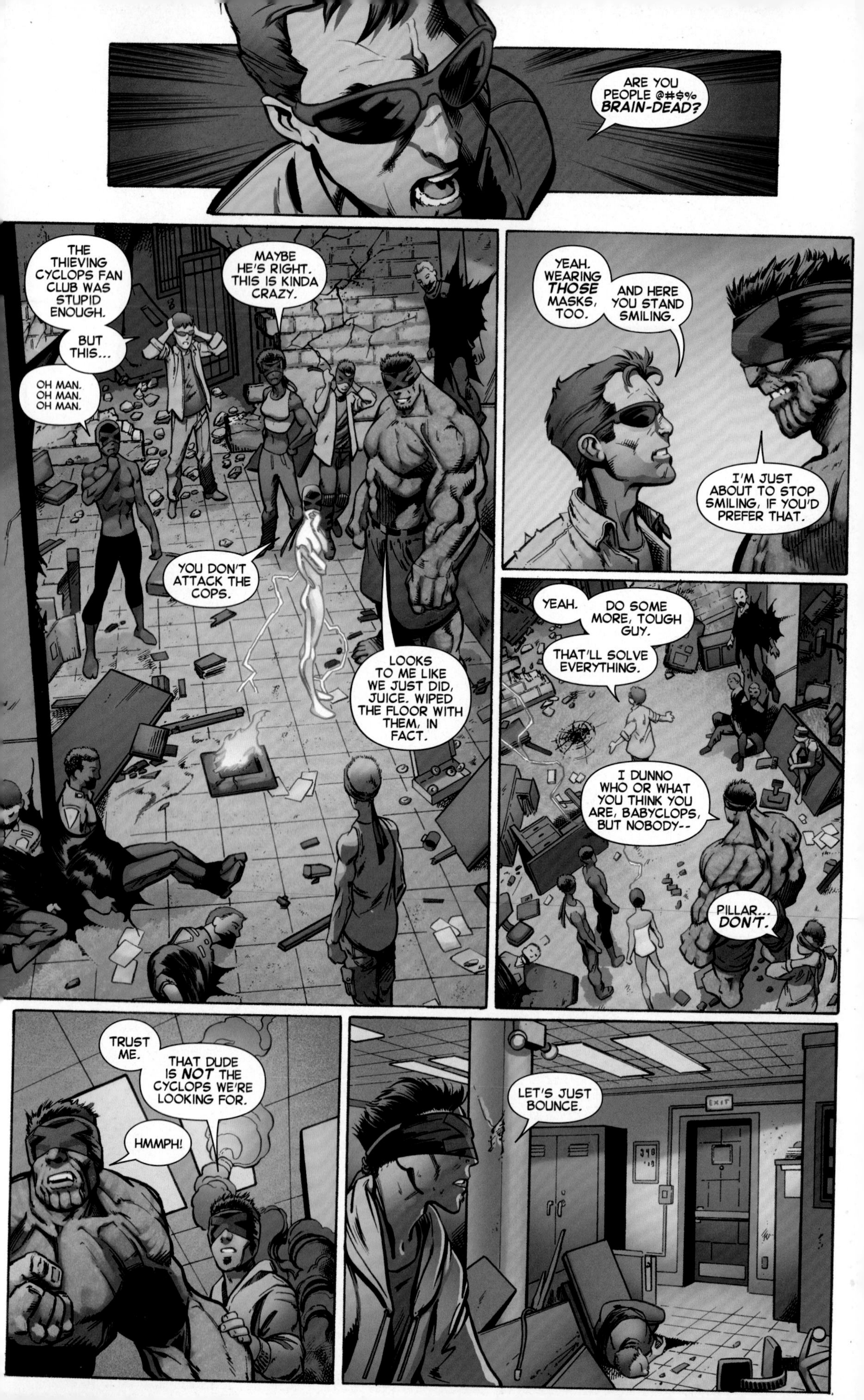
ARE YOU PEOPLE @#$% BRAIN-DEAD?
THE THIEVING CYCLOPS FAN CLUB WAS STUPID ENOUGH.
BUT THIS...
OH MAN. OH MAN. OH MAN.
MAYBE HE'S RIGHT. THIS IS KINDA CRAZY.
YOU DON'T ATTACK THE COPS.
LOOKS TO ME LIKE WE JUST DID, JUICE. WIPED THE FLOOR WITH THEM, IN FACT.
YEAH. WEARING THOSE MASKS, TOO.
AND HERE YOU STAND SMILING.
I'M JUST ABOUT TO STOP SMILING, IF YOU'D PREFER THAT.
YEAH.
DO SOME MORE, TOUGH GUY.
THAT'LL SOLVE EVERYTHING.
I DUNNO WHO OR WHAT YOU THINK YOU ARE, BABYCLOPS, BUT NOBODY--
PILLAR... DON'T.
TRUST ME.
THAT DUDE IS NOT THE CYCLOPS WE'RE LOOKING FOR.
HMMPH!
LET'S JUST BOUNCE.

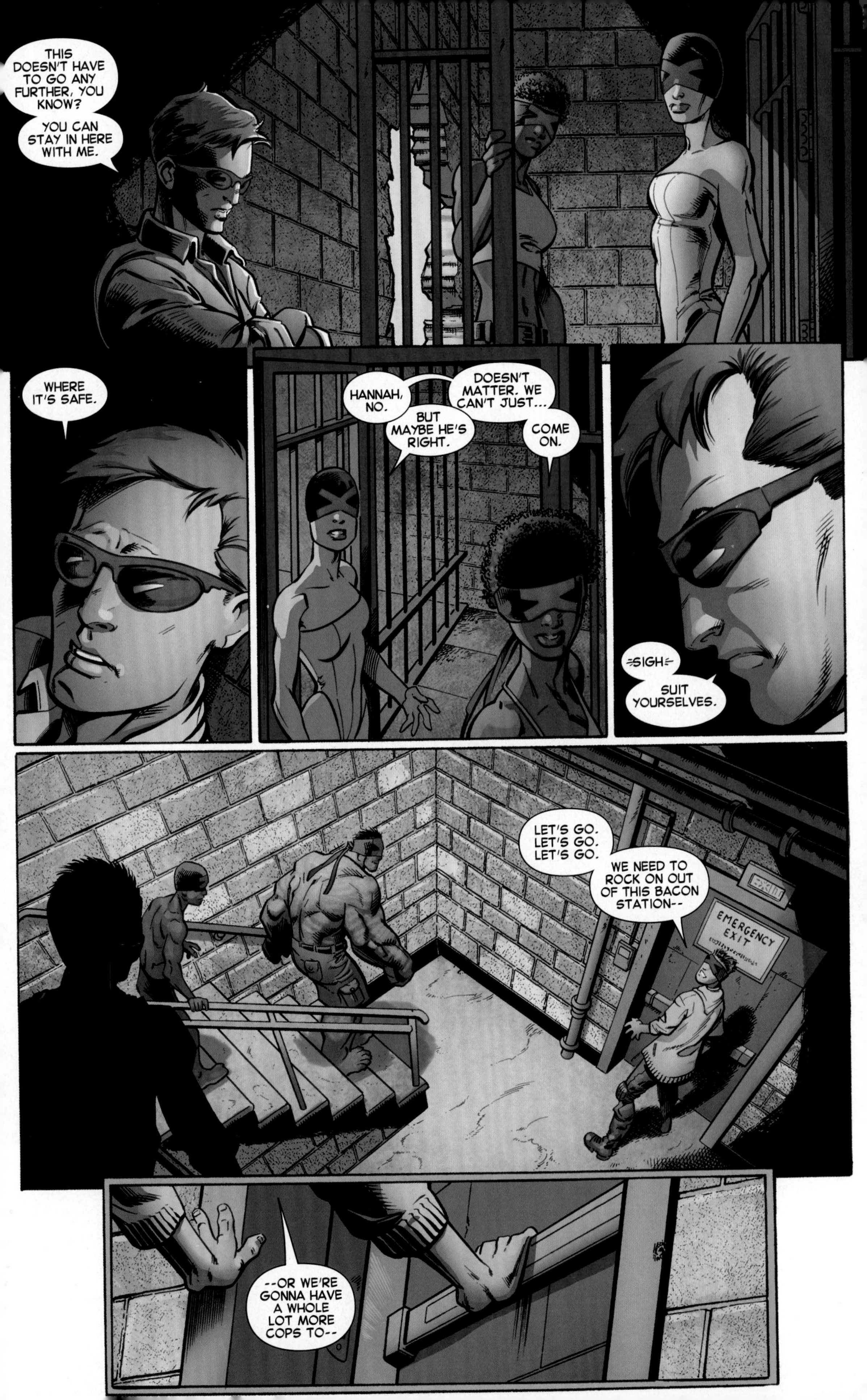
THIS DOESN'T HAVE TO GO ANY FURTHER, YOU KNOW?
YOU CAN STAY IN HERE WITH ME.
WHERE IT'S SAFE.
HANNAH, NO.
DOESN'T MATTER. WE CAN'T JUST...
BUT MAYBE HE'S RIGHT.
COME ON.
=SIGH=
SUIT YOURSELVES.
LET'S GO. LET'S GO. LET'S GO.
WE NEED TO ROCK ON OUT OF THIS BACON STATION--
EMERGENCY EXIT
EXIT
--OR WE'RE GONNA HAVE A WHOLE LOT MORE COPS TO--

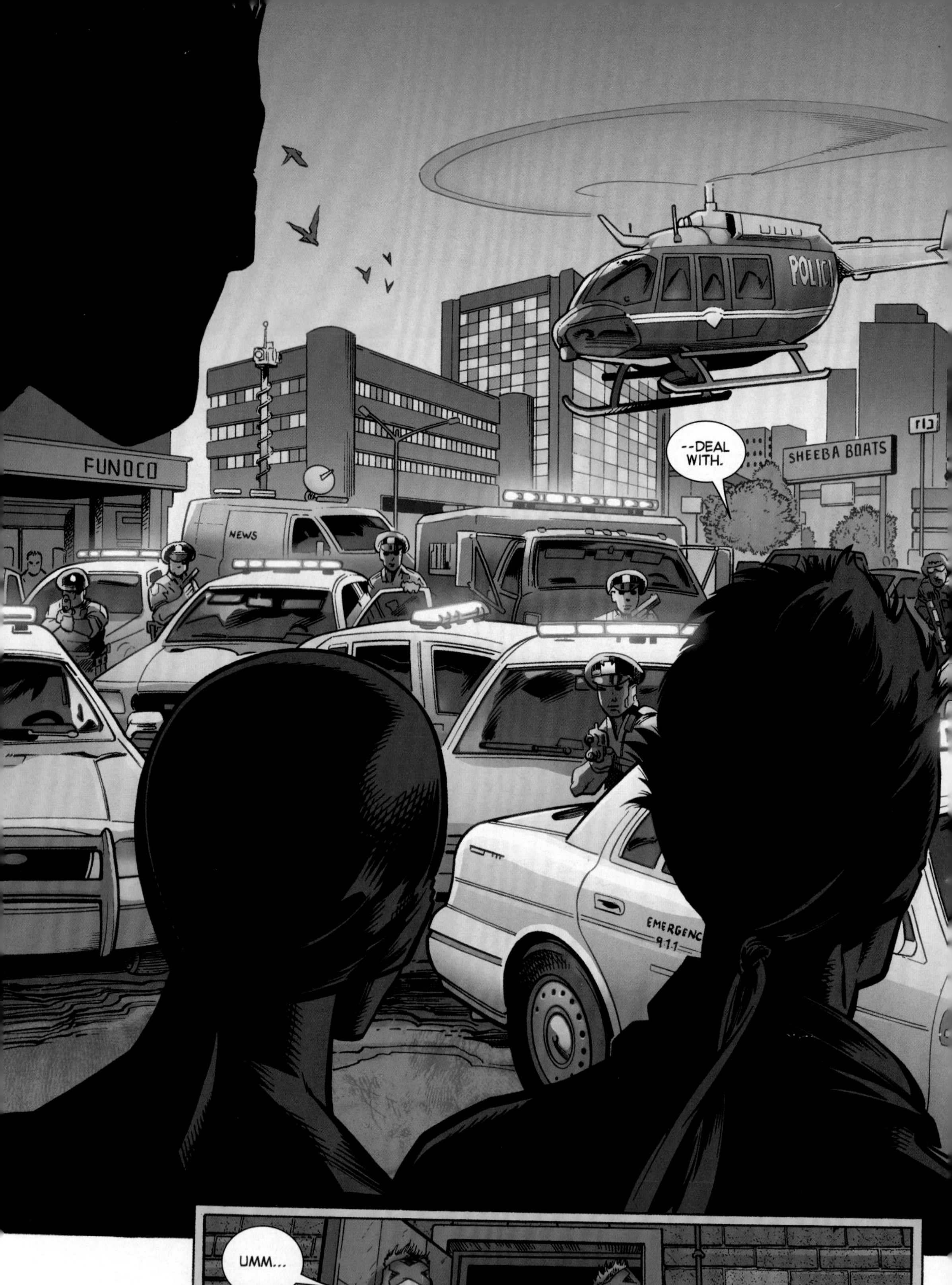
FUNDCO
NEWS
POLICE
SHEEBA BOATS
--DEAL WITH.
EMERGENC
911
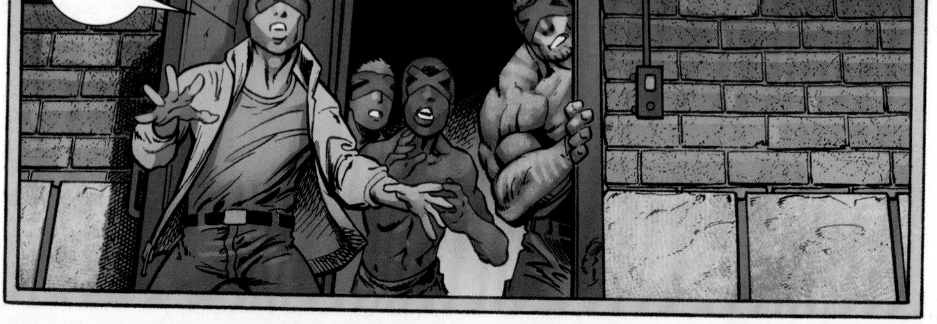
UMM...

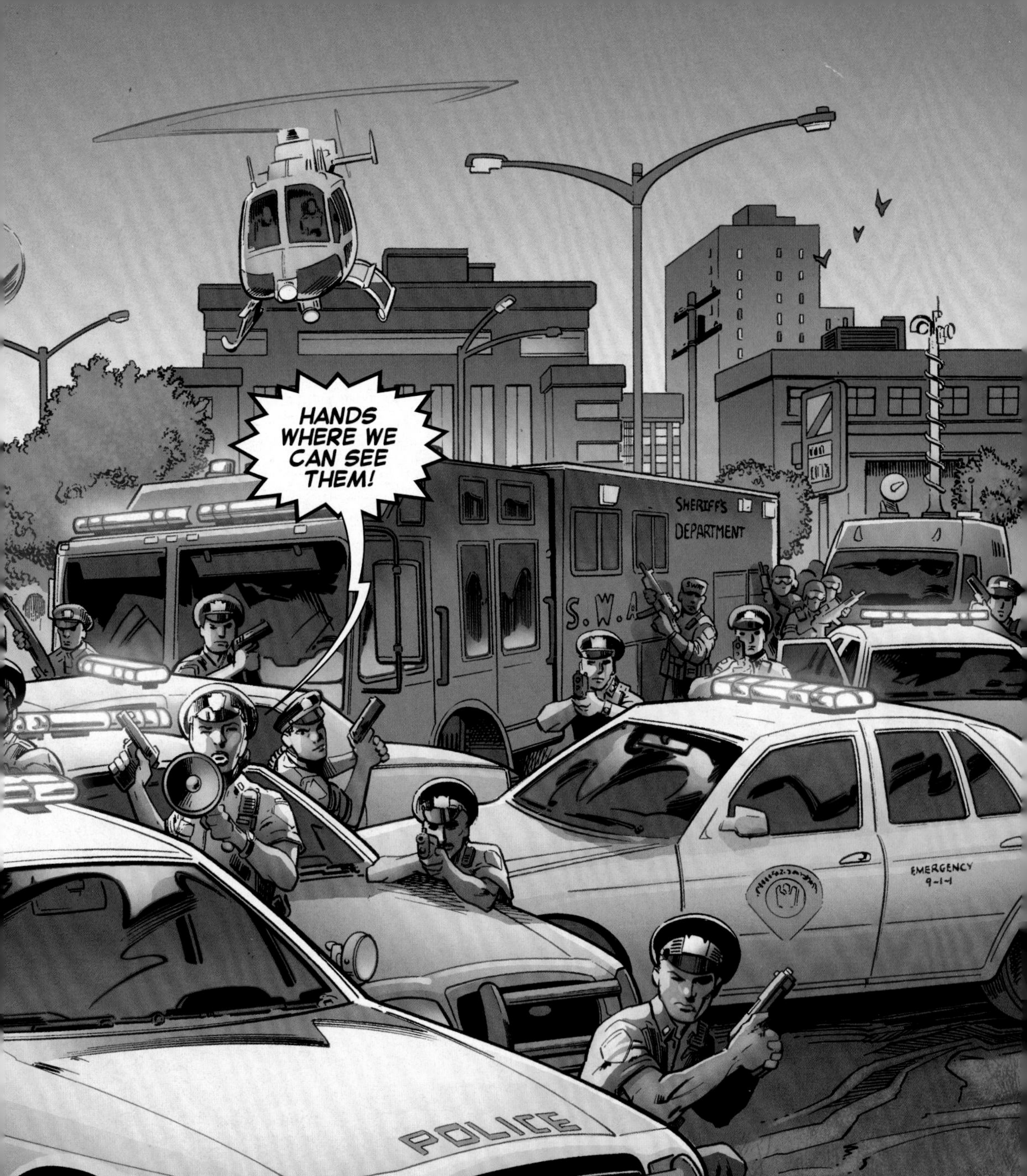
HANDS WHERE WE CAN SEE THEM!
SHERIFF'S DEPARTMENT
S.W.A
SWAT
EMERGENCY 9-1-1
POLICE
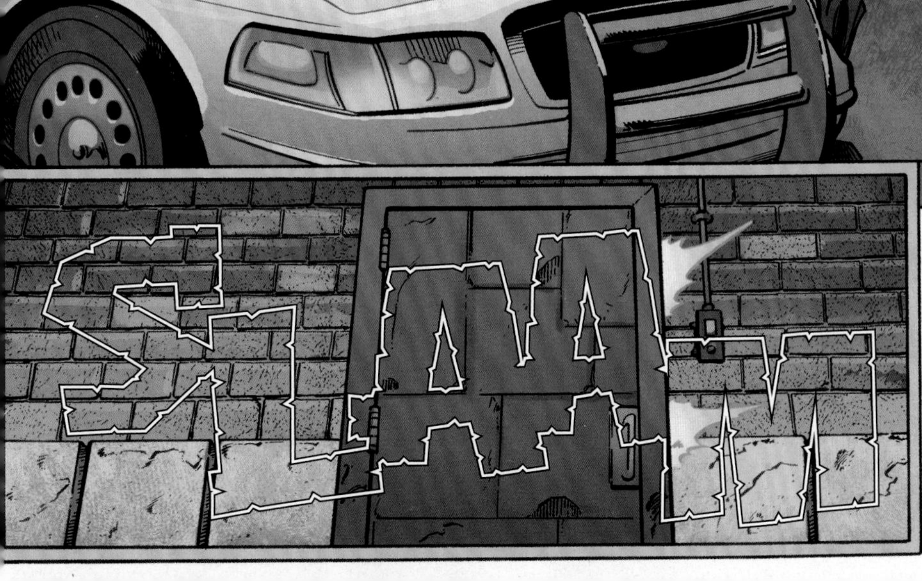
SLAM

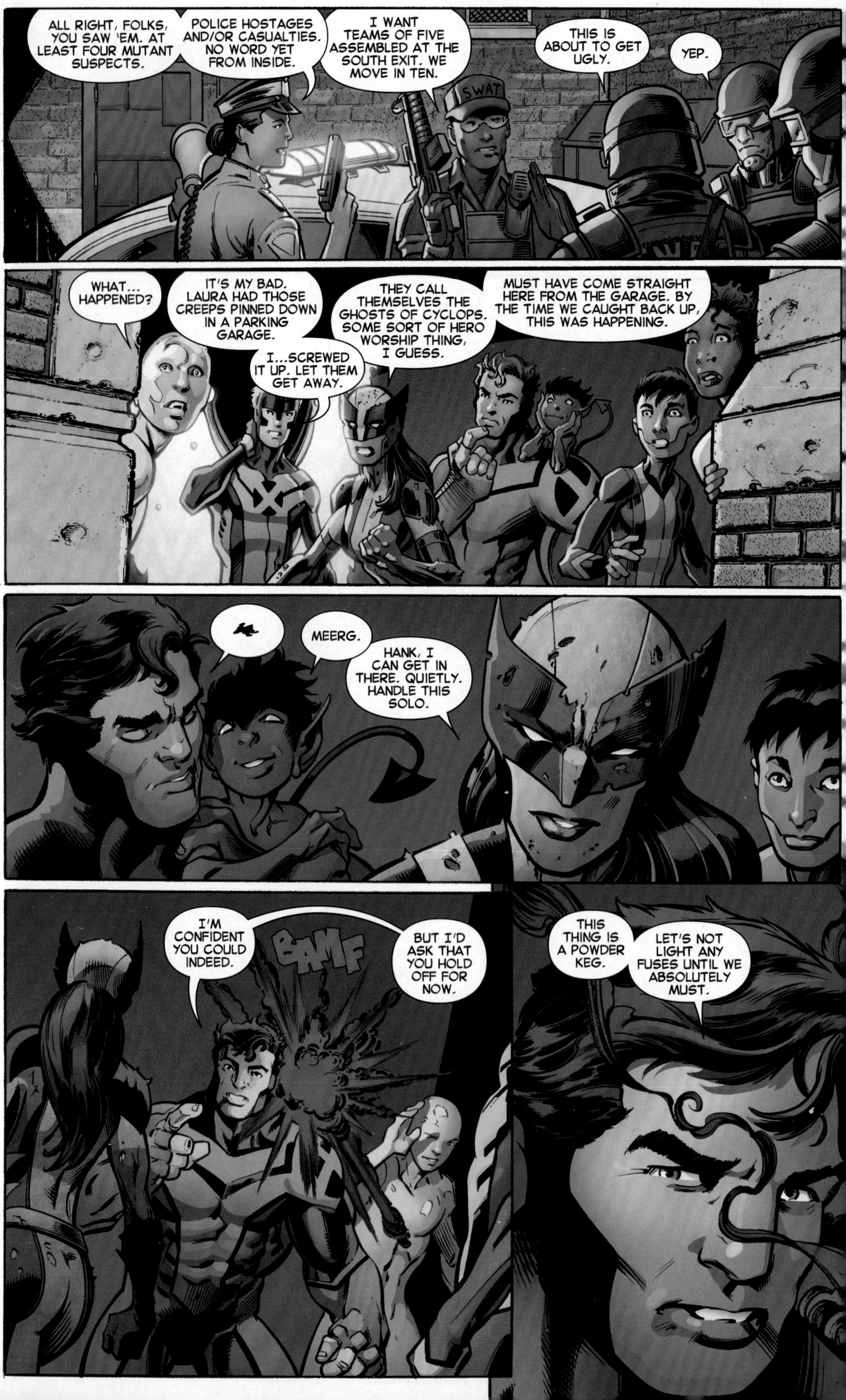
ALL RIGHT, FOLKS, YOU SAW 'EM. AT LEAST FOUR MUTANT SUSPECTS.
POLICE HOSTAGES AND/OR CASUALTIES. NO WORD YET FROM INSIDE.
I WANT TEAMS OF FIVE ASSEMBLED AT THE SOUTH EXIT. WE MOVE IN TEN.
THIS IS ABOUT TO GET UGLY.
YEP.
SWAT
WHAT... HAPPENED?
IT'S MY BAD. LAURA HAD THOSE CREEPS PINNED DOWN IN A PARKING GARAGE.
I...SCREWED IT UP. LET THEM GET AWAY.
THEY CALL THEMSELVES THE GHOSTS OF CYCLOPS. SOME SORT OF HERO WORSHIP THING, I GUESS.
MUST HAVE COME STRAIGHT HERE FROM THE GARAGE. BY THE TIME WE CAUGHT BACK UP, THIS WAS HAPPENING.
MEERG.
HANK, I CAN GET IN THERE. QUIETLY. HANDLE THIS SOLO.
I'M CONFIDENT YOU COULD INDEED.
BAMF
BUT I'D ASK THAT YOU HOLD OFF FOR NOW.
THIS THING IS A POWDER KEG.
LET'S NOT LIGHT ANY FUSES UNTIL WE ABSOLUTELY MUST.

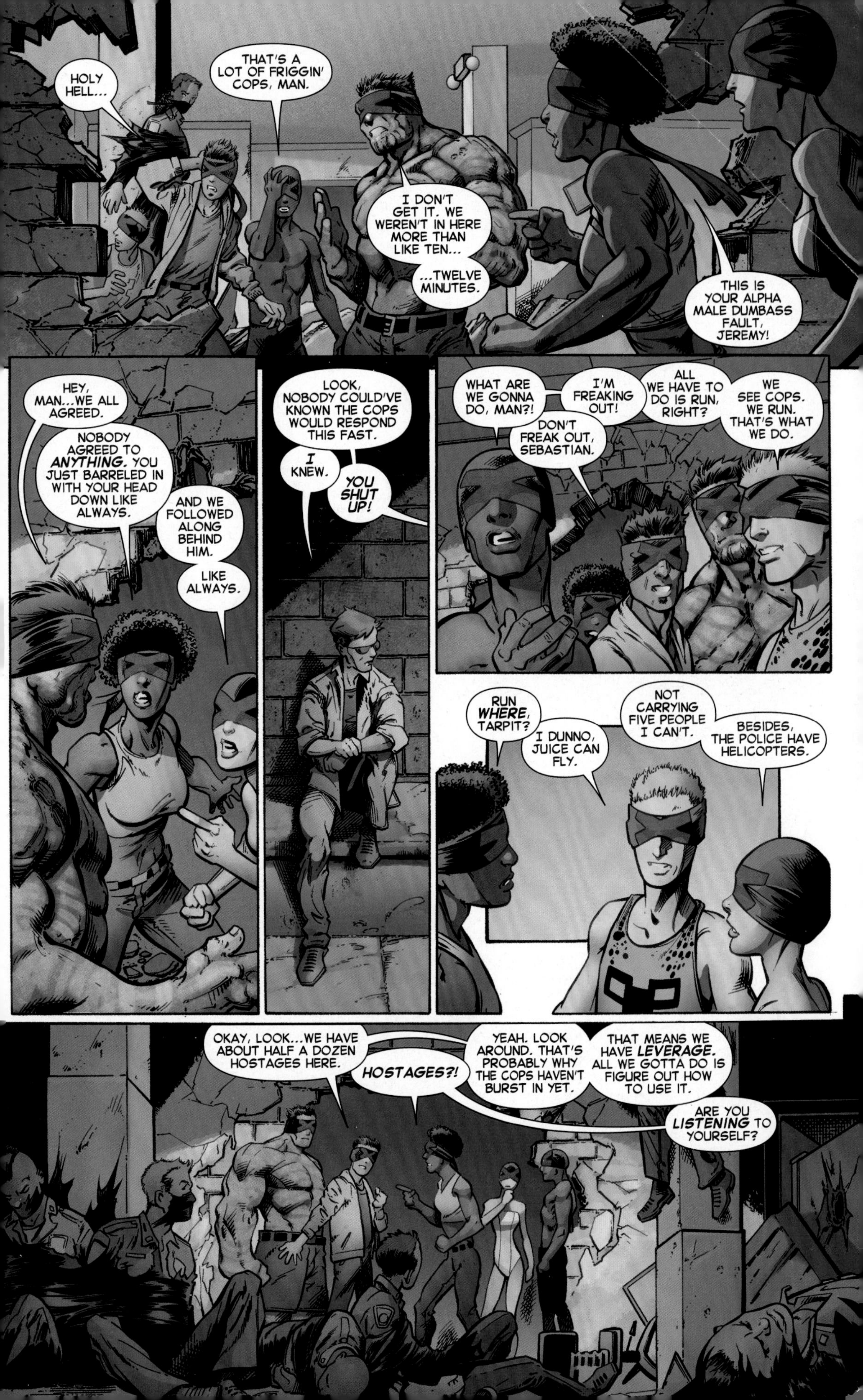
HOLY HELL...
THAT'S A LOT OF FRIGGIN' COPS, MAN.
I DON'T GET IT. WE WEREN'T IN HERE MORE THAN LIKE TEN...
...TWELVE MINUTES.
THIS IS YOUR ALPHA MALE DUMBASS FAULT, JEREMY!
HEY, MAN...WE ALL AGREED.
NOBODY AGREED TO ANYTHING. YOU JUST BARRELED IN WITH YOUR HEAD DOWN LIKE ALWAYS.
AND WE FOLLOWED ALONG BEHIND HIM.
LIKE ALWAYS.
LOOK, NOBODY COULD'VE KNOWN THE COPS WOULD RESPOND THIS FAST.
I KNEW.
YOU SHUT UP!
WHAT ARE WE GONNA DO, MAN?!
I'M FREAKING OUT!
DON'T FREAK OUT, SEBASTIAN.
ALL WE HAVE TO DO IS RUN, RIGHT?
WE SEE COPS. WE RUN. THAT'S WHAT WE DO.
RUN WHERE, TARPIT?
I DUNNO, JUICE CAN FLY.
NOT CARRYING FIVE PEOPLE I CAN'T.
BESIDES, THE POLICE HAVE HELICOPTERS.
OKAY, LOOK...WE HAVE ABOUT HALF A DOZEN HOSTAGES HERE.
HOSTAGES?!
YEAH. LOOK AROUND. THAT'S PROBABLY WHY THE COPS HAVEN'T BURST IN YET.
THAT MEANS WE HAVE LEVERAGE. ALL WE GOTTA DO IS FIGURE OUT HOW TO USE IT.
ARE YOU LISTENING TO YOURSELF?

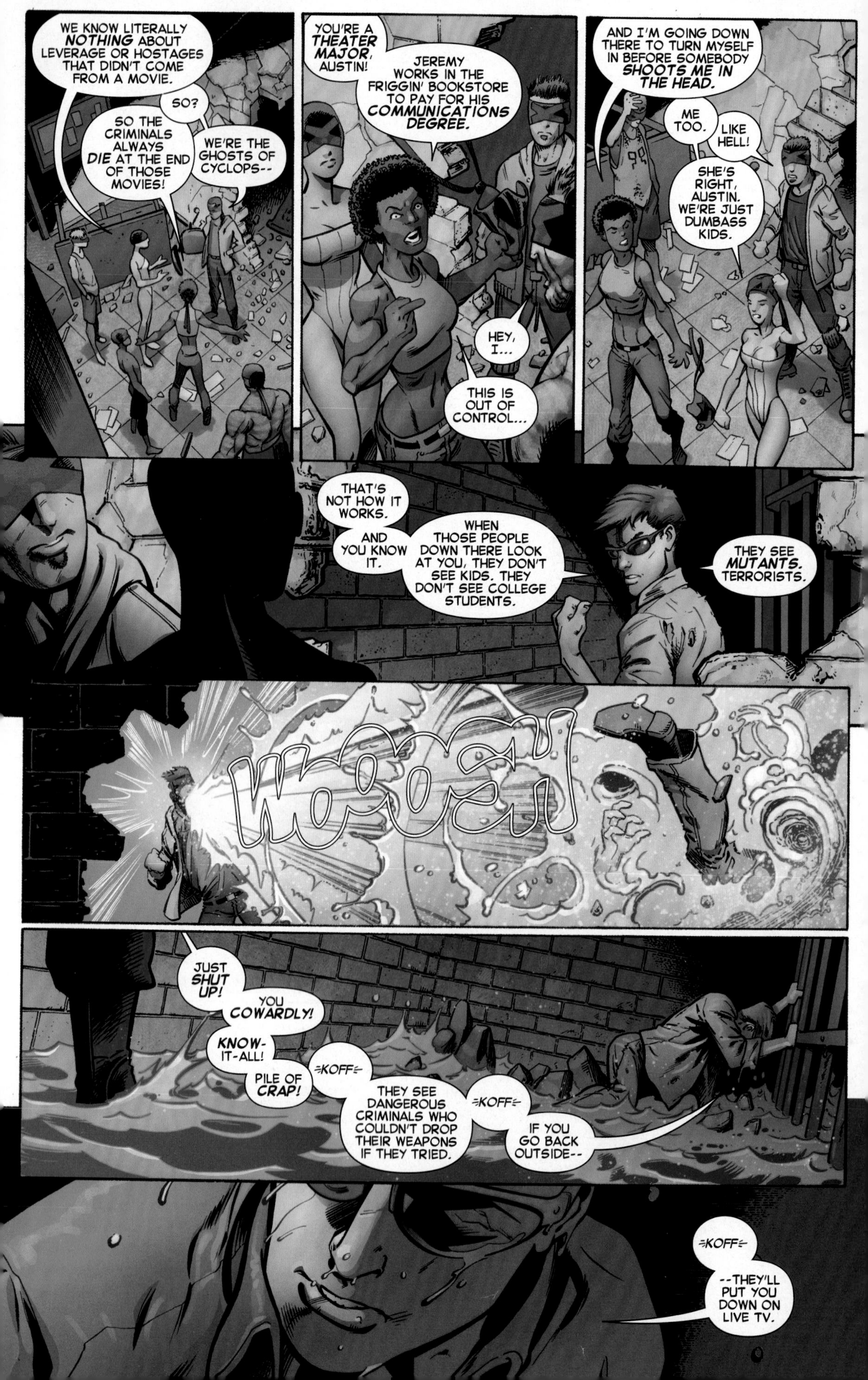
WE KNOW LITERALLY NOTHING ABOUT LEVERAGE OR HOSTAGES THAT DIDN'T COME FROM A MOVIE.
SO?
SO THE CRIMINALS ALWAYS DIE AT THE END OF THOSE MOVIES!
WE'RE THE GHOSTS OF CYCLOPS--
YOU'RE A THEATER MAJOR, AUSTIN!
JEREMY WORKS IN THE FRIGGIN' BOOKSTORE TO PAY FOR HIS COMMUNICATIONS DEGREE.
HEY, I...
THIS IS OUT OF CONTROL...
AND I'M GOING DOWN THERE TO TURN MYSELF IN BEFORE SOMEBODY SHOOTS ME IN THE HEAD.
ME TOO.
LIKE HELL!
SHE'S RIGHT, AUSTIN. WE'RE JUST DUMBASS KIDS.
THAT'S NOT HOW IT WORKS.
AND YOU KNOW IT.
WHEN THOSE PEOPLE DOWN THERE LOOK AT YOU, THEY DON'T SEE KIDS. THEY DON'T SEE COLLEGE STUDENTS.
THEY SEE MUTANTS. TERRORISTS.
WOOSH
JUST SHUT UP!
YOU COWARDLY!
KNOW-IT-ALL!
PILE OF CRAP!
=KOFF=
THEY SEE DANGEROUS CRIMINALS WHO COULDN'T DROP THEIR WEAPONS IF THEY TRIED.
=KOFF=
IF YOU GO BACK OUTSIDE--
=KOFF=
--THEY'LL PUT YOU DOWN ON LIVE TV.

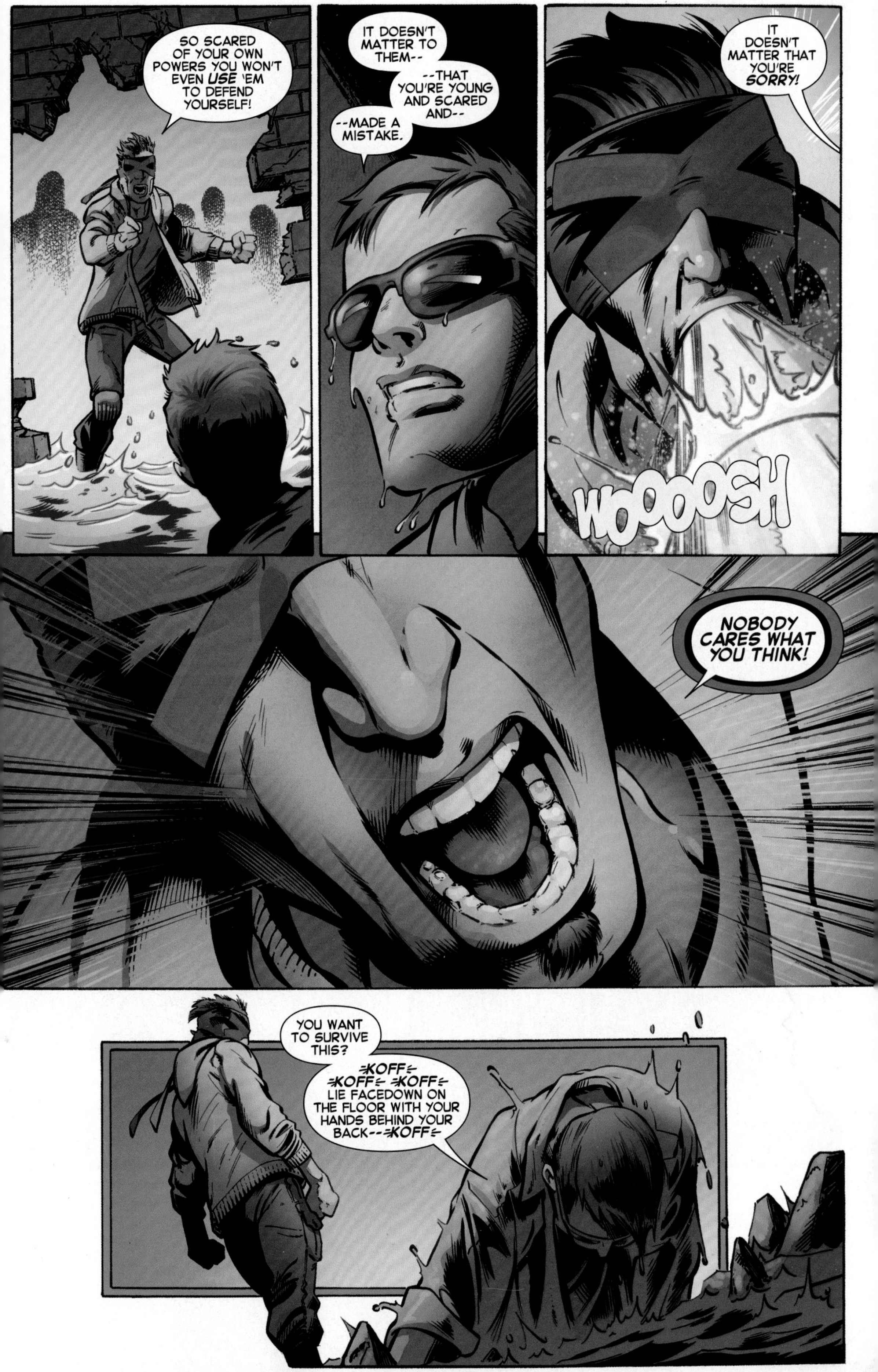
SO SCARED OF YOUR OWN POWERS YOU WON'T EVEN USE 'EM TO DEFEND YOURSELF!
IT DOESN'T MATTER TO THEM--
--THAT YOU'RE YOUNG AND SCARED AND--
--MADE A MISTAKE.
IT DOESN'T MATTER THAT YOU'RE SORRY!
WOOOOSH
NOBODY CARES WHAT YOU THINK!
YOU WANT TO SURVIVE THIS?
=KOFF= =KOFF= =KOFF= LIE FACEDOWN ON THE FLOOR WITH YOUR HANDS BEHIND YOUR BACK--=KOFF=

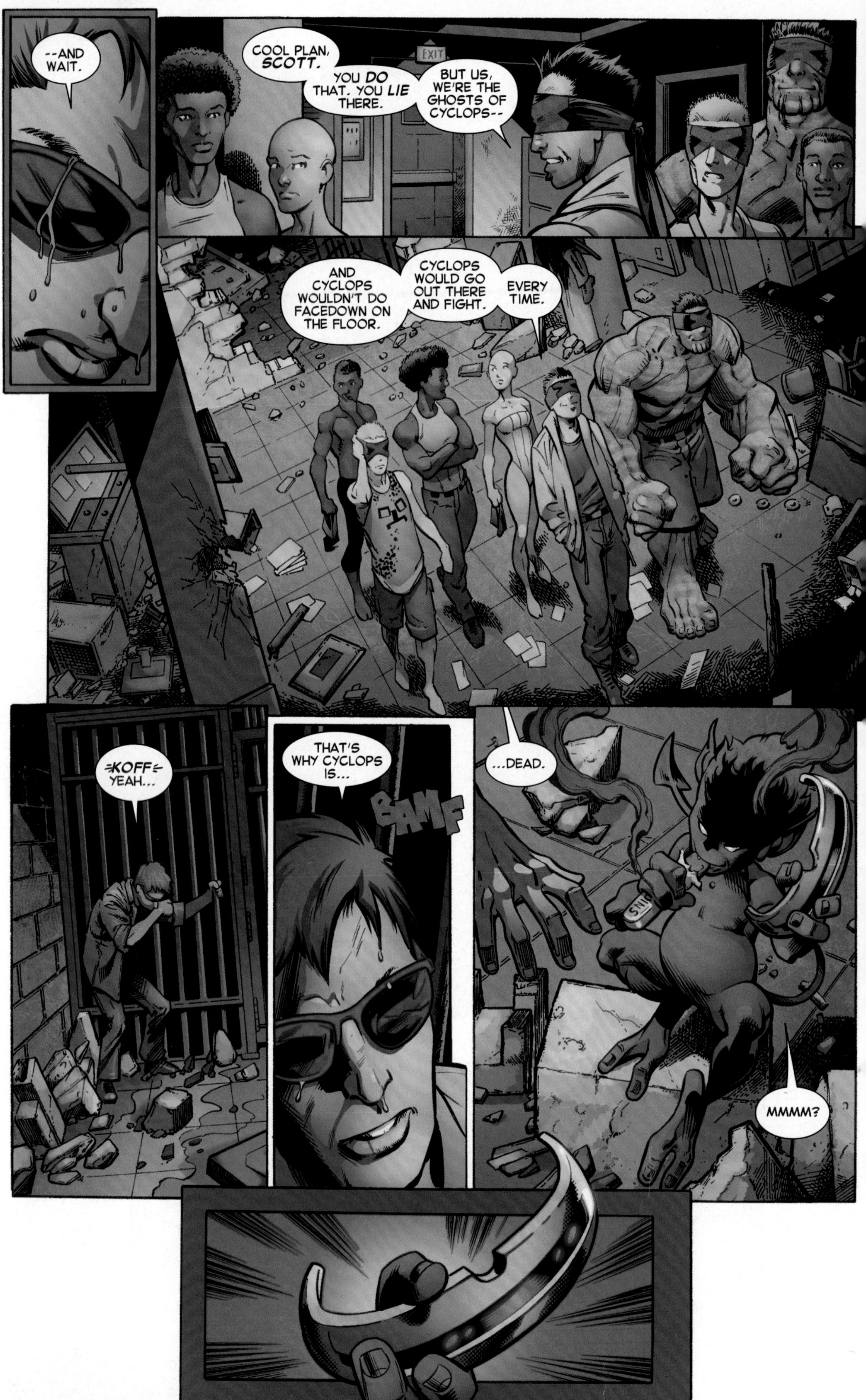
--AND WAIT.
COOL PLAN, SCOTT.
YOU DO THAT. YOU LIE THERE.
BUT US, WE'RE THE GHOSTS OF CYCLOPS--
EXIT
AND CYCLOPS WOULDN'T DO FACEDOWN ON THE FLOOR.
CYCLOPS WOULD GO OUT THERE AND FIGHT.
EVERY TIME.
KOFF YEAH...
THAT'S WHY CYCLOPS IS...
BAMF
...DEAD.
MMMM?

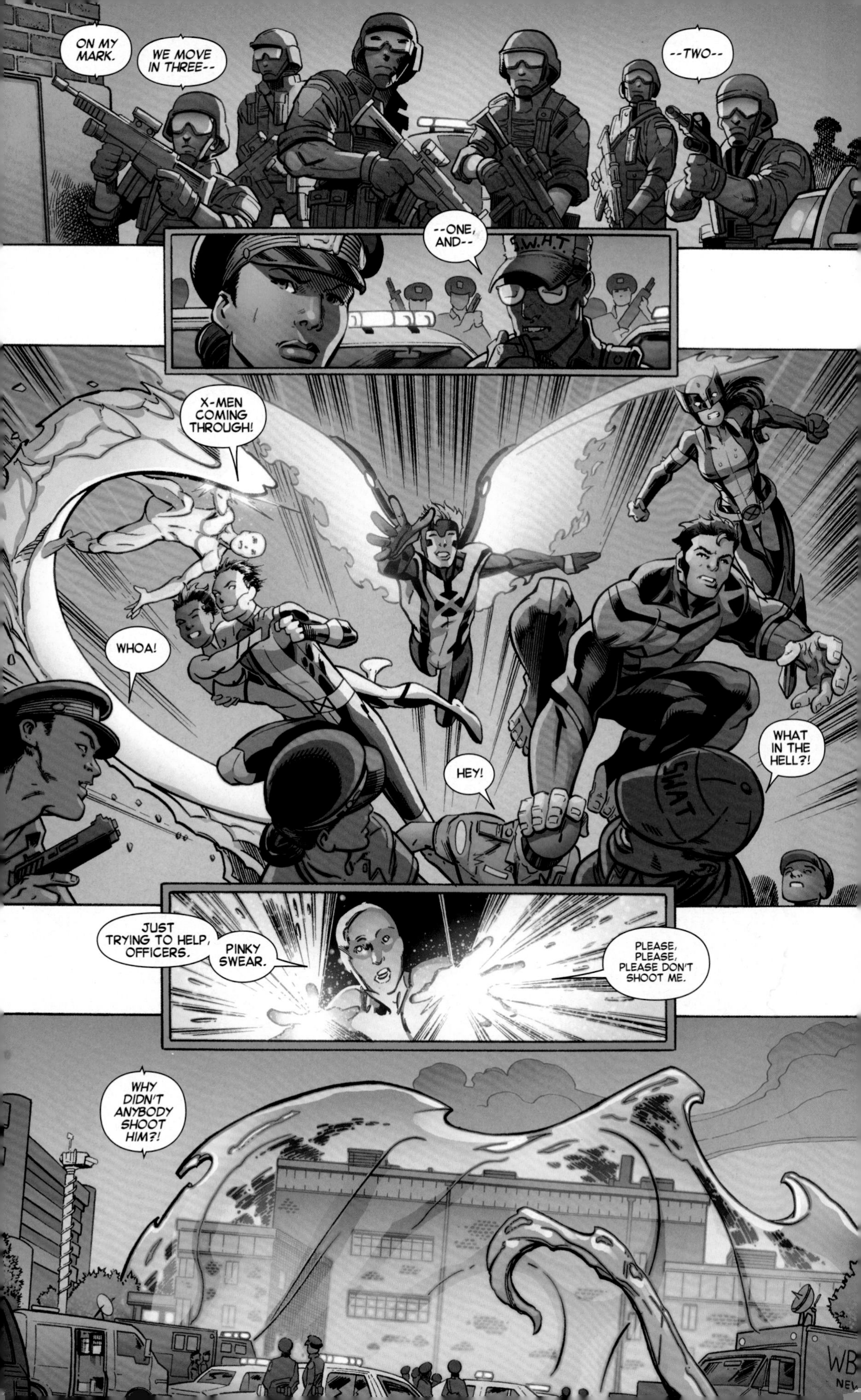

ON MY MARK.
WE MOVE IN THREE--
--TWO--
--ONE, AND--
S.W.A.T.
X-MEN COMING THROUGH!
WHOA!
HEY!
WHAT IN THE HELL?!
SWAT
JUST TRYING TO HELP, OFFICERS.
PINKY SWEAR.
PLEASE, PLEASE, PLEASE DON'T SHOOT ME.
WHY DIDN'T ANYBODY SHOOT HIM?!

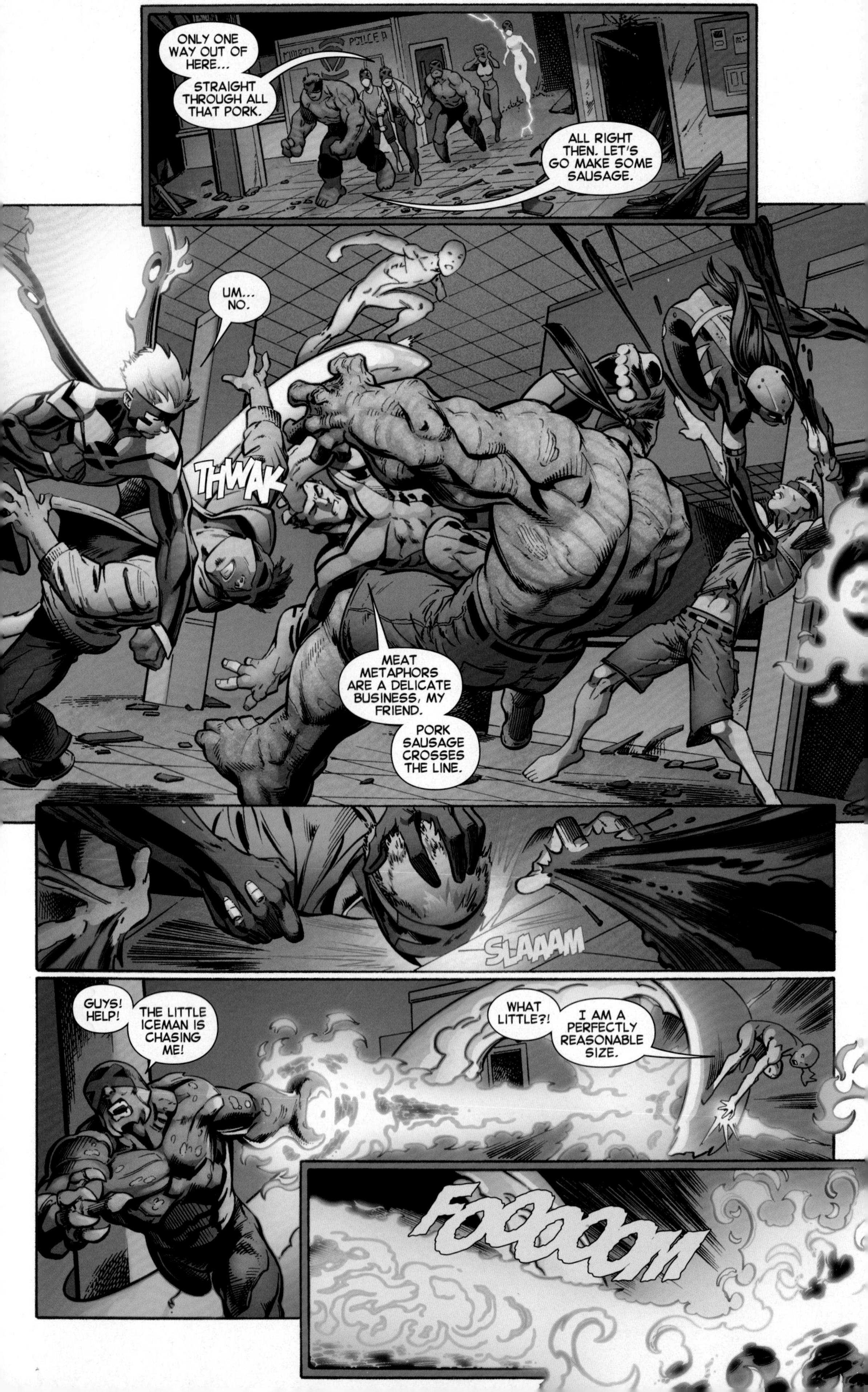
ONLY ONE WAY OUT OF HERE...
STRAIGHT THROUGH ALL THAT PORK.
ALL RIGHT THEN. LET'S GO MAKE SOME SAUSAGE.
UM... NO.
THWAK
MEAT METAPHORS ARE A DELICATE BUSINESS, MY FRIEND.
PORK SAUSAGE CROSSES THE LINE.
SLAAAM
GUYS! HELP!
THE LITTLE ICEMAN IS CHASING ME!
WHAT LITTLE?!
I AM A PERFECTLY REASONABLE SIZE.
FOOOOM

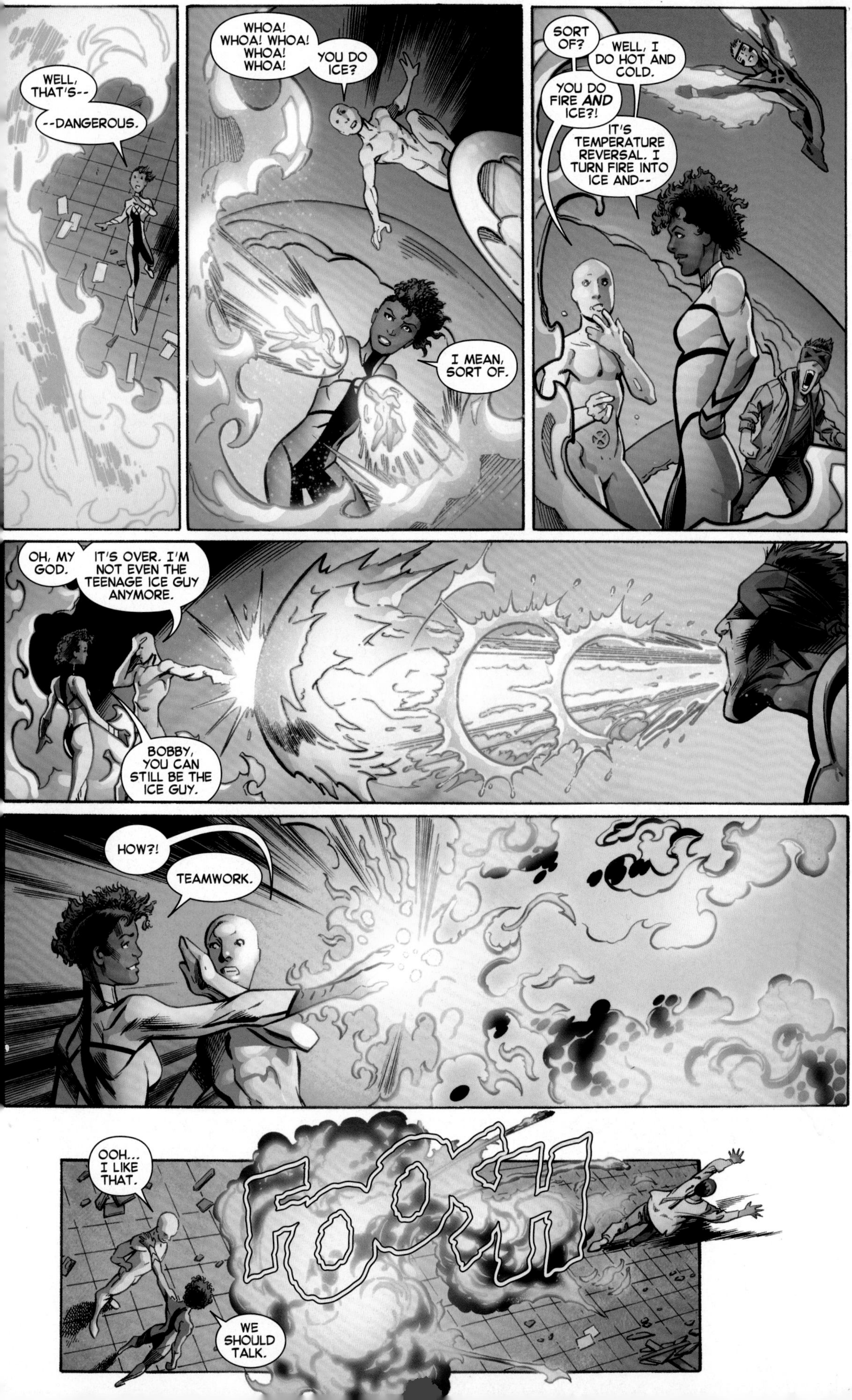
WELL, THAT'S--
--DANGEROUS.
WHOA! WHOA! WHOA! WHOA! WHOA!
YOU DO ICE?
I MEAN, SORT OF.
SORT OF?
WELL, I DO HOT AND COLD.
YOU DO FIRE AND ICE?!
IT'S TEMPERATURE REVERSAL. I TURN FIRE INTO ICE AND--
OH, MY GOD.
IT'S OVER. I'M NOT EVEN THE TEENAGE ICE GUY ANYMORE.
BOBBY, YOU CAN STILL BE THE ICE GUY.
HOW?!
TEAMWORK.
OOH... I LIKE THAT.
FOOM
WE SHOULD TALK.

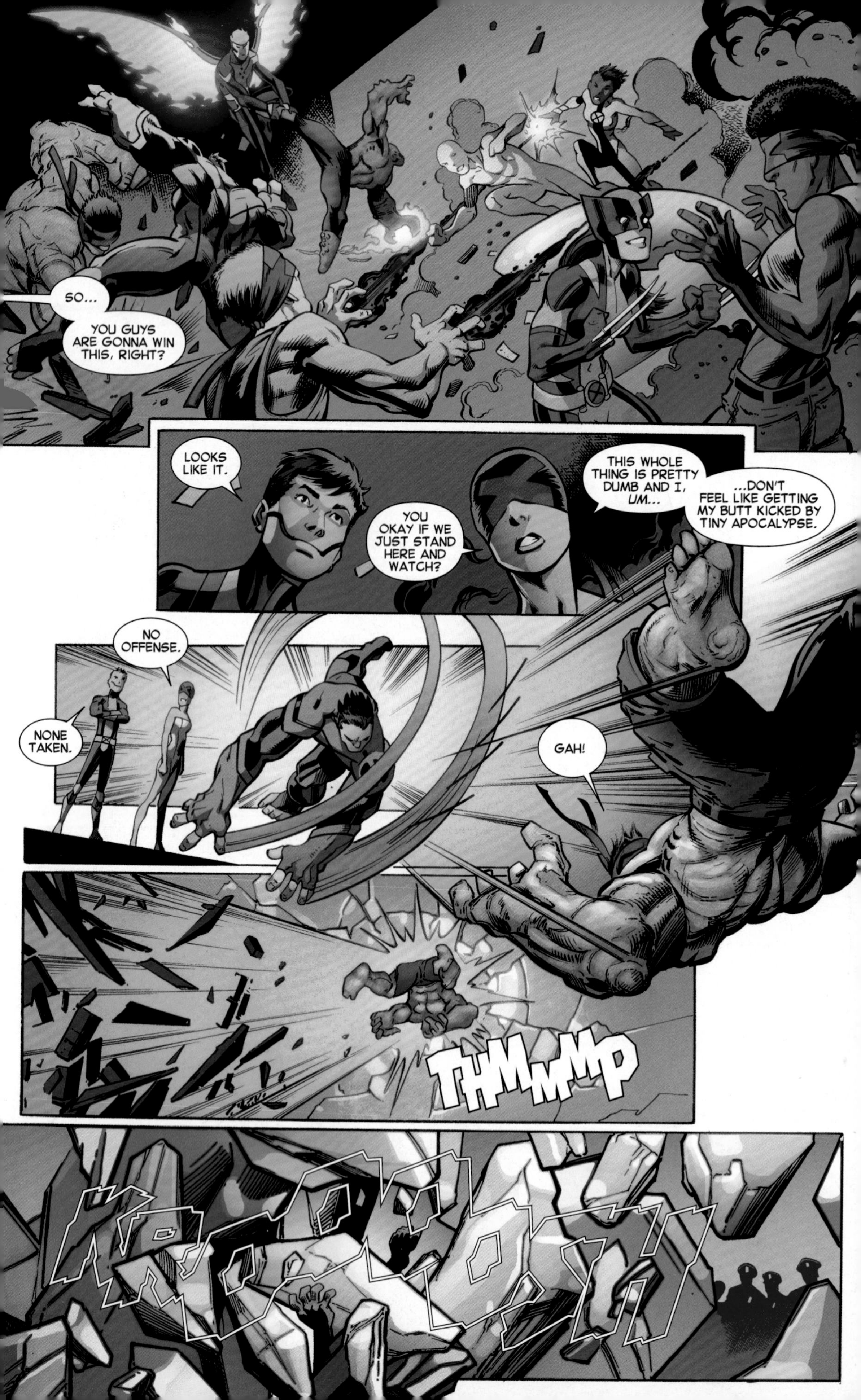
SO...
YOU GUYS ARE GONNA WIN THIS, RIGHT?
LOOKS LIKE IT.
YOU OKAY IF WE JUST STAND HERE AND WATCH?
THIS WHOLE THING IS PRETTY DUMB AND I, UM...
...DON'T FEEL LIKE GETTING MY BUTT KICKED BY TINY APOCALYPSE.
NO OFFENSE.
NONE TAKEN.
GAH!
THMMMP

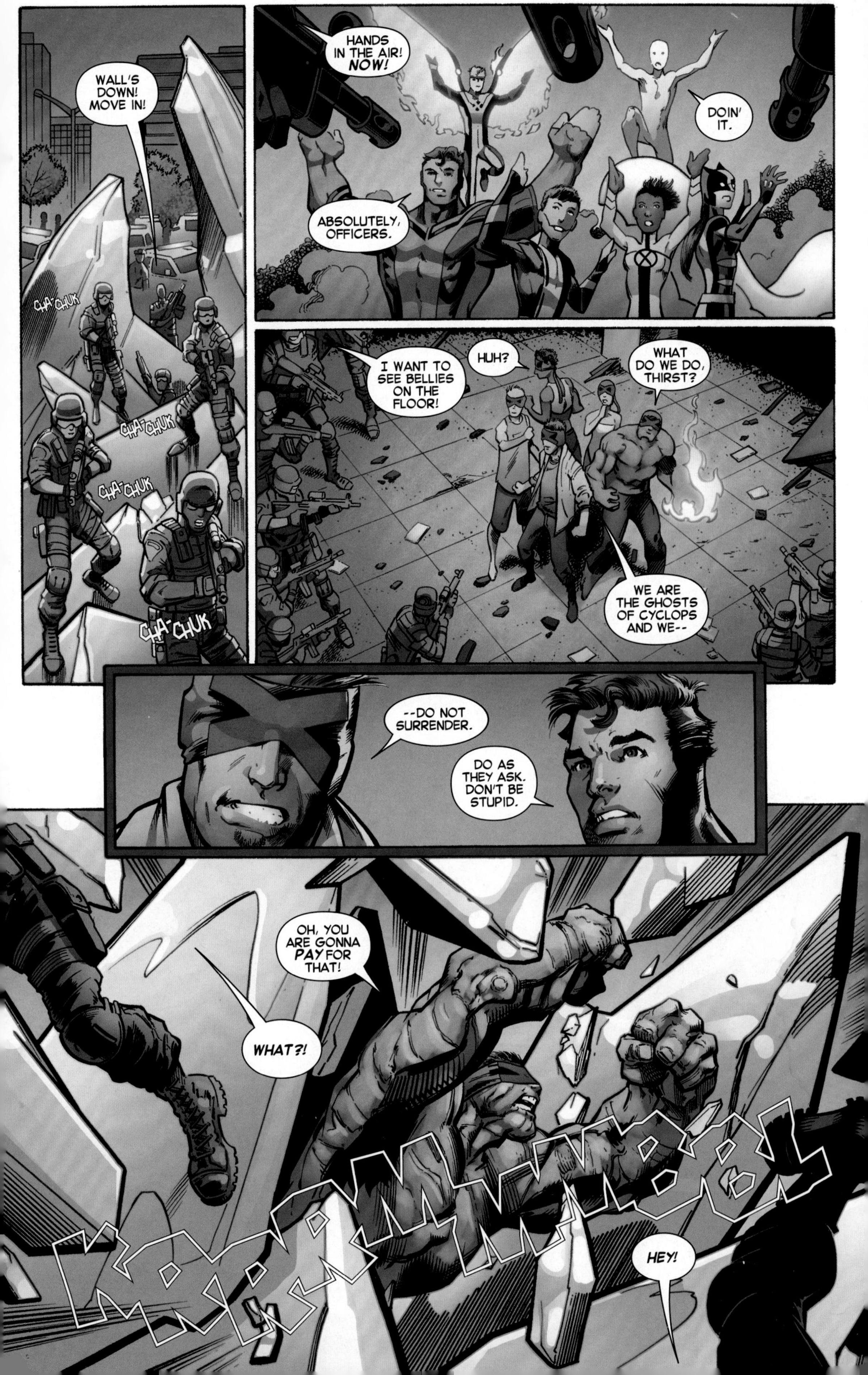

WALL'S DOWN! MOVE IN!
CHA-CHUK
CHA-CHUK
CHA-CHUK
CHA-CHUK
HANDS IN THE AIR! NOW!
ABSOLUTELY, OFFICERS.
DOIN' IT.
I WANT TO SEE BELLIES ON THE FLOOR!
HUH?
WHAT DO WE DO, THIRST?
WE ARE THE GHOSTS OF CYCLOPS AND WE--
--DO NOT SURRENDER.
DO AS THEY ASK. DON'T BE STUPID.
OH, YOU ARE GONNA PAY FOR THAT!
WHAT?!
HEY!

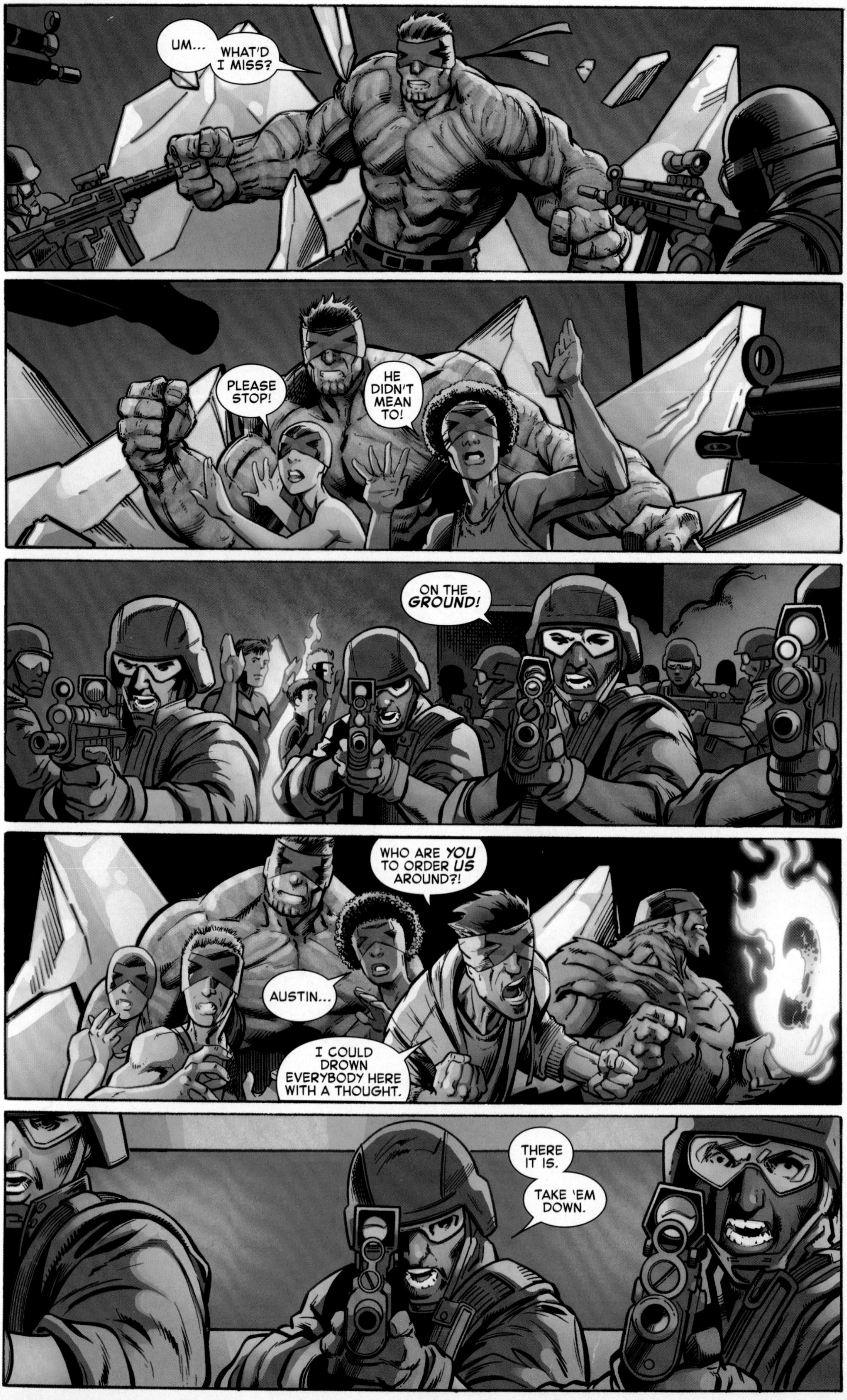
UM...
WHAT'D I MISS?
PLEASE STOP!
HE DIDN'T MEAN TO!
ON THE GROUND!
WHO ARE YOU TO ORDER US AROUND?!
AUSTIN...
I COULD DROWN EVERYBODY HERE WITH A THOUGHT.
THERE IT IS.
TAKE 'EM DOWN.

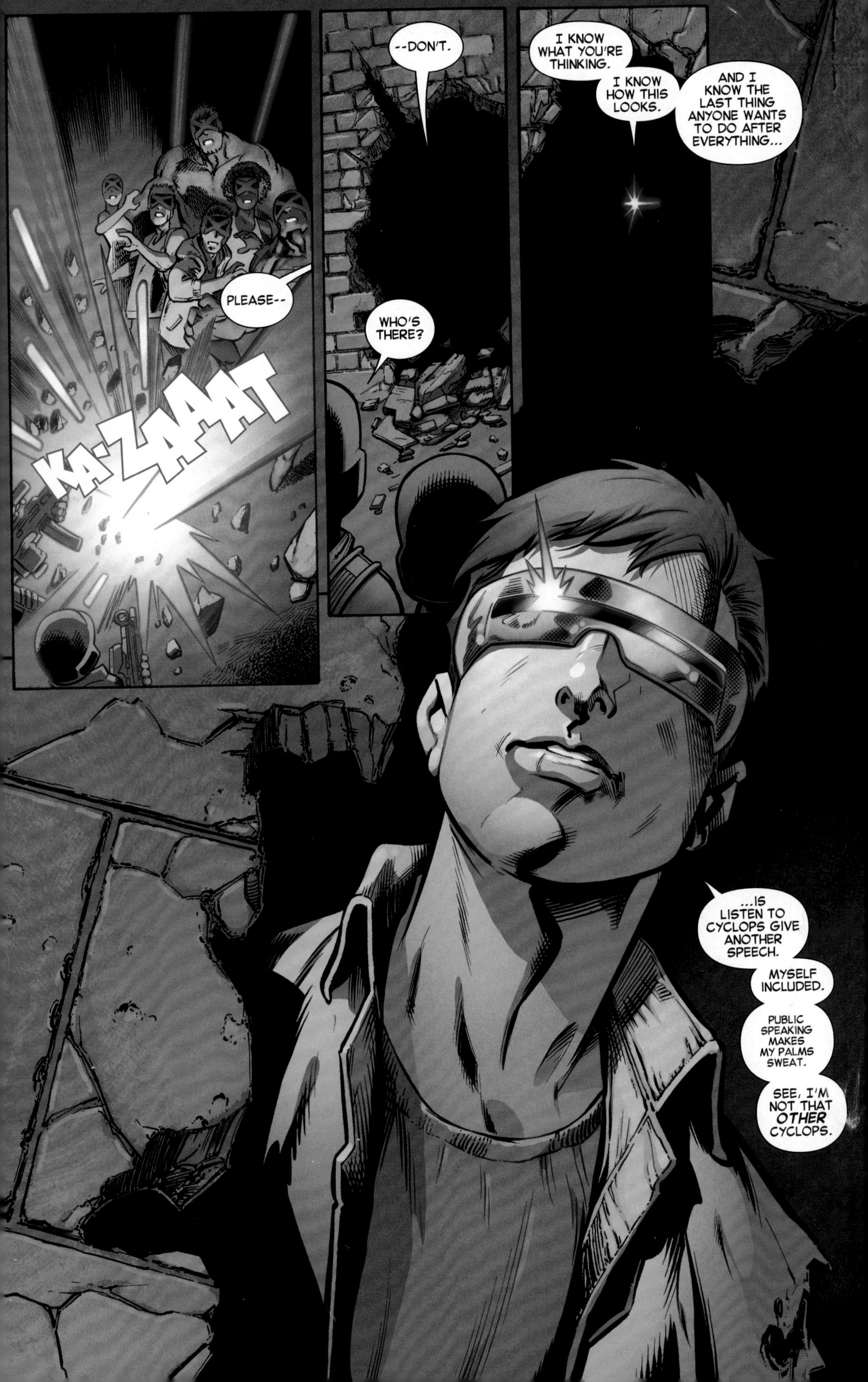
PLEASE--
KA-ZAAAT
--DON'T.
WHO'S THERE?
I KNOW WHAT YOU'RE THINKING.
I KNOW HOW THIS LOOKS.
AND I KNOW THE LAST THING ANYONE WANTS TO DO AFTER EVERYTHING...
...IS LISTEN TO CYCLOPS GIVE ANOTHER SPEECH.
MYSELF INCLUDED.
PUBLIC SPEAKING MAKES MY PALMS SWEAT.
SEE, I'M NOT THAT *OTHER* CYCLOPS.

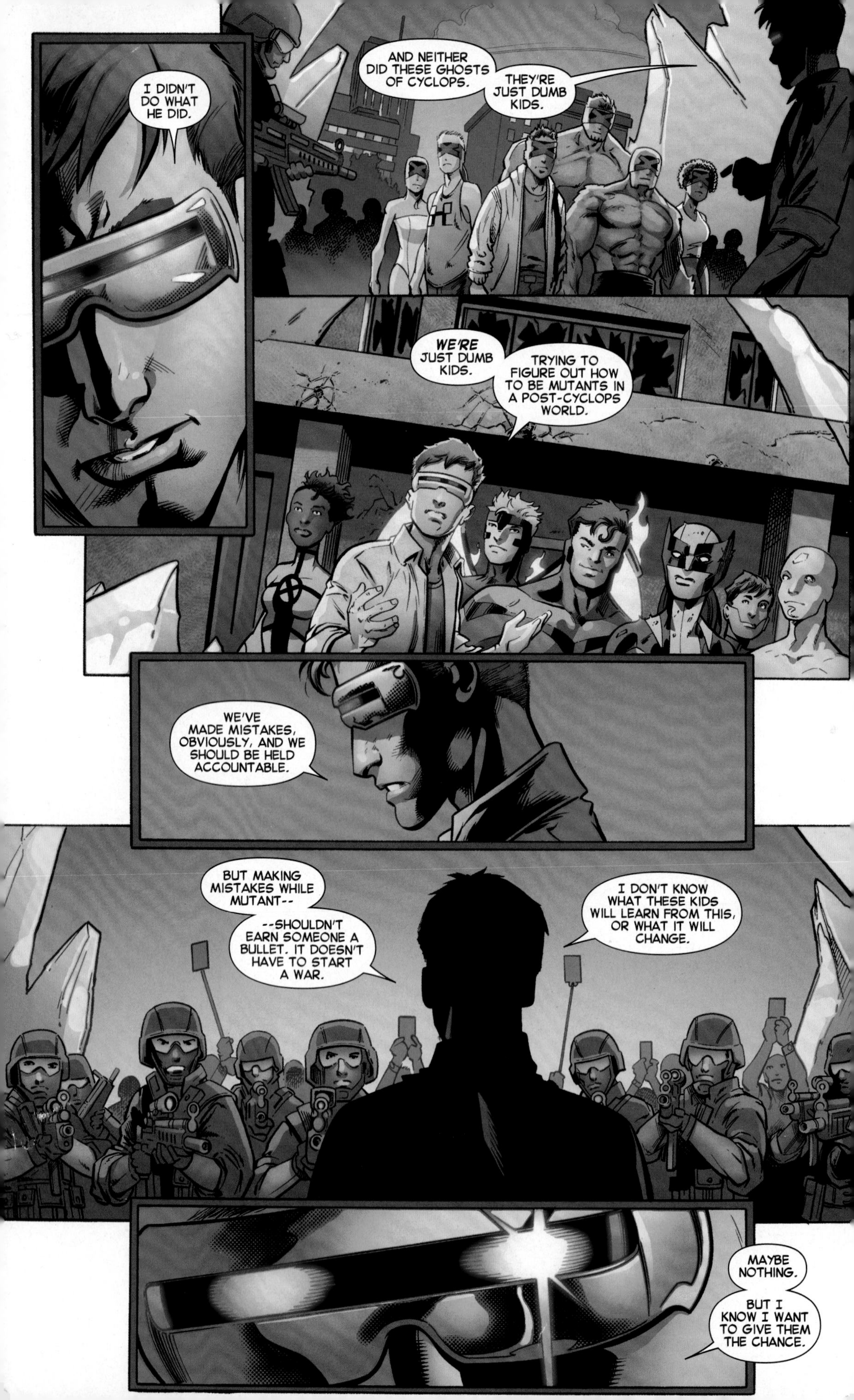
I DIDN'T DO WHAT HE DID.
AND NEITHER DID THESE GHOSTS OF CYCLOPS.
THEY'RE JUST DUMB KIDS.
WE'RE JUST DUMB KIDS.
TRYING TO FIGURE OUT HOW TO BE MUTANTS IN A POST-CYCLOPS WORLD.
WE'VE MADE MISTAKES, OBVIOUSLY, AND WE SHOULD BE HELD ACCOUNTABLE.
BUT MAKING MISTAKES WHILE MUTANT--
--SHOULDN'T EARN SOMEONE A BULLET. IT DOESN'T HAVE TO START A WAR.
I DON'T KNOW WHAT THESE KIDS WILL LEARN FROM THIS, OR WHAT IT WILL CHANGE.
MAYBE NOTHING.
BUT I KNOW I WANT TO GIVE THEM THE CHANCE.

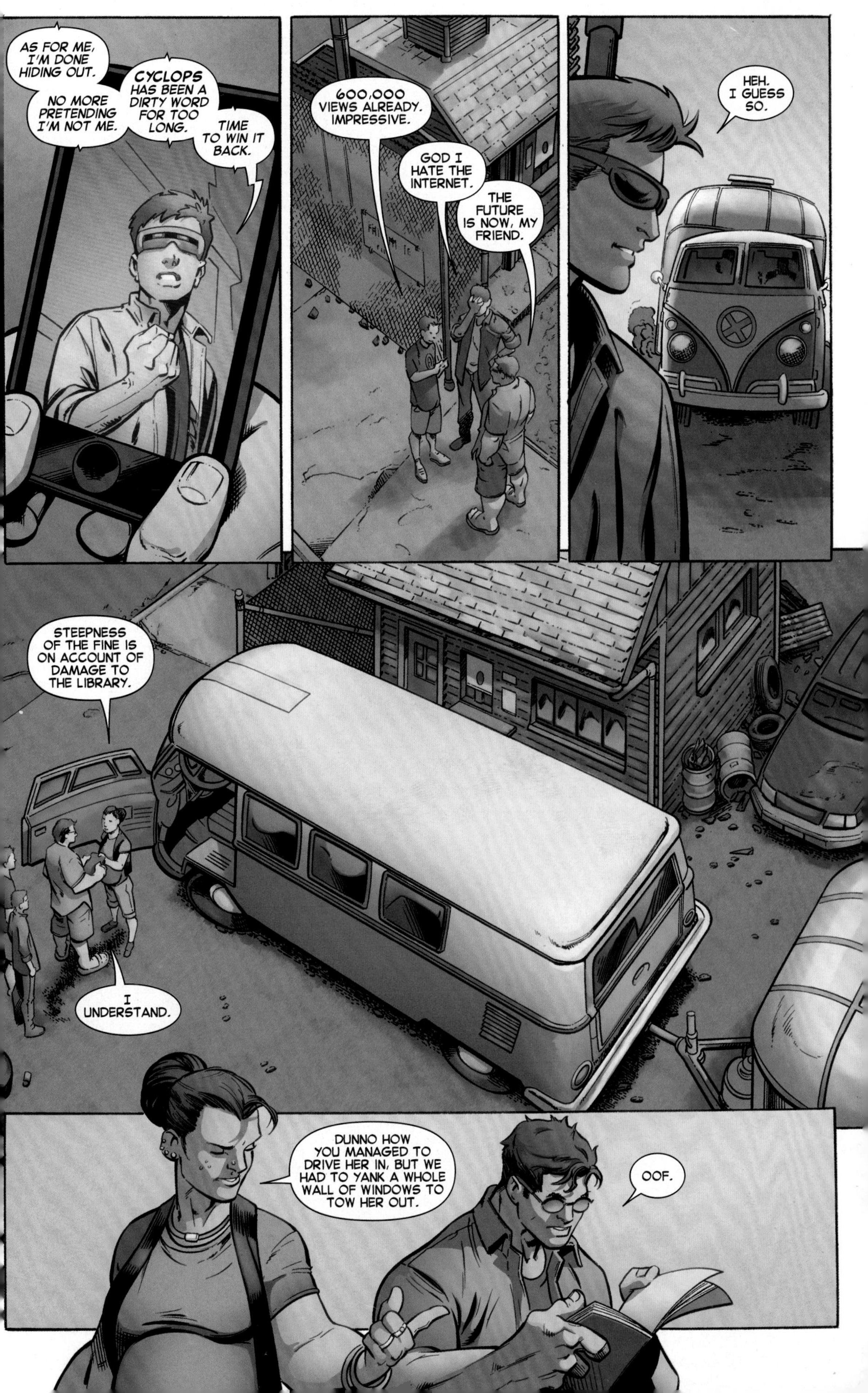

AS FOR ME, I'M DONE HIDING OUT.
NO MORE PRETENDING I'M NOT ME.
CYCLOPS HAS BEEN A DIRTY WORD FOR TOO LONG.
TIME TO WIN IT BACK.
600,000 VIEWS ALREADY. IMPRESSIVE.
GOD I HATE THE INTERNET.
THE FUTURE IS NOW, MY FRIEND.
HEH. I GUESS SO.
STEEPNESS OF THE FINE IS ON ACCOUNT OF DAMAGE TO THE LIBRARY.
I UNDERSTAND.
DUNNO HOW YOU MANAGED TO DRIVE HER IN, BUT WE HAD TO YANK A WHOLE WALL OF WINDOWS TO TOW HER OUT.
OOF.

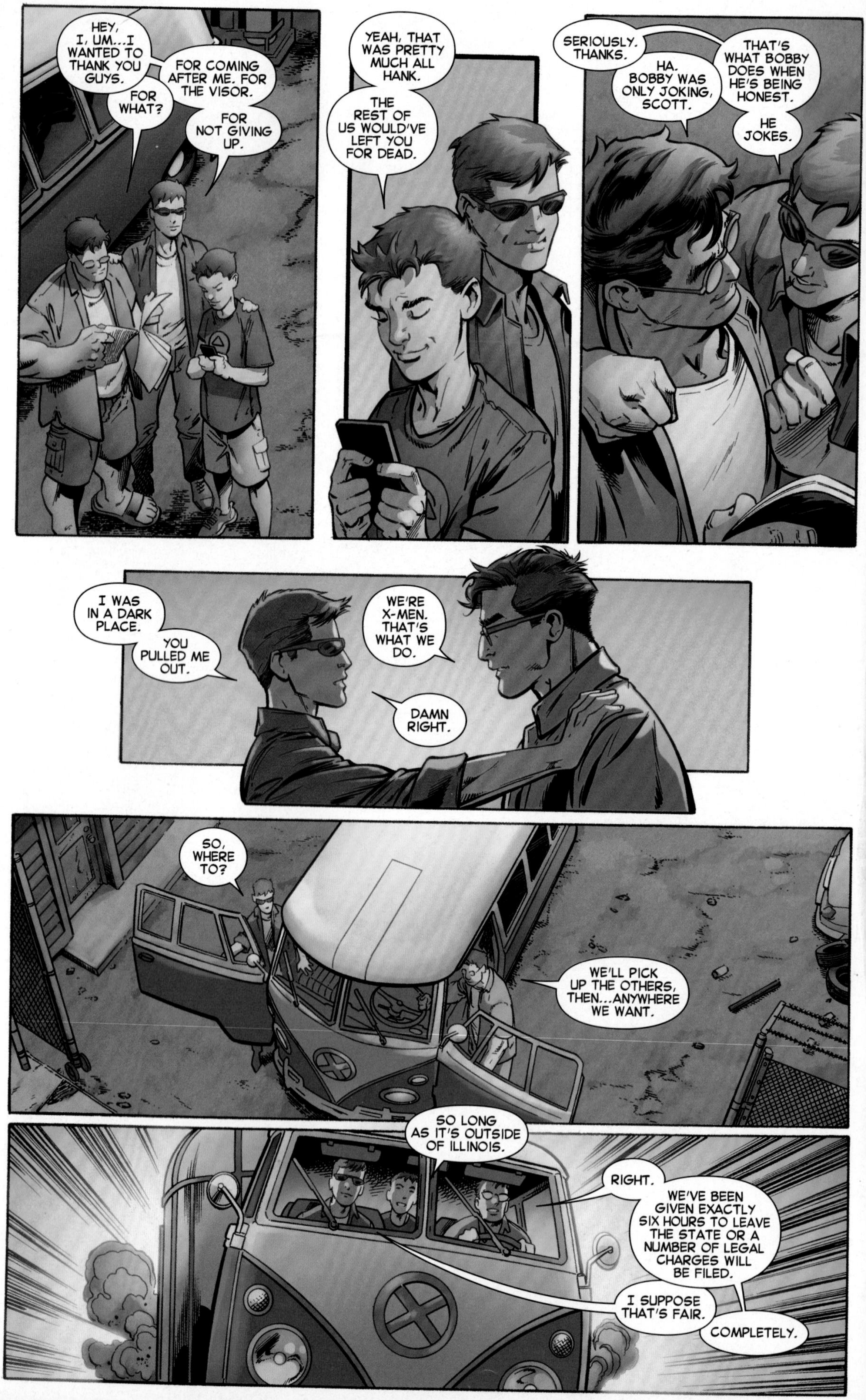
HEY, I, UM...I WANTED TO THANK YOU GUYS.
FOR WHAT?
FOR COMING AFTER ME. FOR THE VISOR.
FOR NOT GIVING UP.
YEAH, THAT WAS PRETTY MUCH ALL HANK.
THE REST OF US WOULD'VE LEFT YOU FOR DEAD.
SERIOUSLY. THANKS.
HA. BOBBY WAS ONLY JOKING, SCOTT.
THAT'S WHAT BOBBY DOES WHEN HE'S BEING HONEST.
HE JOKES.
I WAS IN A DARK PLACE.
YOU PULLED ME OUT.
WE'RE X-MEN. THAT'S WHAT WE DO.
DAMN RIGHT.
SO, WHERE TO?
WE'LL PICK UP THE OTHERS, THEN...ANYWHERE WE WANT.
SO LONG AS IT'S OUTSIDE OF ILLINOIS.
RIGHT.
WE'VE BEEN GIVEN EXACTLY SIX HOURS TO LEAVE THE STATE OR A NUMBER OF LEGAL CHARGES WILL BE FILED.
I SUPPOSE THAT'S FAIR.
COMPLETELY.

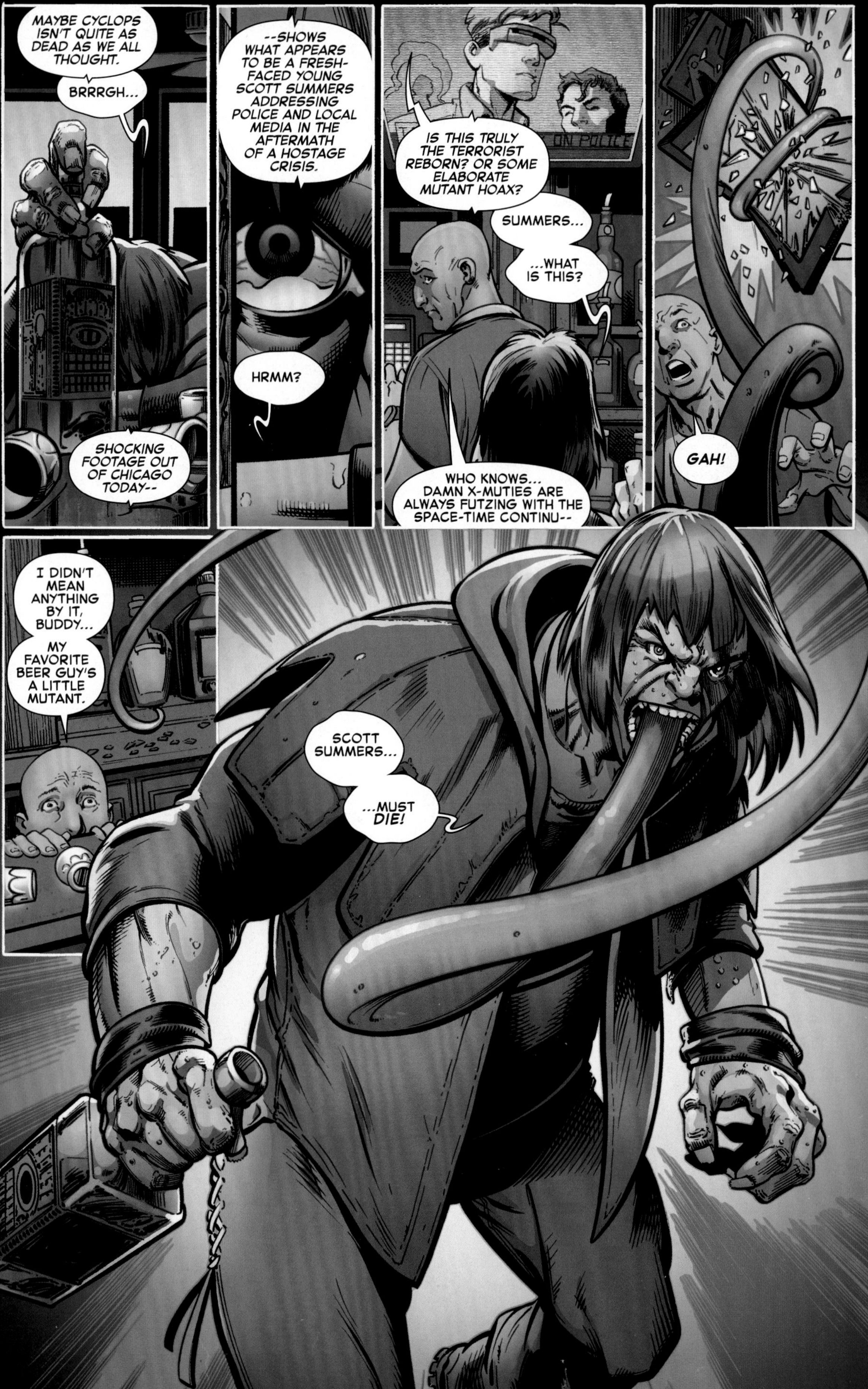
MAYBE CYCLOPS ISN'T QUITE AS DEAD AS WE ALL THOUGHT.
BRRRGH...
SHOCKING FOOTAGE OUT OF CHICAGO TODAY--
--SHOWS WHAT APPEARS TO BE A FRESH-FACED YOUNG SCOTT SUMMERS ADDRESSING POLICE AND LOCAL MEDIA IN THE AFTERMATH OF A HOSTAGE CRISIS.
HRMM?
IS THIS TRULY THE TERRORIST REBORN? OR SOME ELABORATE MUTANT HOAX?
SUMMERS...
...WHAT IS THIS?
WHO KNOWS... DAMN X-MUTIES ARE ALWAYS FUTZING WITH THE SPACE-TIME CONTINU--
GAH!
I DIDN'T MEAN ANYTHING BY IT, BUDDY...
MY FAVORITE BEER GUY'S A LITTLE MUTANT.
SCOTT SUMMERS...
...MUST DIE!

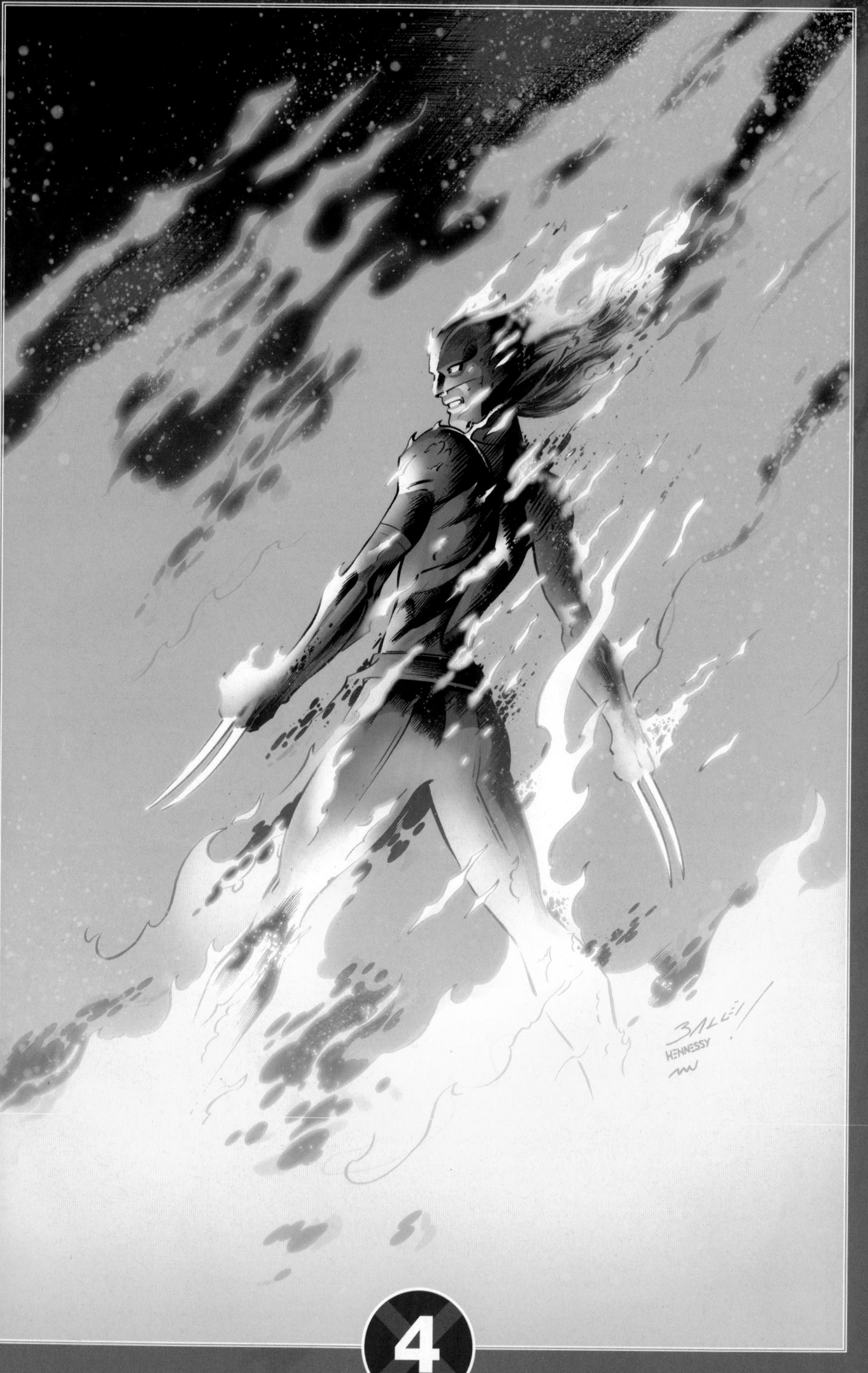
HENNESSY
4

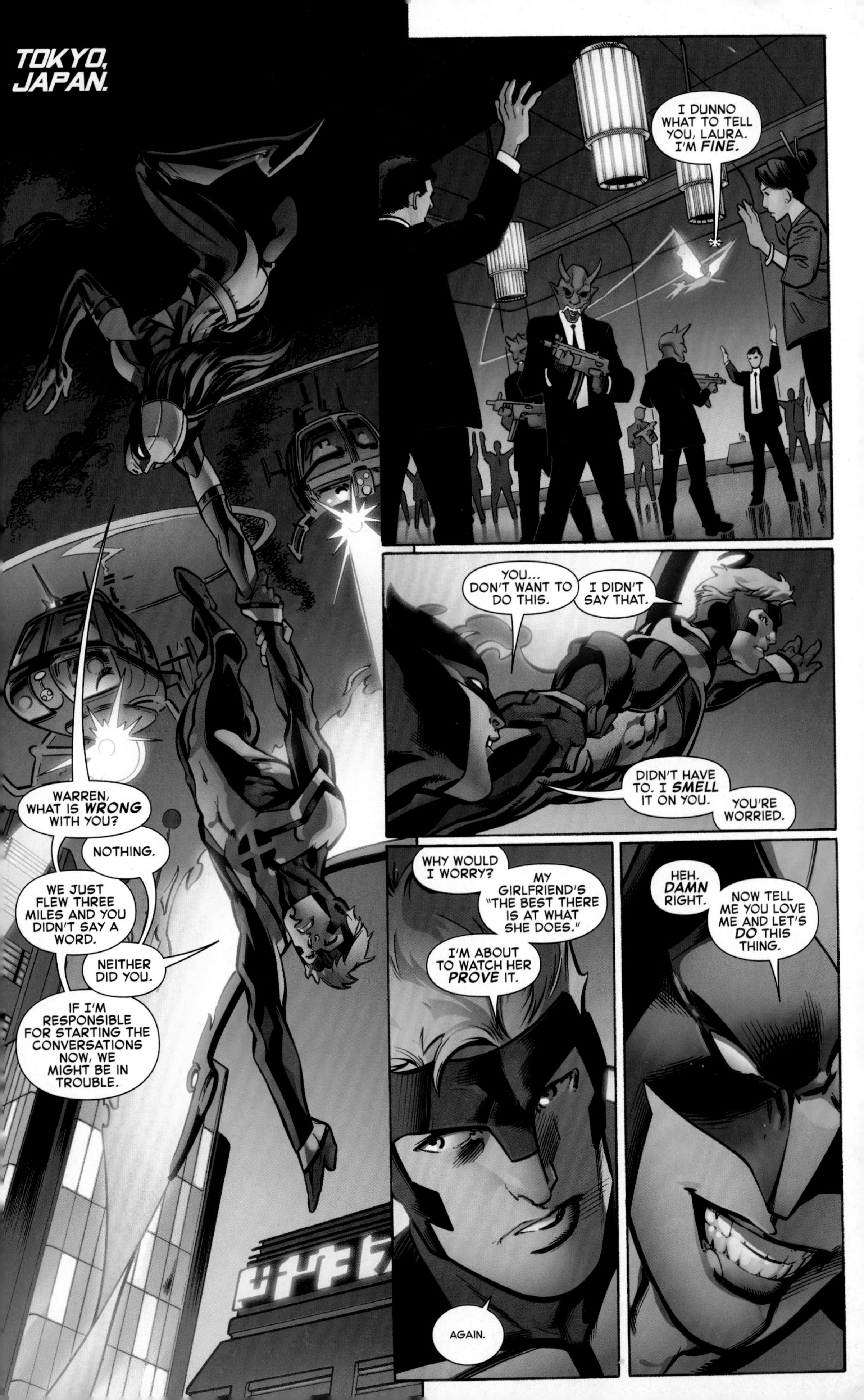
TOKYO, JAPAN.
I DUNNO WHAT TO TELL YOU, LAURA. I'M FINE.
WARREN, WHAT IS WRONG WITH YOU?
NOTHING.
WE JUST FLEW THREE MILES AND YOU DIDN'T SAY A WORD.
NEITHER DID YOU.
IF I'M RESPONSIBLE FOR STARTING THE CONVERSATIONS NOW, WE MIGHT BE IN TROUBLE.
YOU... DON'T WANT TO DO THIS.
I DIDN'T SAY THAT.
DIDN'T HAVE TO. I SMELL IT ON YOU.
YOU'RE WORRIED.
WHY WOULD I WORRY?
MY GIRLFRIEND'S "THE BEST THERE IS AT WHAT SHE DOES."
I'M ABOUT TO WATCH HER PROVE IT.
AGAIN.
HEH. DAMN RIGHT.
NOW TELL ME YOU LOVE ME AND LET'S DO THIS THING.

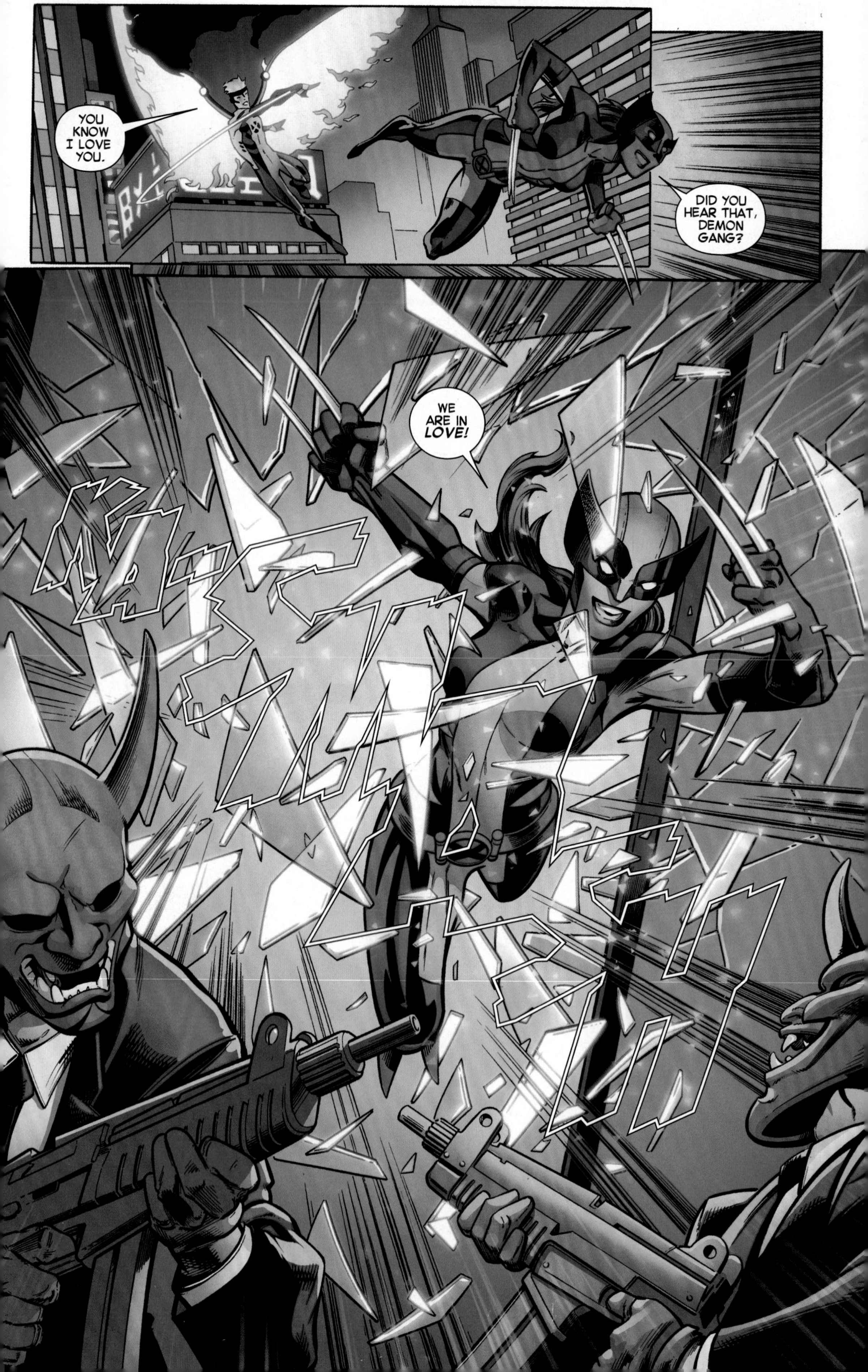
YOU KNOW I LOVE YOU.
DID YOU HEAR THAT, DEMON GANG?
WE ARE IN *LOVE!*

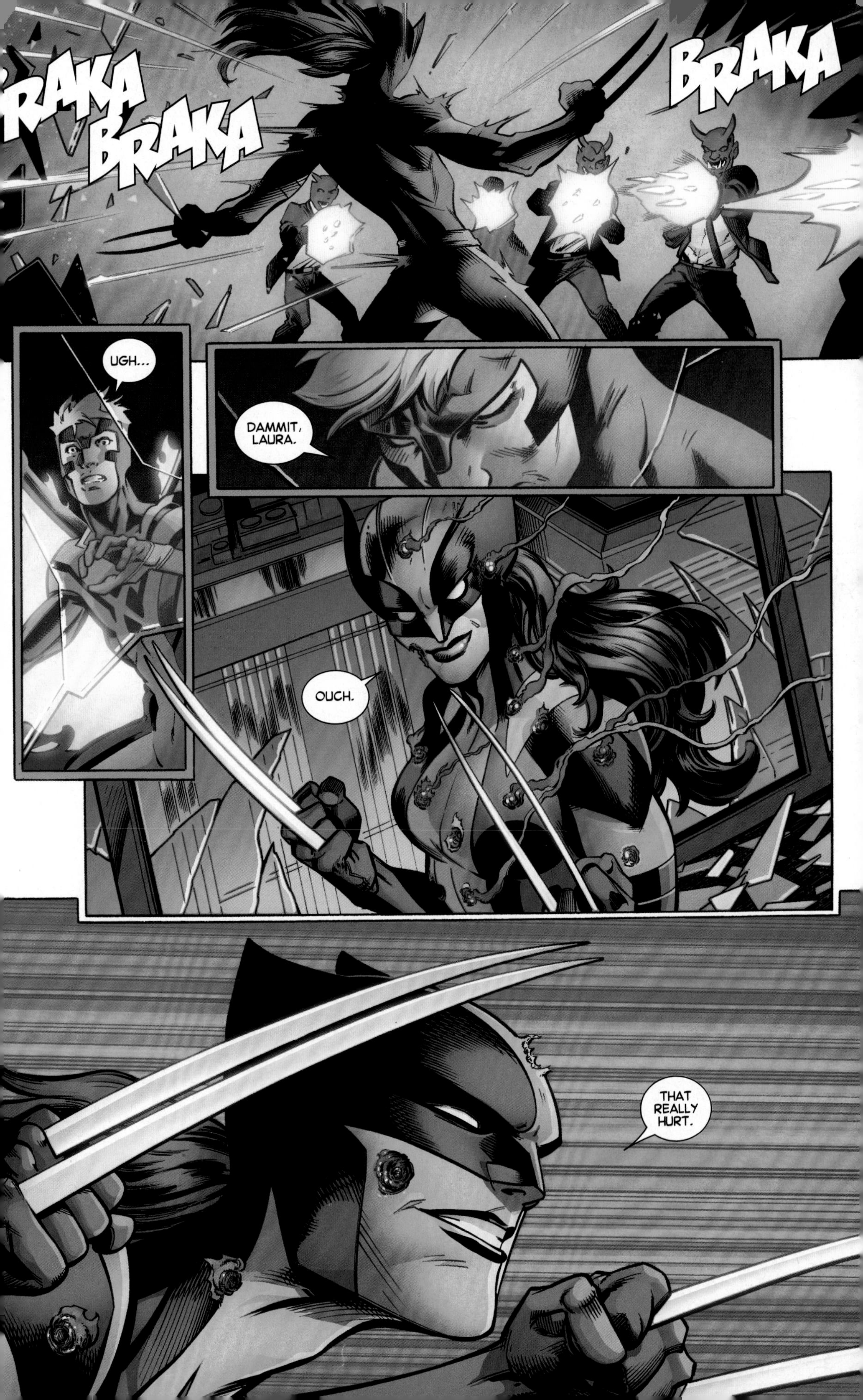
RAKA
BRAKA
BRAKA
UGH...
DAMMIT, LAURA.
OUCH.
THAT REALLY HURT.

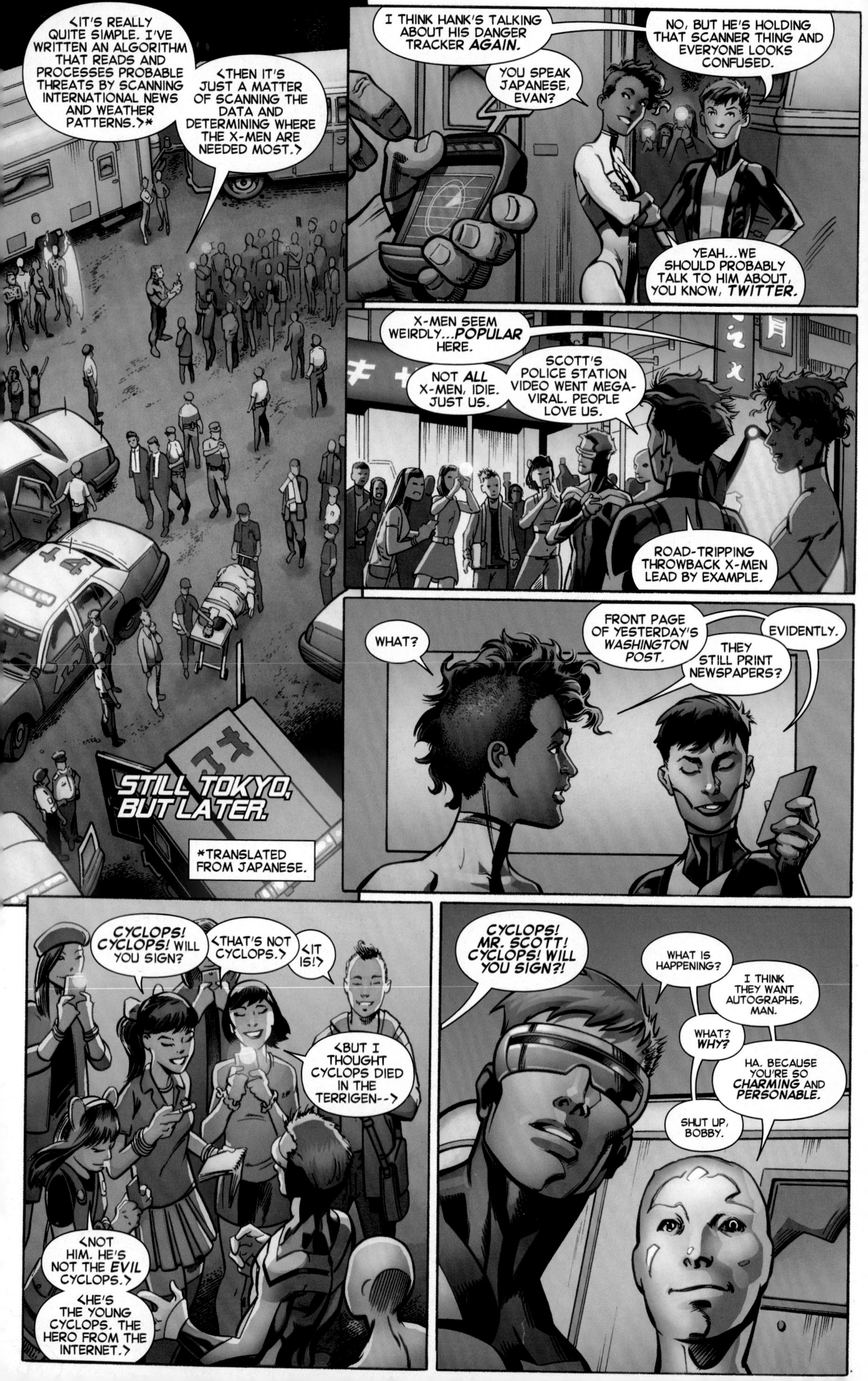

<IT'S REALLY QUITE SIMPLE. I'VE WRITTEN AN ALGORITHM THAT READS AND PROCESSES PROBABLE THREATS BY SCANNING INTERNATIONAL NEWS AND WEATHER PATTERNS.>*
<THEN IT'S JUST A MATTER OF SCANNING THE DATA AND DETERMINING WHERE THE X-MEN ARE NEEDED MOST.>
STILL TOKYO, BUT LATER.
*TRANSLATED FROM JAPANESE.
I THINK HANK'S TALKING ABOUT HIS DANGER TRACKER AGAIN.
YOU SPEAK JAPANESE, EVAN?
NO, BUT HE'S HOLDING THAT SCANNER THING AND EVERYONE LOOKS CONFUSED.
YEAH...WE SHOULD PROBABLY TALK TO HIM ABOUT, YOU KNOW, TWITTER.
X-MEN SEEM WEIRDLY...POPULAR HERE.
NOT ALL X-MEN, IDIE. JUST US.
SCOTT'S POLICE STATION VIDEO WENT MEGA-VIRAL. PEOPLE LOVE US.
ROAD-TRIPPING THROWBACK X-MEN LEAD BY EXAMPLE.
WHAT?
FRONT PAGE OF YESTERDAY'S WASHINGTON POST.
THEY STILL PRINT NEWSPAPERS?
EVIDENTLY.
CYCLOPS! CYCLOPS! WILL YOU SIGN?
<THAT'S NOT CYCLOPS.>
<IT IS!>
<BUT I THOUGHT CYCLOPS DIED IN THE TERRIGEN-->
<NOT HIM. HE'S NOT THE EVIL CYCLOPS.>
<HE'S THE YOUNG CYCLOPS. THE HERO FROM THE INTERNET.>
CYCLOPS! MR. SCOTT! CYCLOPS! WILL YOU SIGN?!
WHAT IS HAPPENING?
I THINK THEY WANT AUTOGRAPHS, MAN.
WHAT? WHY?
HA. BECAUSE YOU'RE SO CHARMING AND PERSONABLE.
SHUT UP, BOBBY.

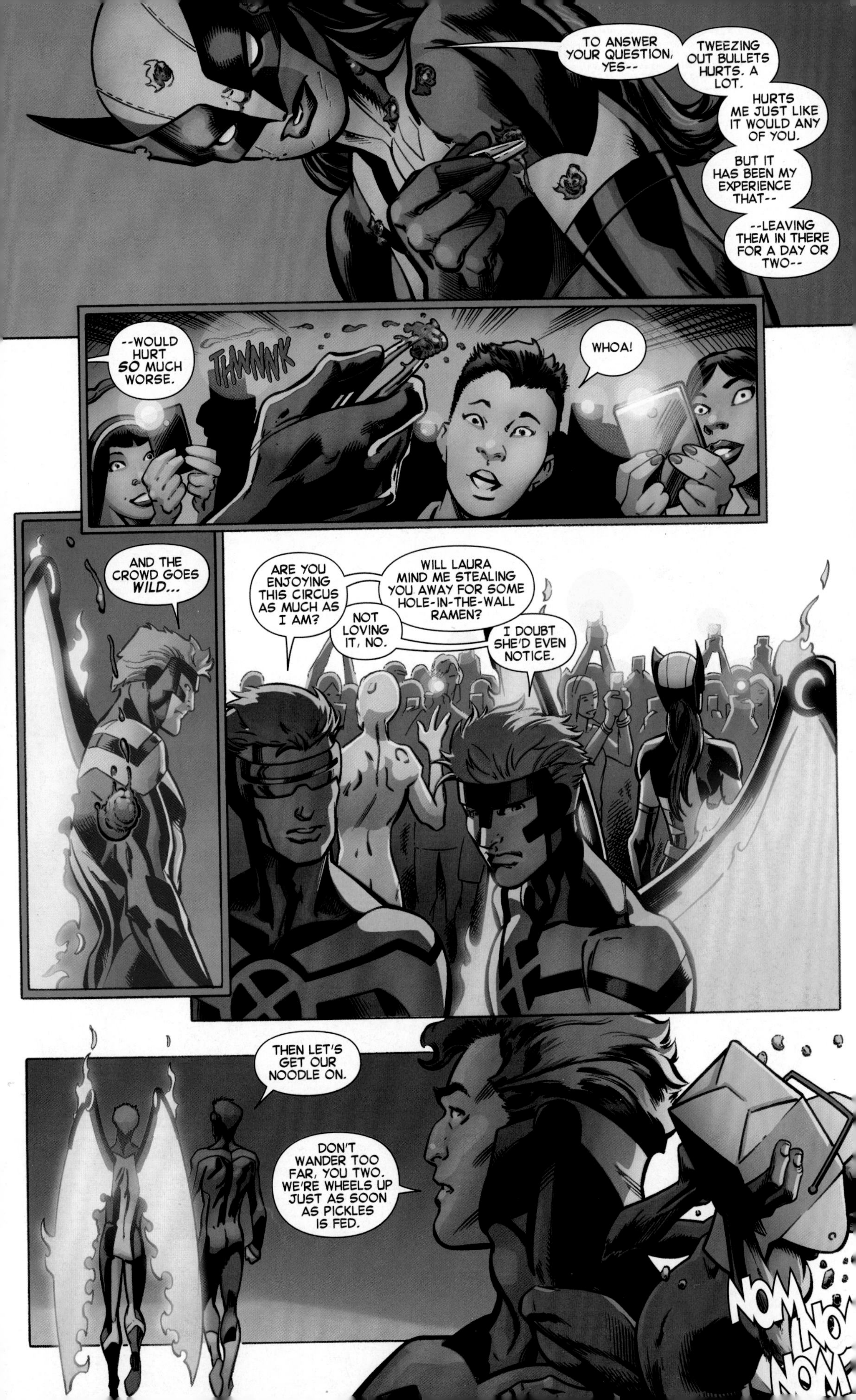
TO ANSWER YOUR QUESTION, YES--
TWEEZING OUT BULLETS HURTS. A LOT.
HURTS ME JUST LIKE IT WOULD ANY OF YOU.
BUT IT HAS BEEN MY EXPERIENCE THAT--
--LEAVING THEM IN THERE FOR A DAY OR TWO--
--WOULD HURT SO MUCH WORSE.
THWNNK
WHOA!
AND THE CROWD GOES WILD...
ARE YOU ENJOYING THIS CIRCUS AS MUCH AS I AM?
WILL LAURA MIND ME STEALING YOU AWAY FOR SOME HOLE-IN-THE-WALL RAMEN?
NOT LOVING IT, NO.
I DOUBT SHE'D EVEN NOTICE.
THEN LET'S GET OUR NOODLE ON.
DON'T WANDER TOO FAR, YOU TWO. WE'RE WHEELS UP JUST AS SOON AS PICKLES IS FED.
NOM

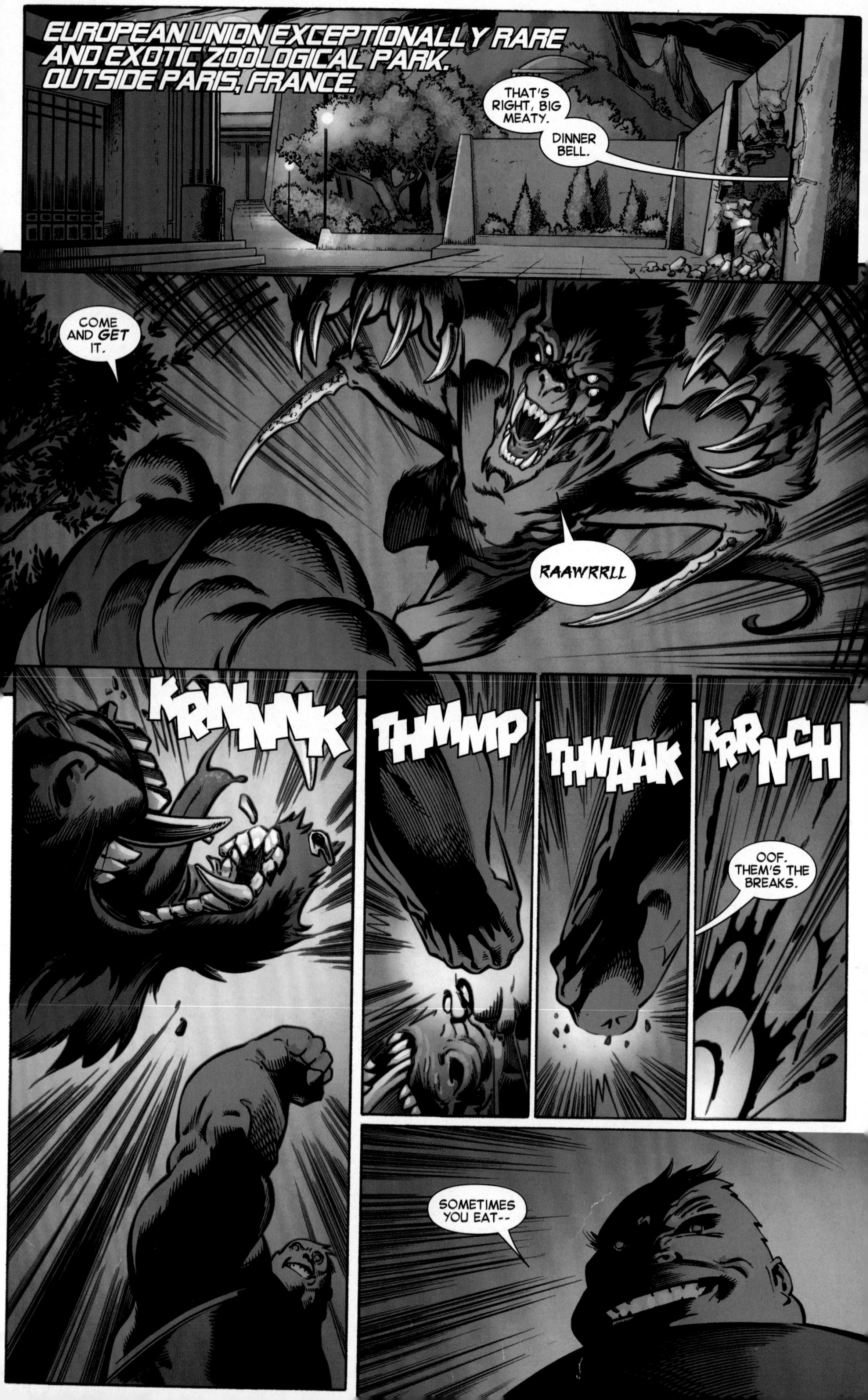

EUROPEAN UNION EXCEPTIONALLY RARE AND EXOTIC ZOOLOGICAL PARK. OUTSIDE PARIS, FRANCE.
THAT'S RIGHT, BIG MEATY.
DINNER BELL.
COME AND GET IT.
RAAWRRLL
KRNNNK
THMMP
THWAAK
KRRNCH
OOF. THEM'S THE BREAKS.
SOMETIMES YOU EAT--

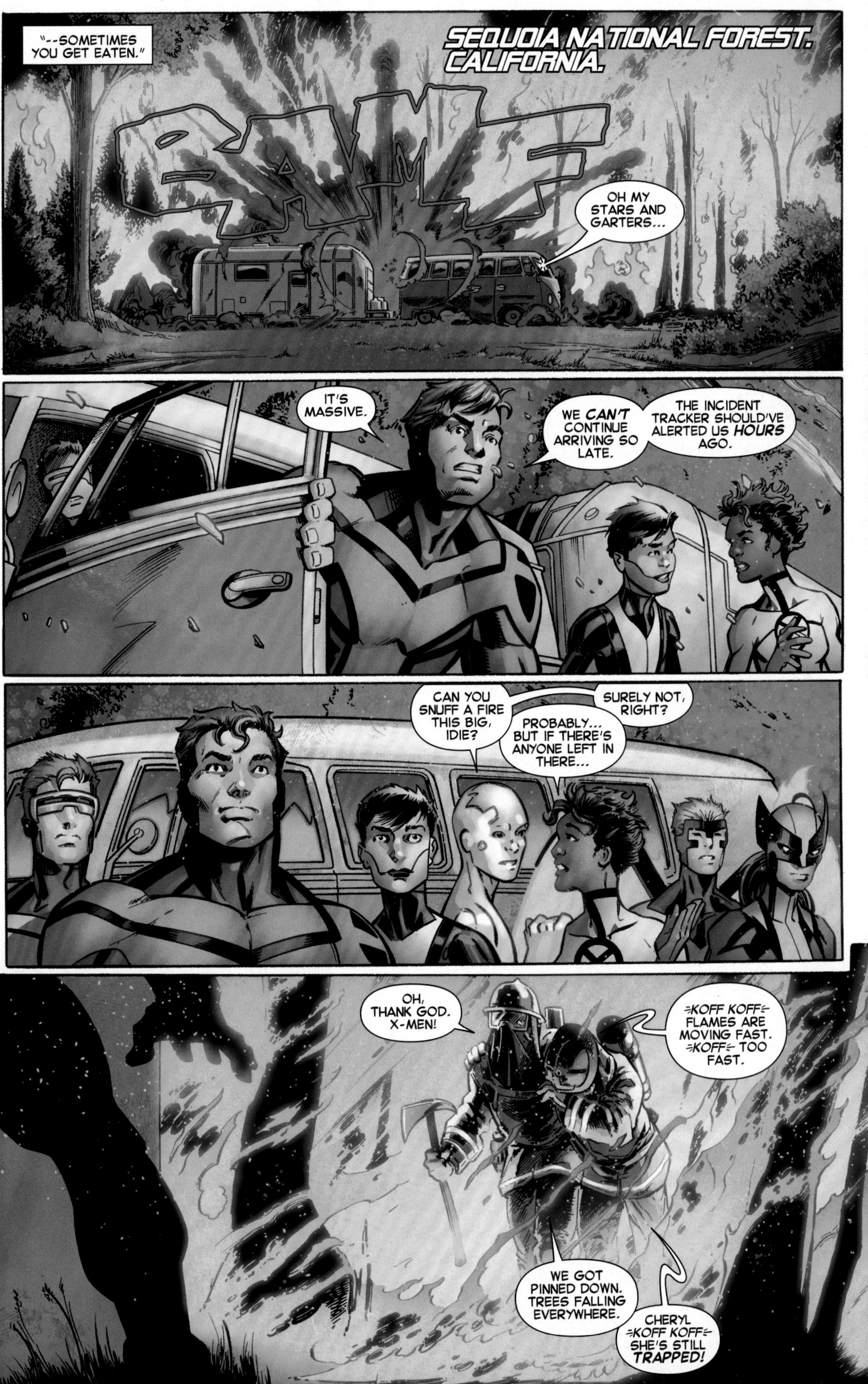
"--SOMETIMES YOU GET EATEN."
SEQUOIA NATIONAL FOREST. CALIFORNIA.
OH MY STARS AND GARTERS...
IT'S MASSIVE.
WE CAN'T CONTINUE ARRIVING SO LATE.
THE INCIDENT TRACKER SHOULD'VE ALERTED US HOURS AGO.
CAN YOU SNUFF A FIRE THIS BIG, IDIE?
SURELY NOT, RIGHT?
PROBABLY... BUT IF THERE'S ANYONE LEFT IN THERE...
OH, THANK GOD. X-MEN!
=KOFF KOFF= FLAMES ARE MOVING FAST. =KOFF= TOO FAST.
WE GOT PINNED DOWN. TREES FALLING EVERYWHERE.
CHERYL =KOFF KOFF= SHE'S STILL TRAPPED!

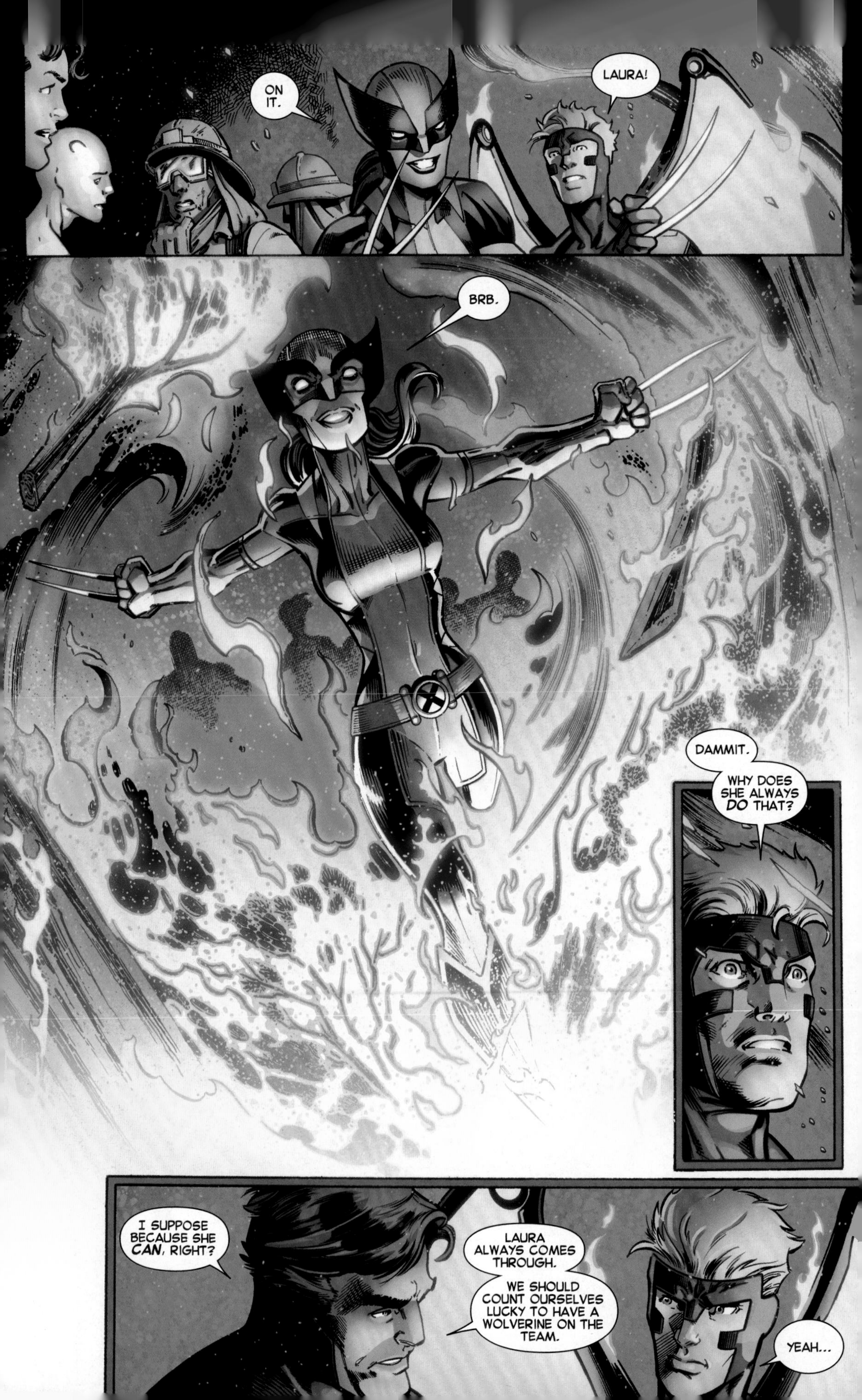
ON IT.
LAURA!
BRB.
DAMMIT.
WHY DOES SHE ALWAYS DO THAT?
I SUPPOSE BECAUSE SHE CAN, RIGHT?
LAURA ALWAYS COMES THROUGH.
WE SHOULD COUNT OURSELVES LUCKY TO HAVE A WOLVERINE ON THE TEAM.
YEAH...

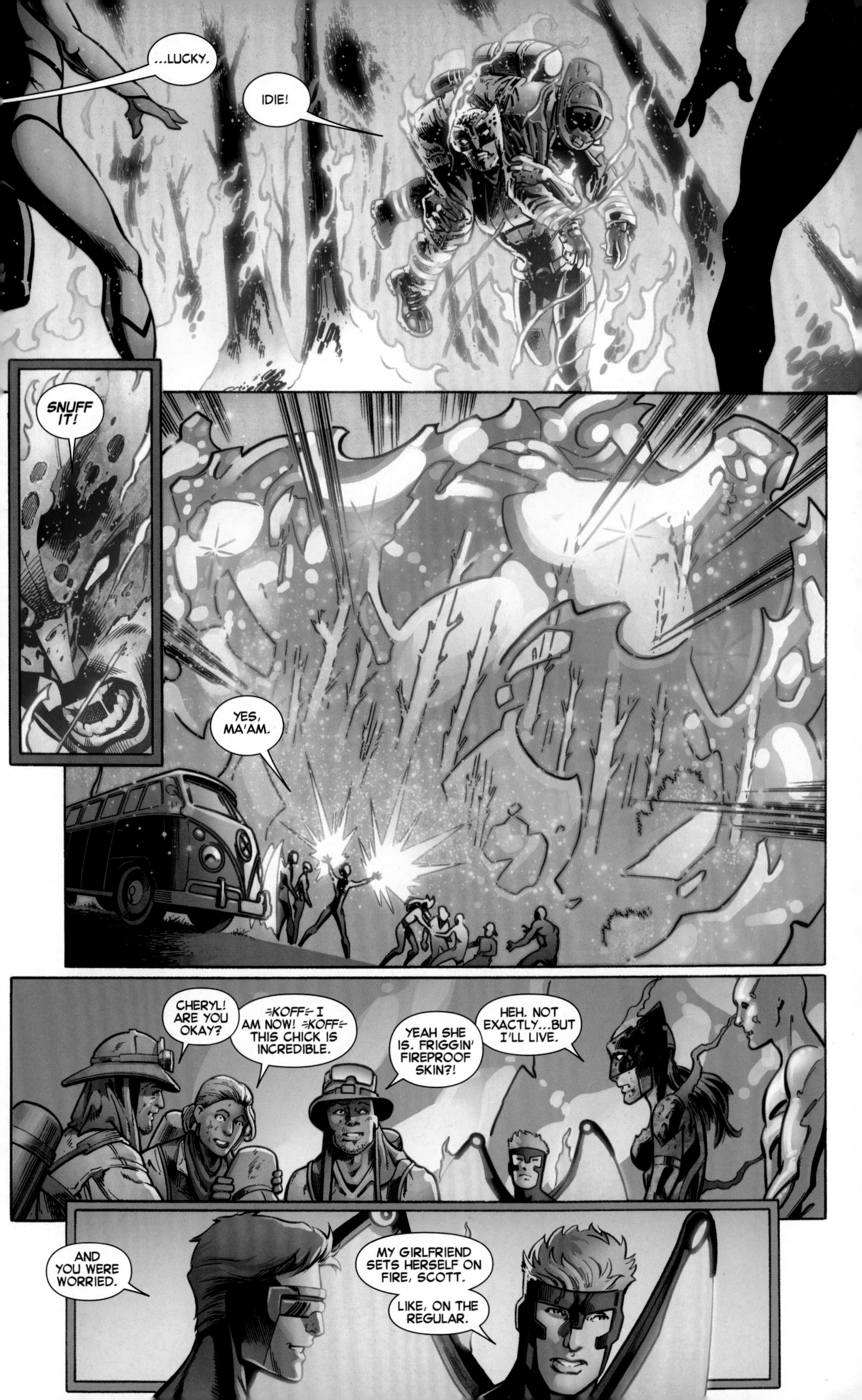
...LUCKY.
IDIE!
SNUFF IT!
YES, MA'AM.
CHERYL! ARE YOU OKAY?
=KOFF= I AM NOW! =KOFF= THIS CHICK IS INCREDIBLE.
YEAH SHE IS. FRIGGIN' FIREPROOF SKIN?!
HEH. NOT EXACTLY...BUT I'LL LIVE.
AND YOU WERE WORRIED.
MY GIRLFRIEND SETS HERSELF ON FIRE, SCOTT.
LIKE, ON THE REGULAR.

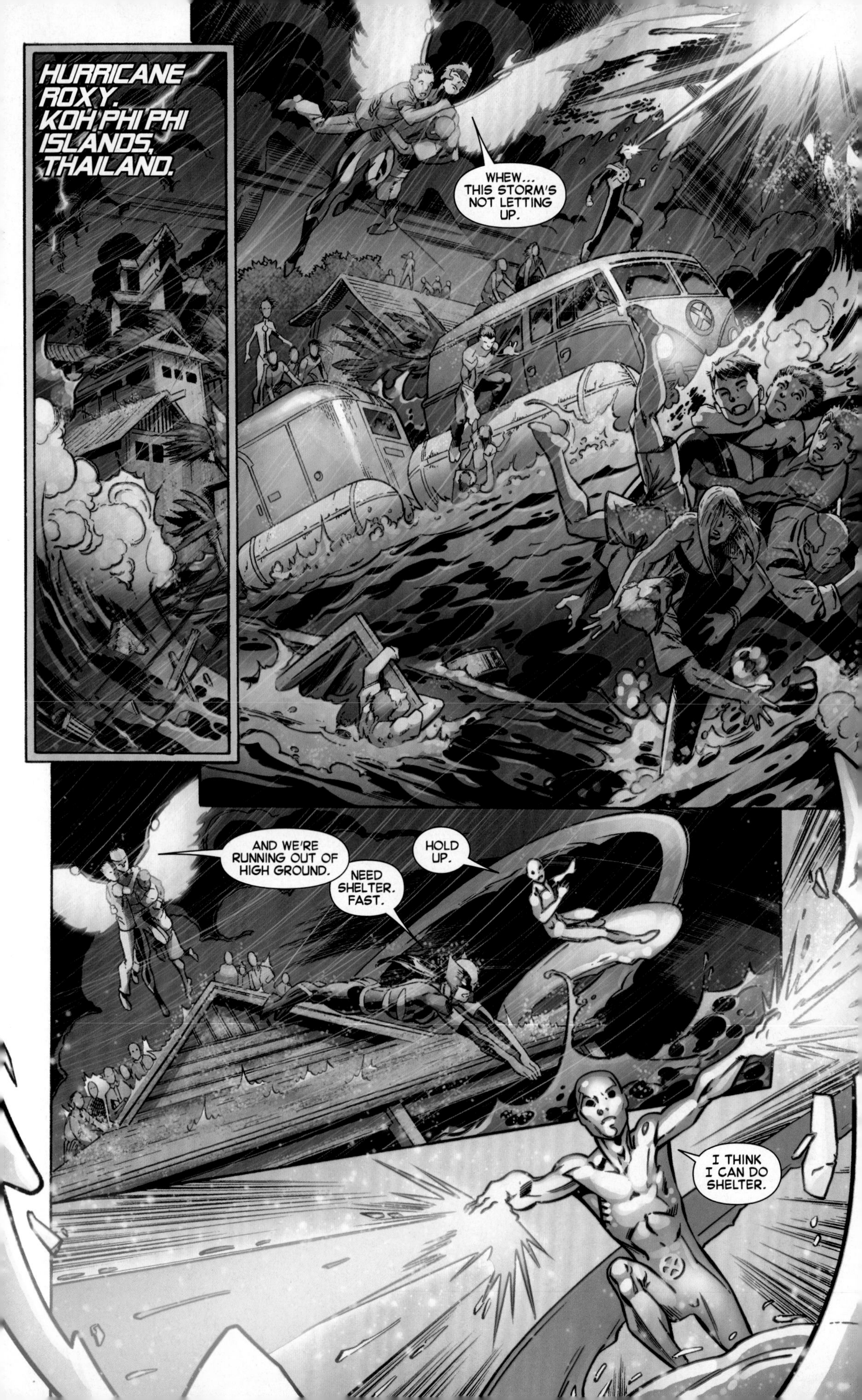
HURRICANE ROXY. KOH PHI PHI ISLANDS, THAILAND.
WHEW... THIS STORM'S NOT LETTING UP.
AND WE'RE RUNNING OUT OF HIGH GROUND.
NEED SHELTER. FAST.
HOLD UP.
I THINK I CAN DO SHELTER.

WHOA...

INCREDIBLE.

YEAH, IT IS...GO BOBBY.

NICE WORK THERE, ROBERT. QUICK THINKING.

KINDA HUGE, HUH?.

IT'S LIKE I'M GETTING... *ICIER* ALL THE TIME.

WAIT. WAIT. WAIT. WAIT.

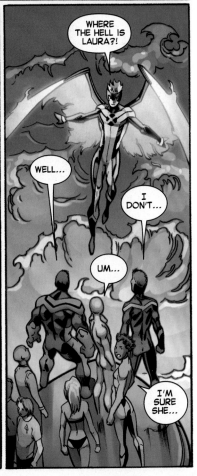

WHERE THE HELL IS LAURA?!

WELL...

I DON'T...

UM...

I'M SURE SHE...

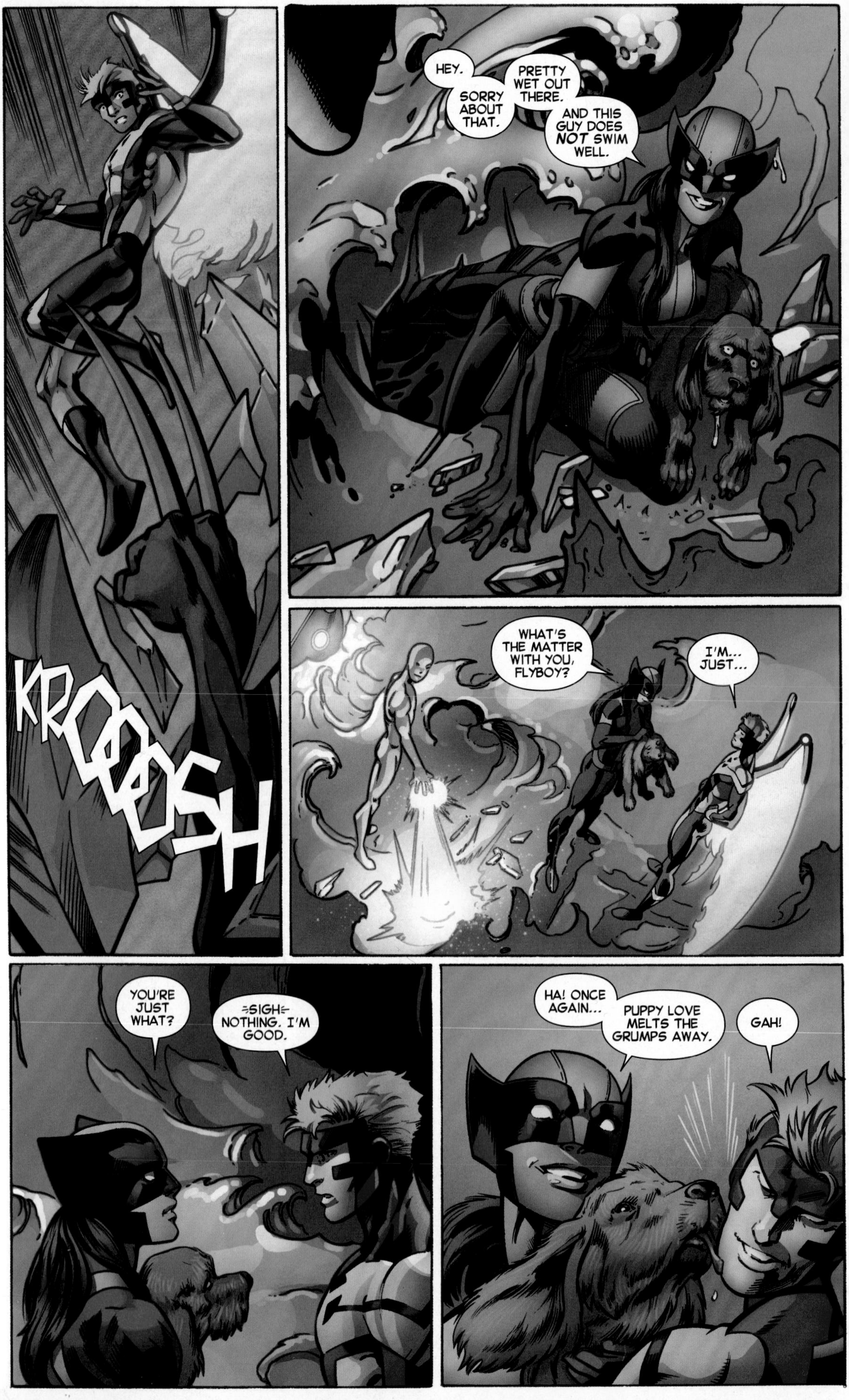
KROOOSH
HEY.
SORRY ABOUT THAT.
PRETTY WET OUT THERE.
AND THIS GUY DOES NOT SWIM WELL.
WHAT'S THE MATTER WITH YOU, FLYBOY?
I'M... JUST...
YOU'RE JUST WHAT?
=SIGH= NOTHING. I'M GOOD.
HA! ONCE AGAIN...
PUPPY LOVE MELTS THE GRUMPS AWAY.
GAH!

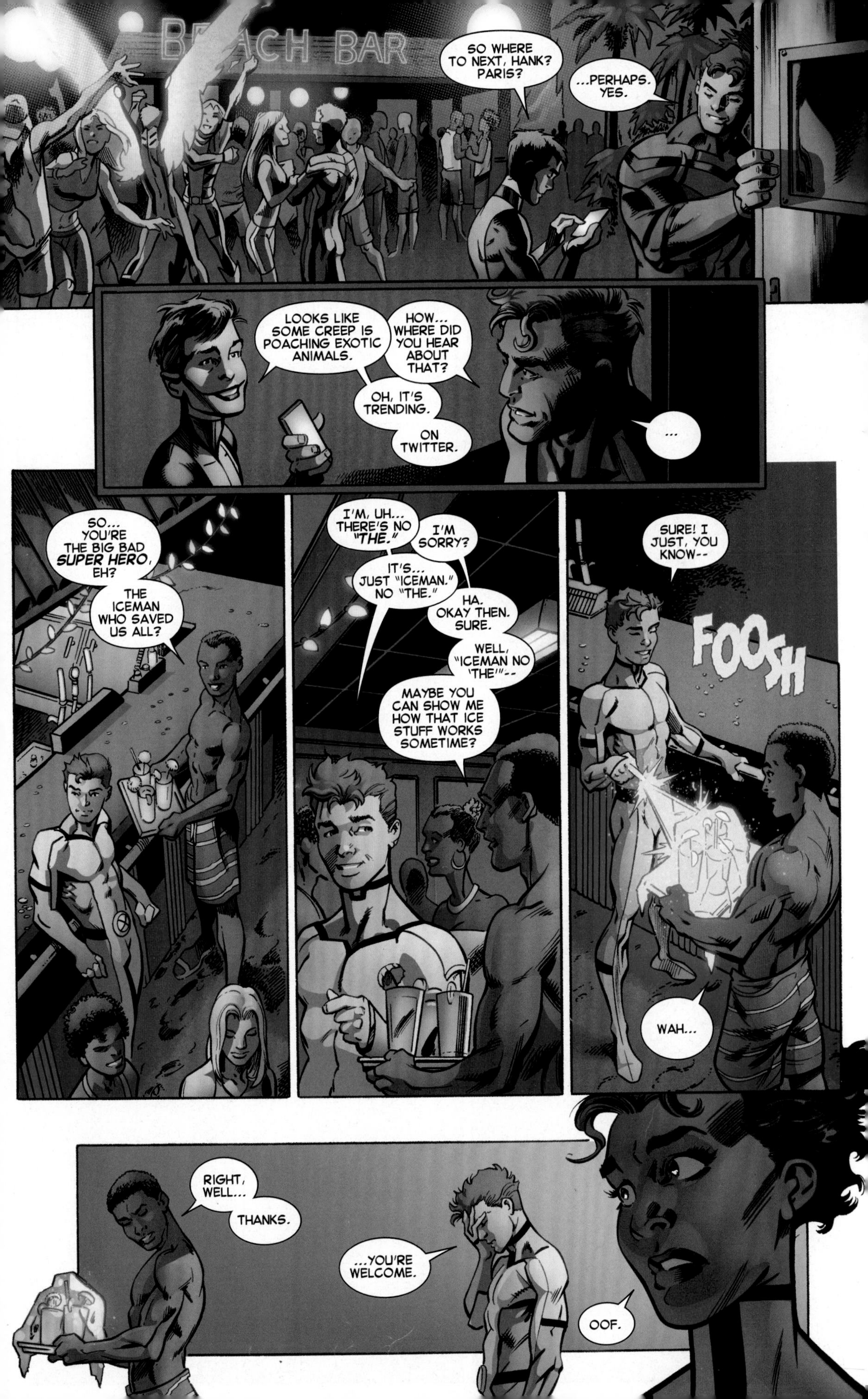
BEACH BAR
SO WHERE TO NEXT, HANK? PARIS?
...PERHAPS. YES.
LOOKS LIKE SOME CREEP IS POACHING EXOTIC ANIMALS.
HOW... WHERE DID YOU HEAR ABOUT THAT?
OH, IT'S TRENDING.
ON TWITTER.
...
SO... YOU'RE THE BIG BAD SUPER HERO, EH?
THE ICEMAN WHO SAVED US ALL?
I'M, UH... THERE'S NO "THE."
I'M SORRY?
IT'S... JUST "ICEMAN." NO "THE."
HA. OKAY THEN. SURE.
WELL, "ICEMAN NO 'THE'"--
MAYBE YOU CAN SHOW ME HOW THAT ICE STUFF WORKS SOMETIME?
SURE! I JUST, YOU KNOW--
FOOSH
WAH...
RIGHT, WELL...
THANKS.
...YOU'RE WELCOME.
OOF.

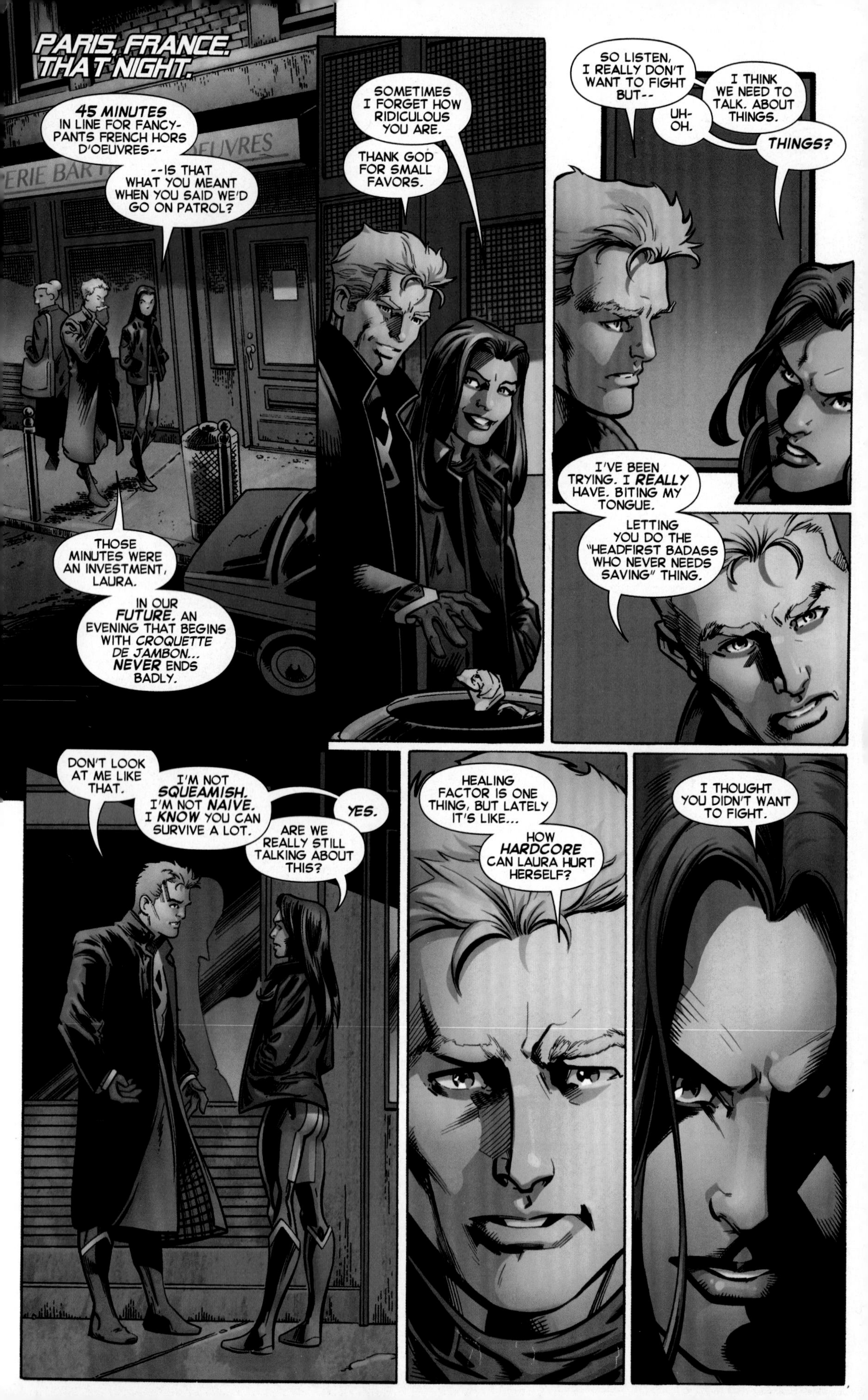
PARIS, FRANCE. THAT NIGHT.
45 MINUTES IN LINE FOR FANCY-PANTS FRENCH HORS D'OEUVRES--
--IS THAT WHAT YOU MEANT WHEN YOU SAID WE'D GO ON PATROL?
THOSE MINUTES WERE AN INVESTMENT, LAURA.
IN OUR FUTURE. AN EVENING THAT BEGINS WITH CROQUETTE DE JAMBON... NEVER ENDS BADLY.
SOMETIMES I FORGET HOW RIDICULOUS YOU ARE.
THANK GOD FOR SMALL FAVORS.
SO LISTEN, I REALLY DON'T WANT TO FIGHT BUT--
UH-OH.
I THINK WE NEED TO TALK. ABOUT THINGS.
THINGS?
I'VE BEEN TRYING. I REALLY HAVE. BITING MY TONGUE.
LETTING YOU DO THE "HEADFIRST BADASS WHO NEVER NEEDS SAVING" THING.
DON'T LOOK AT ME LIKE THAT.
I'M NOT SQUEAMISH. I'M NOT NAIVE. I KNOW YOU CAN SURVIVE A LOT.
YES.
ARE WE REALLY STILL TALKING ABOUT THIS?
HEALING FACTOR IS ONE THING, BUT LATELY IT'S LIKE...
HOW HARDCORE CAN LAURA HURT HERSELF?
I THOUGHT YOU DIDN'T WANT TO FIGHT.

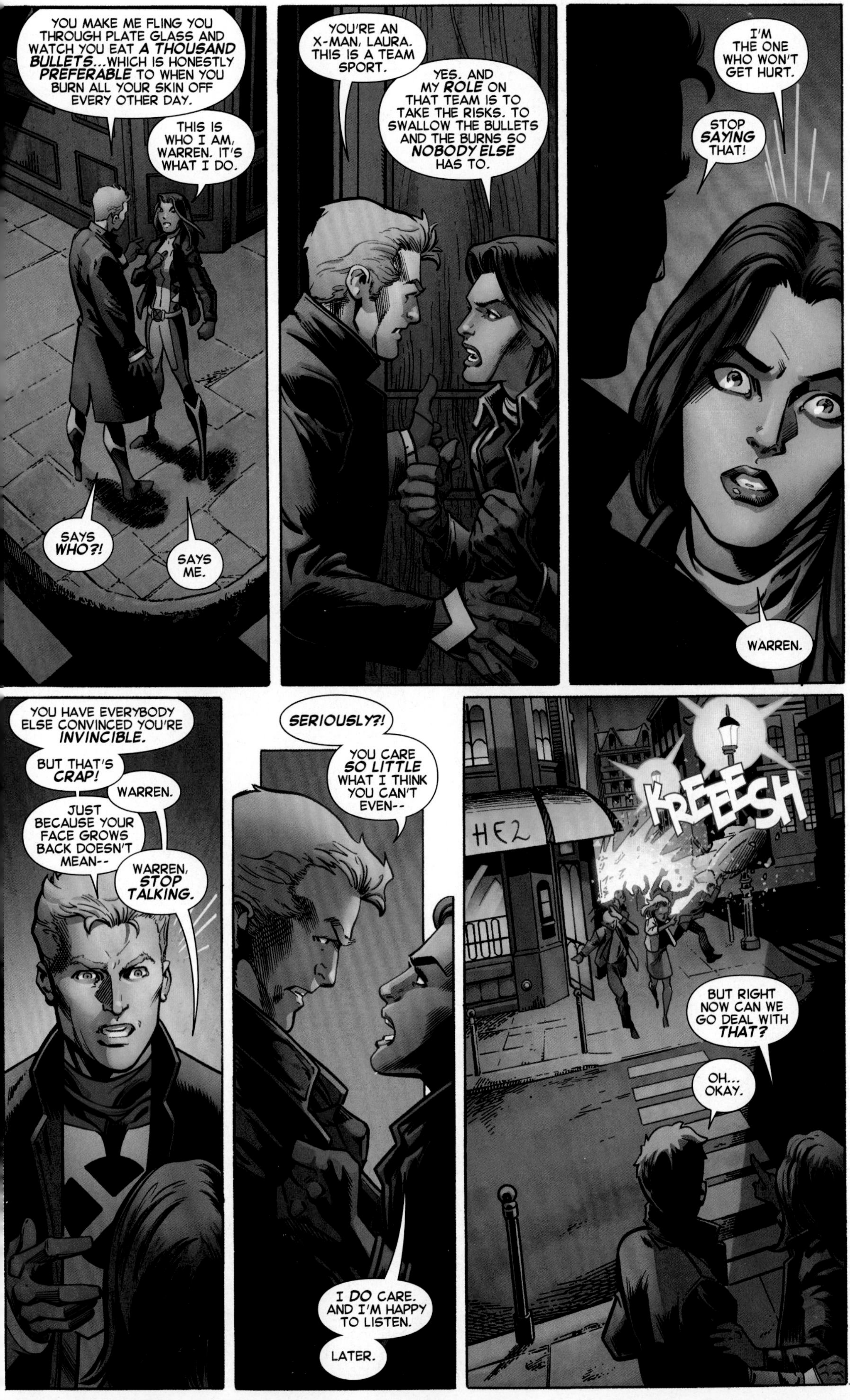
YOU MAKE ME FLING YOU THROUGH PLATE GLASS AND WATCH YOU EAT A THOUSAND BULLETS...WHICH IS HONESTLY PREFERABLE TO WHEN YOU BURN ALL YOUR SKIN OFF EVERY OTHER DAY.
THIS IS WHO I AM, WARREN. IT'S WHAT I DO.
SAYS WHO?!
SAYS ME.
YOU'RE AN X-MAN, LAURA. THIS IS A TEAM SPORT.
YES. AND MY ROLE ON THAT TEAM IS TO TAKE THE RISKS. TO SWALLOW THE BULLETS AND THE BURNS SO NOBODY ELSE HAS TO.
I'M THE ONE WHO WON'T GET HURT.
STOP SAYING THAT!
WARREN.
YOU HAVE EVERYBODY ELSE CONVINCED YOU'RE INVINCIBLE.
BUT THAT'S CRAP!
WARREN.
JUST BECAUSE YOUR FACE GROWS BACK DOESN'T MEAN--
WARREN, STOP TALKING.
SERIOUSLY?!
YOU CARE SO LITTLE WHAT I THINK YOU CAN'T EVEN--
I DO CARE. AND I'M HAPPY TO LISTEN.
LATER.
KREEESH
BUT RIGHT NOW CAN WE GO DEAL WITH THAT?
OH... OKAY.

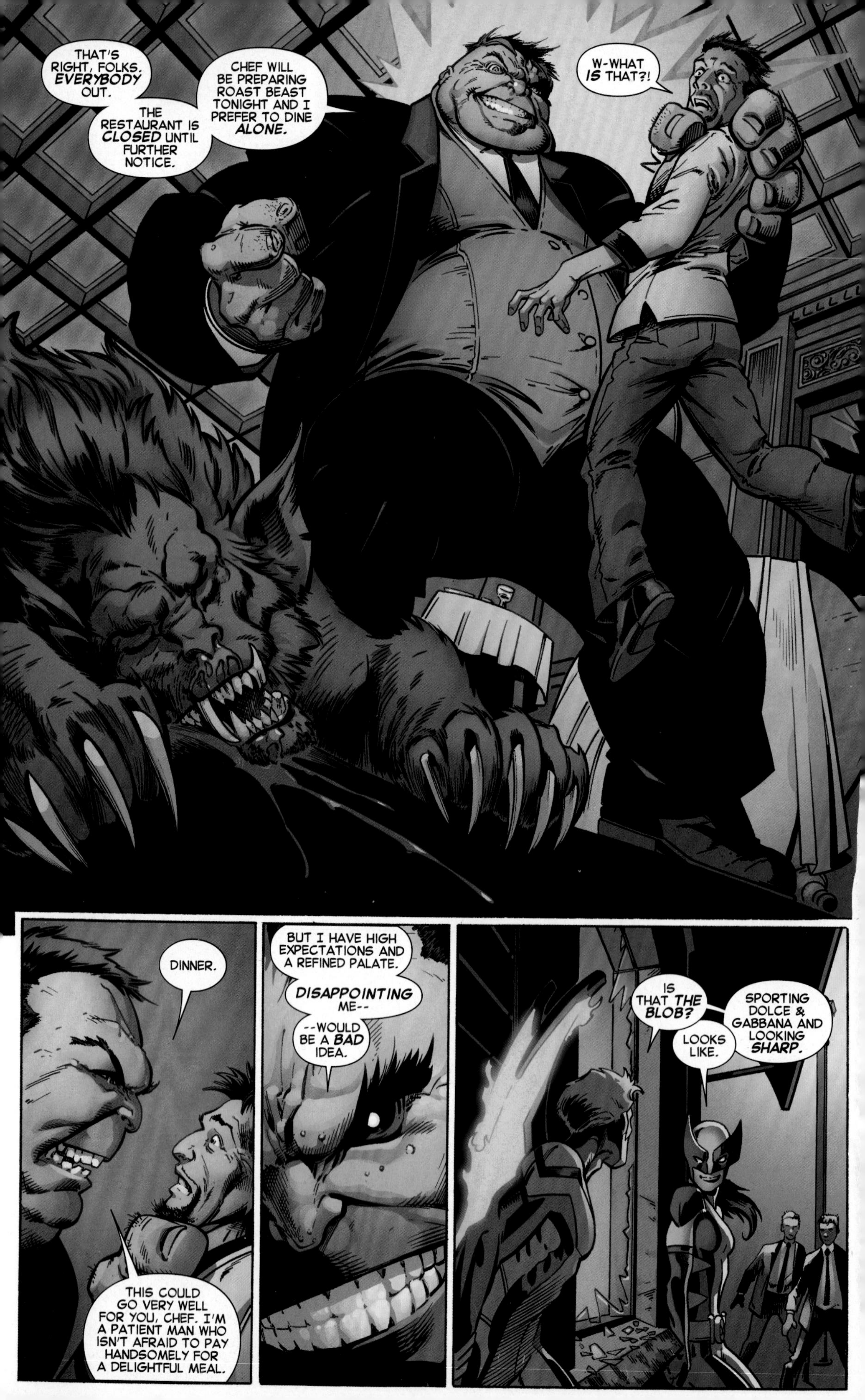
THAT'S RIGHT, FOLKS. EVERYBODY OUT.
THE RESTAURANT IS CLOSED UNTIL FURTHER NOTICE.
CHEF WILL BE PREPARING ROAST BEAST TONIGHT AND I PREFER TO DINE ALONE.
W-WHAT IS THAT?!
DINNER.
THIS COULD GO VERY WELL FOR YOU, CHEF. I'M A PATIENT MAN WHO ISN'T AFRAID TO PAY HANDSOMELY FOR A DELIGHTFUL MEAL.
BUT I HAVE HIGH EXPECTATIONS AND A REFINED PALATE.
DISAPPOINTING ME--
--WOULD BE A BAD IDEA.
IS THAT THE BLOB?
SPORTING DOLCE & GABBANA AND LOOKING SHARP.
LOOKS LIKE.

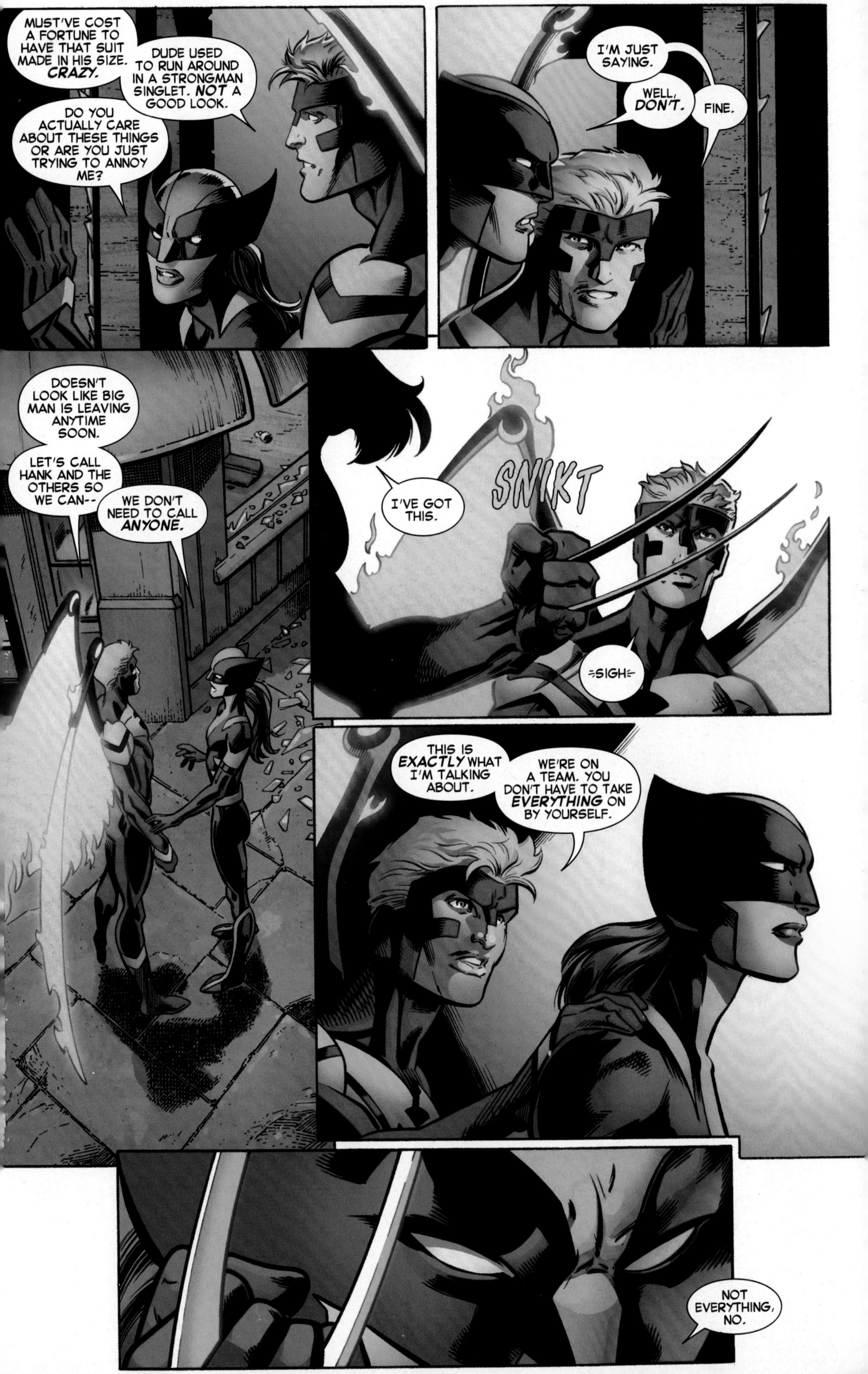

MUST'VE COST A FORTUNE TO HAVE THAT SUIT MADE IN HIS SIZE. *CRAZY.*
DUDE USED TO RUN AROUND IN A STRONGMAN SINGLET. *NOT* A GOOD LOOK.
DO YOU ACTUALLY CARE ABOUT THESE THINGS OR ARE YOU JUST TRYING TO ANNOY ME?
I'M JUST SAYING.
WELL, *DON'T.*
FINE.
DOESN'T LOOK LIKE BIG MAN IS LEAVING ANYTIME SOON.
LET'S CALL HANK AND THE OTHERS SO WE CAN--
WE DON'T NEED TO CALL *ANYONE.*
I'VE GOT THIS.
SNIKT
=SIGH=
THIS IS *EXACTLY* WHAT I'M TALKING ABOUT.
WE'RE ON A TEAM. YOU DON'T HAVE TO TAKE *EVERYTHING* ON BY YOURSELF.
NOT EVERYTHING, NO.

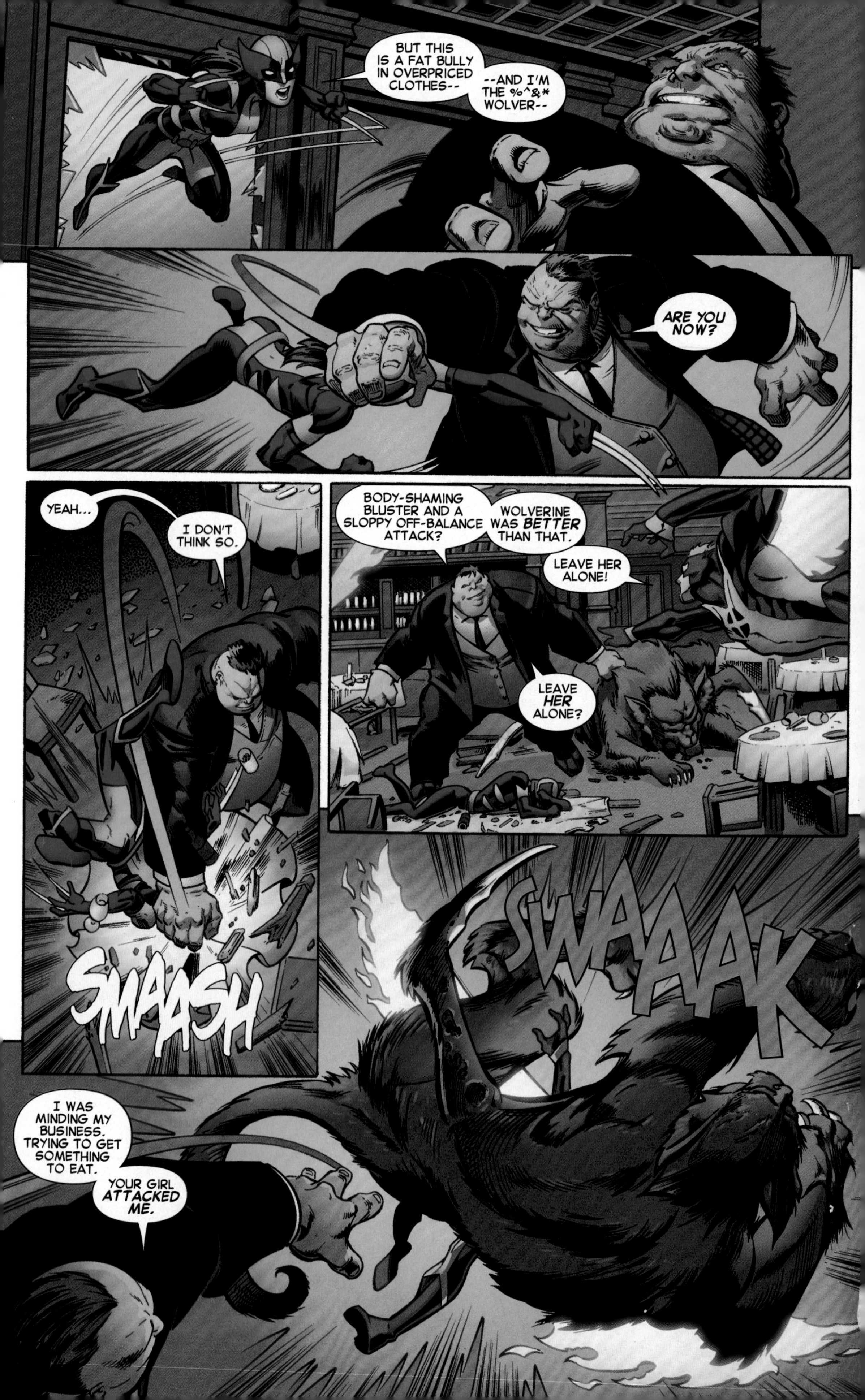

BUT THIS IS A FAT BULLY IN OVERPRICED CLOTHES--
--AND I'M THE %^&* WOLVER--
ARE YOU NOW?
YEAH...
I DON'T THINK SO.
SMAASH
BODY-SHAMING BLUSTER AND A SLOPPY OFF-BALANCE ATTACK?
WOLVERINE WAS BETTER THAN THAT.
LEAVE HER ALONE!
LEAVE HER ALONE?
SWAAAK
I WAS MINDING MY BUSINESS. TRYING TO GET SOMETHING TO EAT.
YOUR GIRL ATTACKED ME.

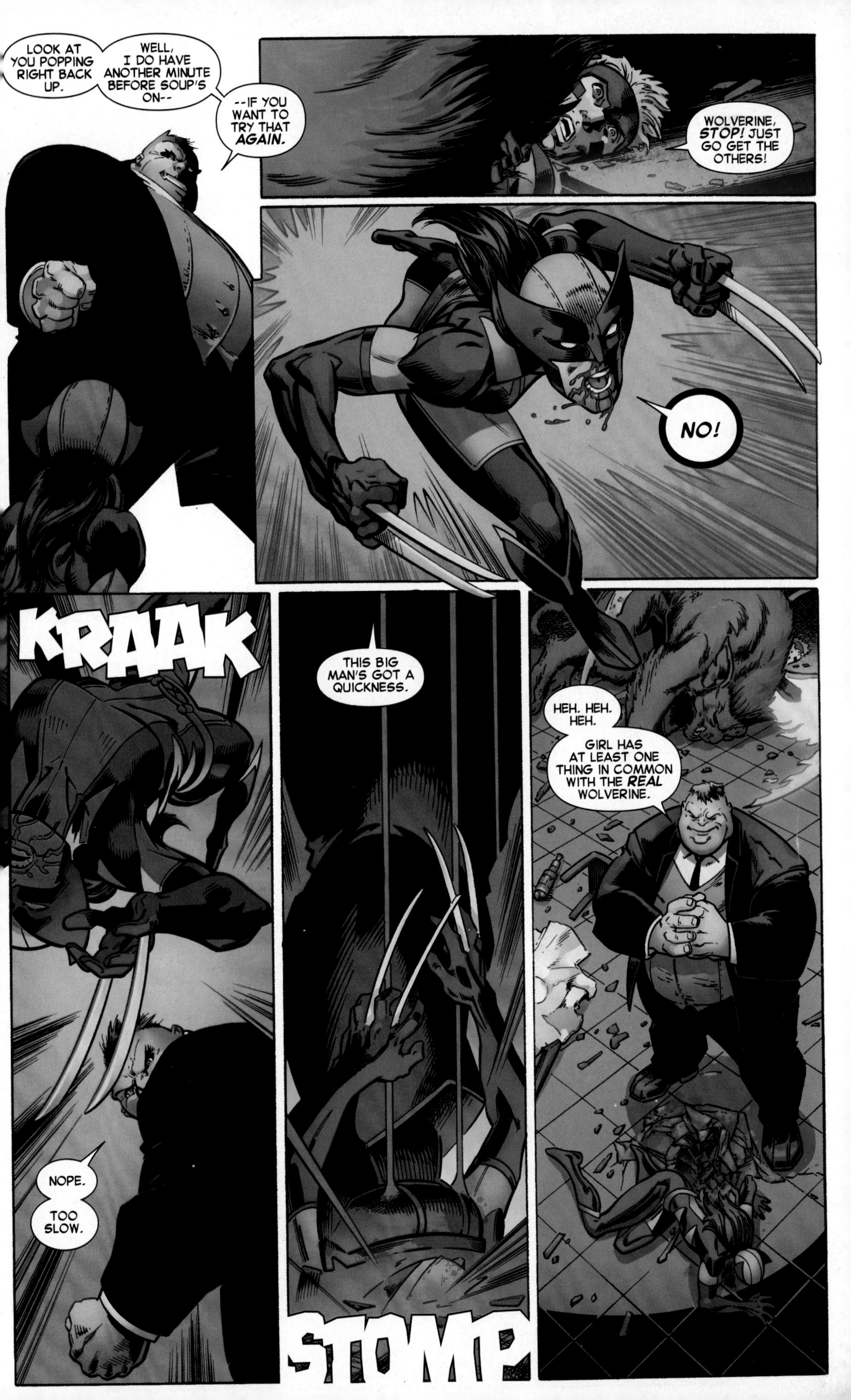
LOOK AT YOU POPPING RIGHT BACK UP.
WELL, I DO HAVE ANOTHER MINUTE BEFORE SOUP'S ON--
--IF YOU WANT TO TRY THAT AGAIN.
WOLVERINE, STOP! JUST GO GET THE OTHERS!
NO!
KRAAK
NOPE.
TOO SLOW.
THIS BIG MAN'S GOT A QUICKNESS.
STOMP
HEH. HEH. HEH.
GIRL HAS AT LEAST ONE THING IN COMMON WITH THE REAL WOLVERINE.

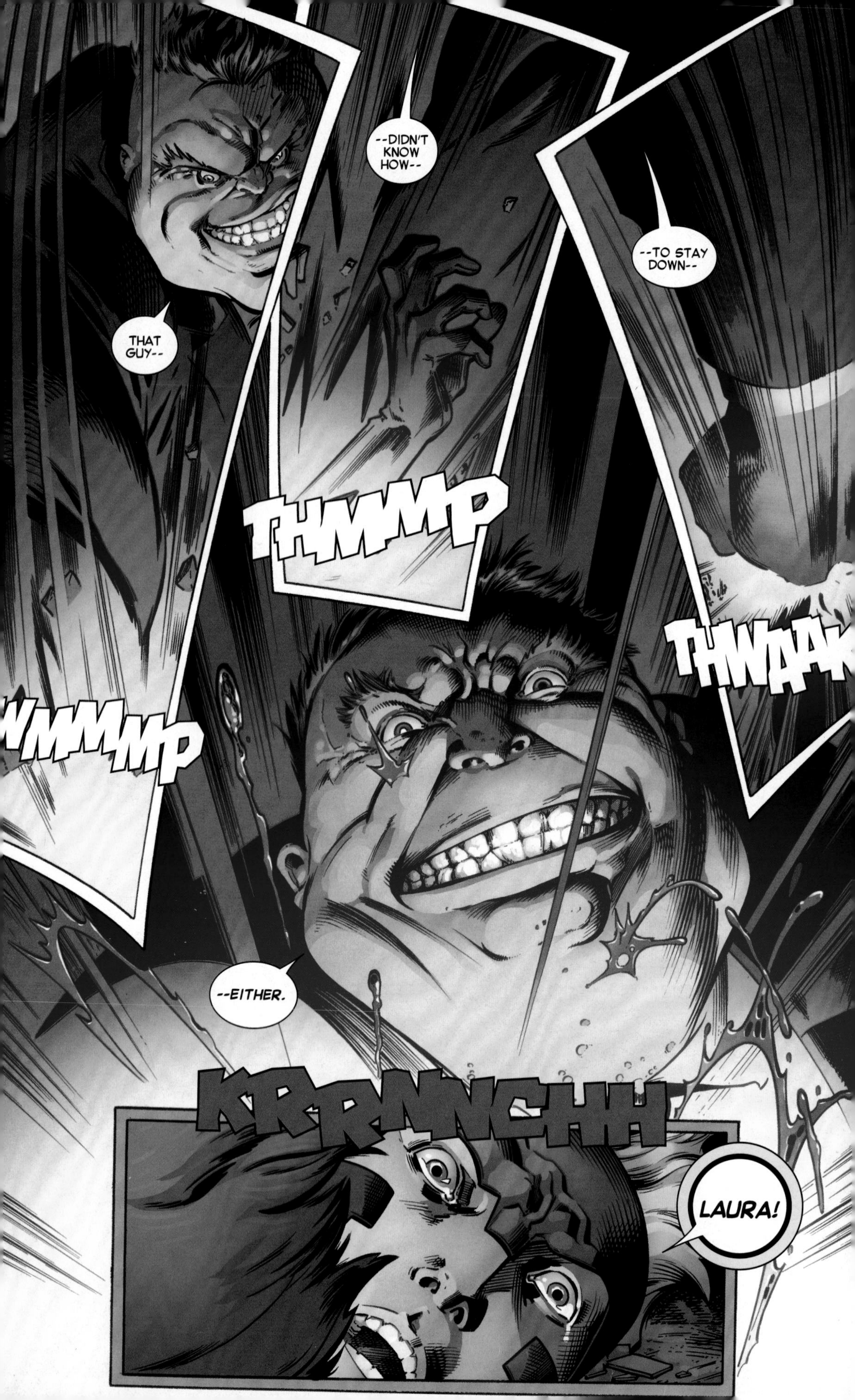
THAT GUY--
--DIDN'T KNOW HOW--
--TO STAY DOWN--
THMMP
THWAAK
WMMMP
--EITHER.
KRRNNCHH
LAURA!

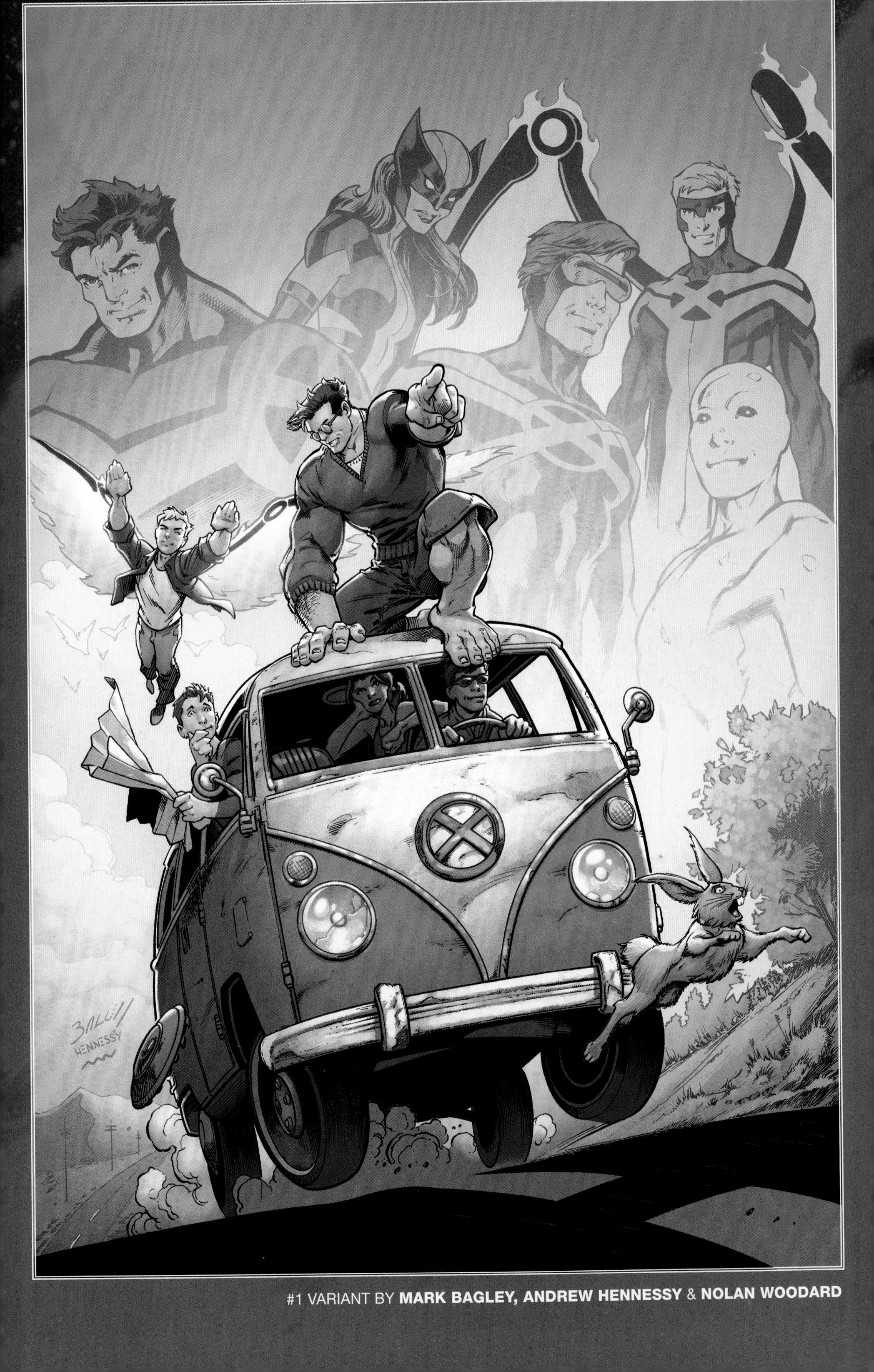
HENNESSY

#1 VARIANT BY **MARK BAGLEY, ANDREW HENNESSY** & **NOLAN WOODARD**

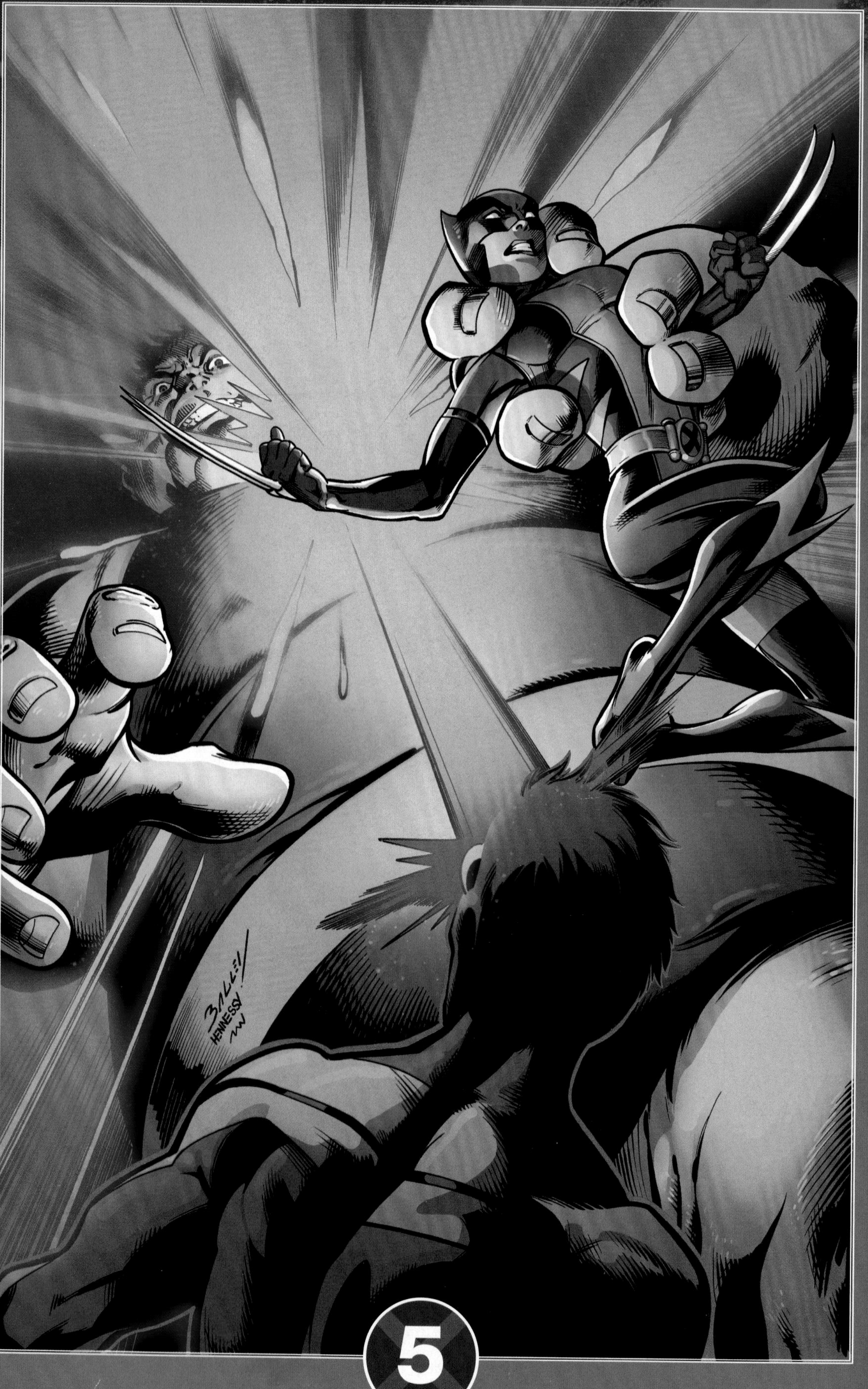

5

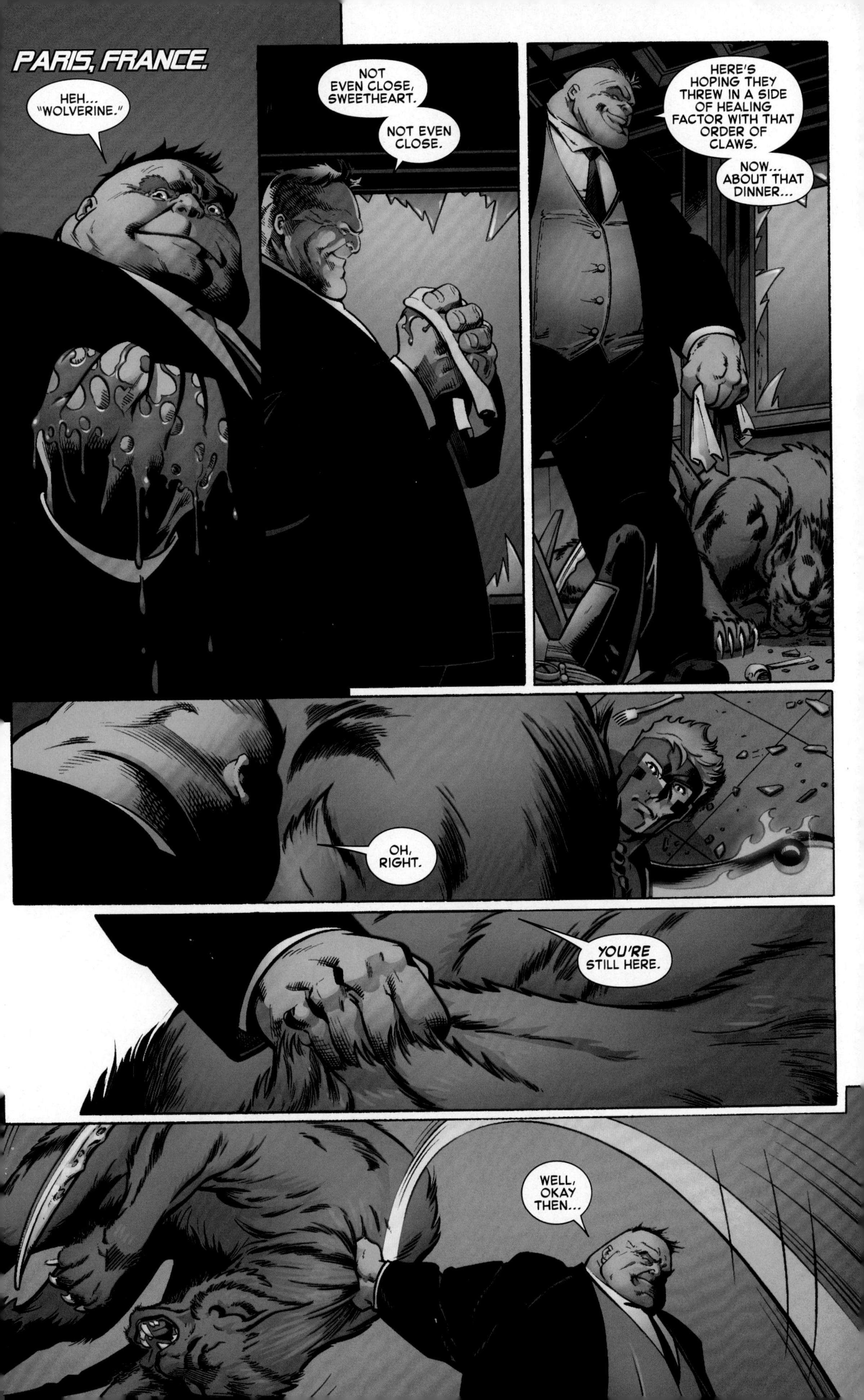
PARIS, FRANCE.
HEH... "WOLVERINE."
NOT EVEN CLOSE, SWEETHEART.
NOT EVEN CLOSE.
HERE'S HOPING THEY THREW IN A SIDE OF HEALING FACTOR WITH THAT ORDER OF CLAWS.
NOW... ABOUT THAT DINNER...
OH, RIGHT.
YOU'RE STILL HERE.
WELL, OKAY THEN...

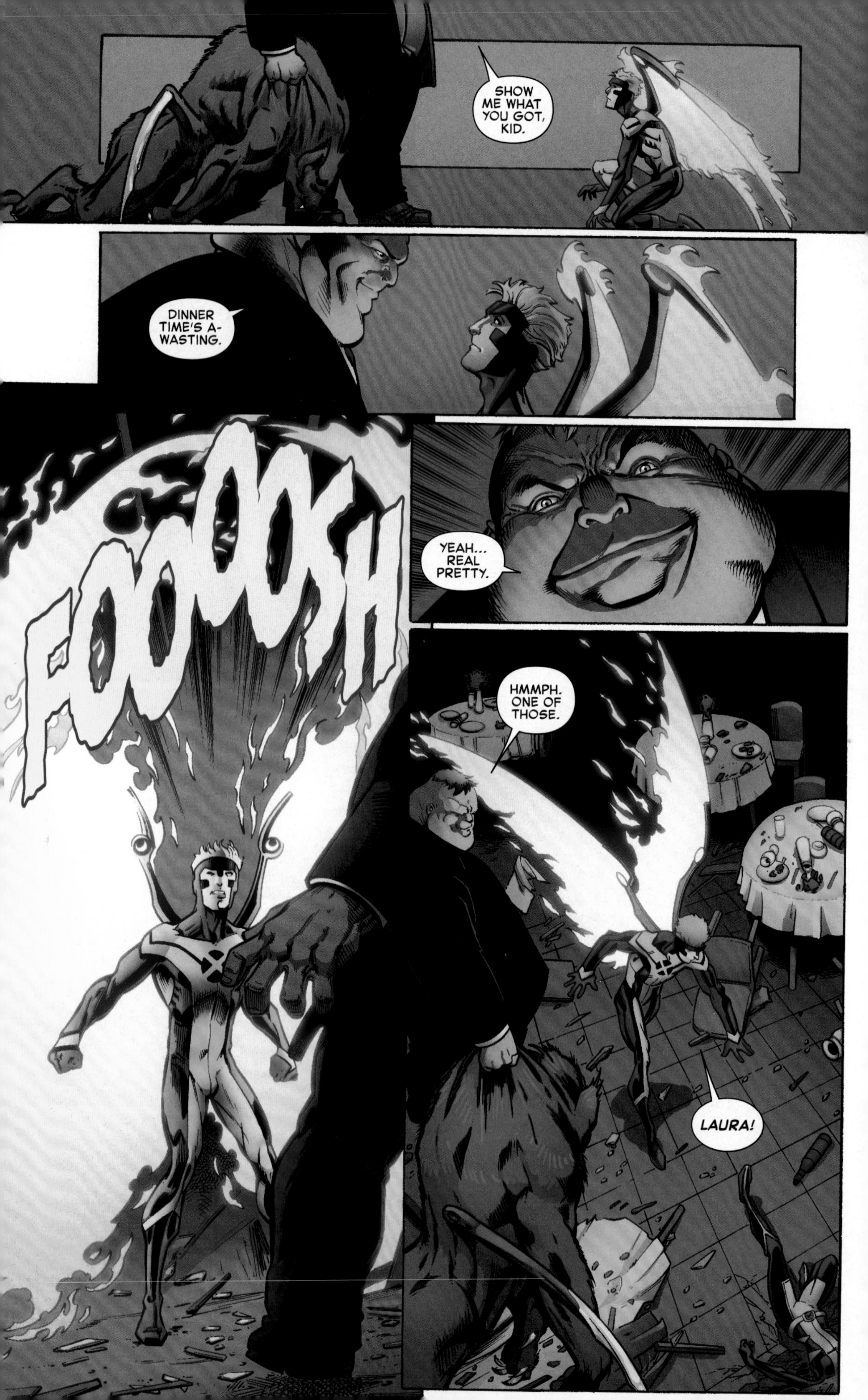
SHOW ME WHAT YOU GOT, KID.
DINNER TIME'S A-WASTING.
FOOOSH
YEAH... REAL PRETTY.
HMMPH. ONE OF THOSE.
LAURA!

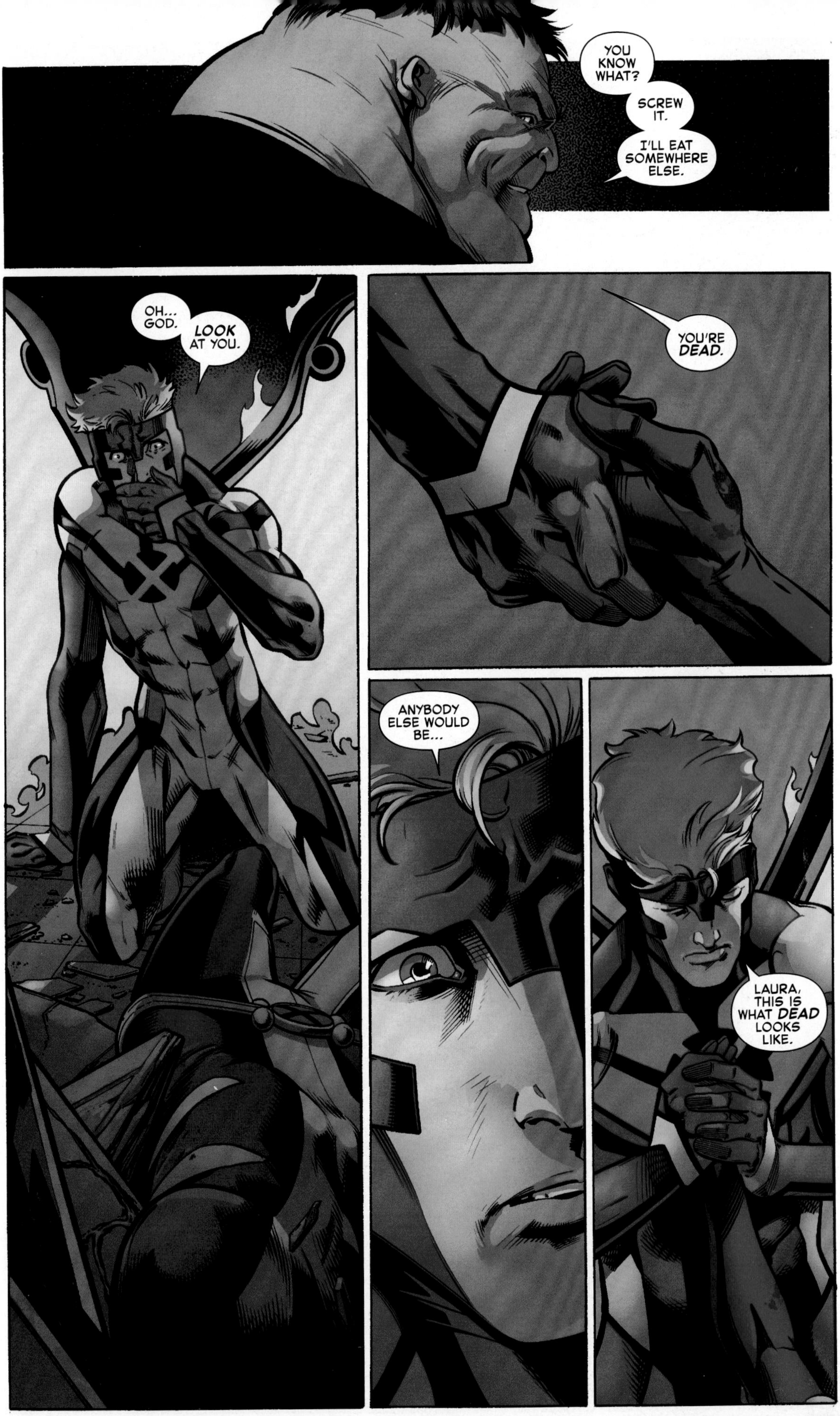
YOU KNOW WHAT?
SCREW IT.
I'LL EAT SOMEWHERE ELSE.
OH... GOD. LOOK AT YOU.
YOU'RE DEAD.
ANYBODY ELSE WOULD BE...
LAURA, THIS IS WHAT DEAD LOOKS LIKE.

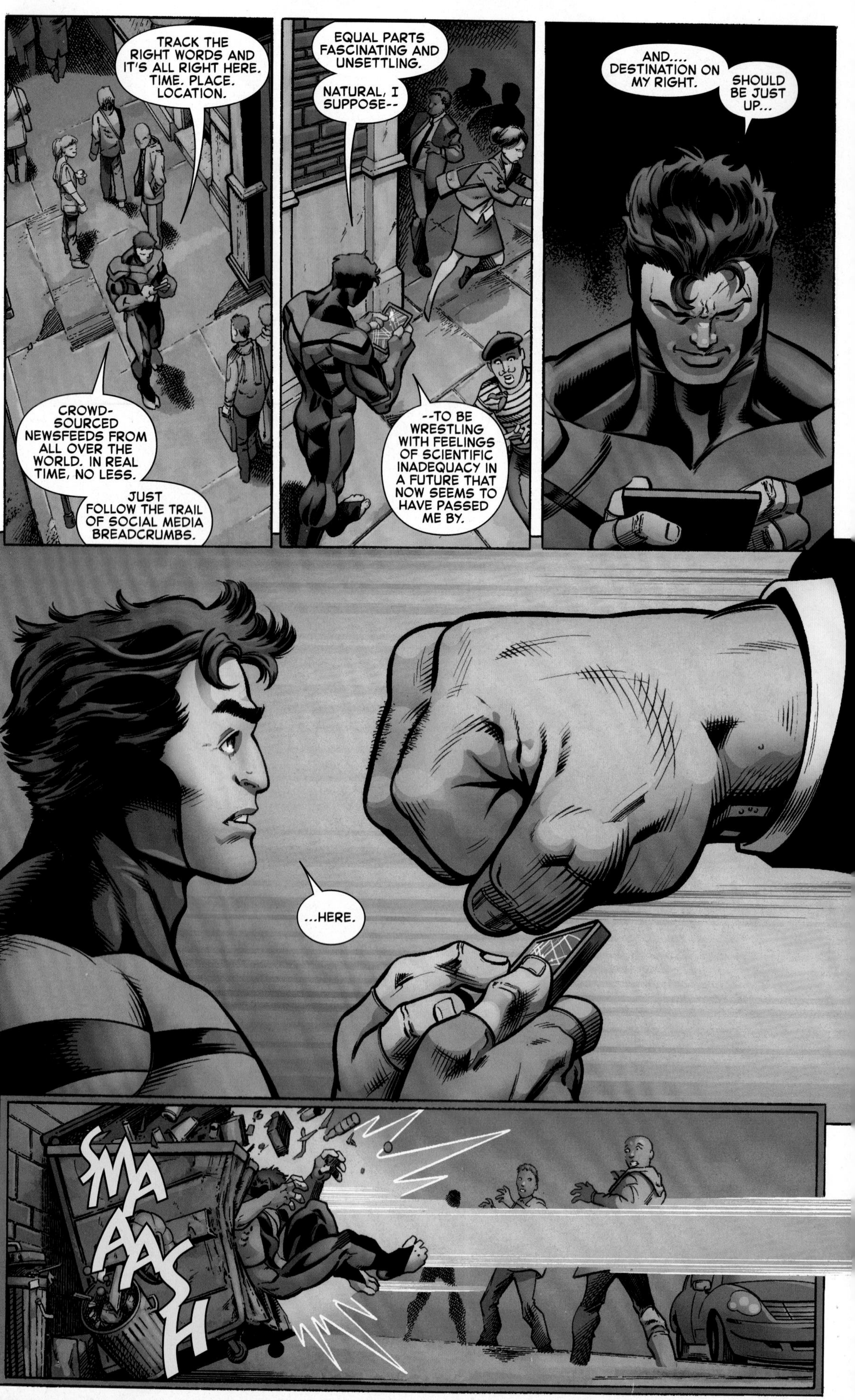

TRACK THE RIGHT WORDS AND IT'S ALL RIGHT HERE. TIME. PLACE. LOCATION.
CROWD-SOURCED NEWSFEEDS FROM ALL OVER THE WORLD. IN REAL TIME, NO LESS.
JUST FOLLOW THE TRAIL OF SOCIAL MEDIA BREADCRUMBS.
EQUAL PARTS FASCINATING AND UNSETTLING.
NATURAL, I SUPPOSE--
--TO BE WRESTLING WITH FEELINGS OF SCIENTIFIC INADEQUACY IN A FUTURE THAT NOW SEEMS TO HAVE PASSED ME BY.
AND.... DESTINATION ON MY RIGHT.
SHOULD BE JUST UP...
...HERE.
SMAAASH

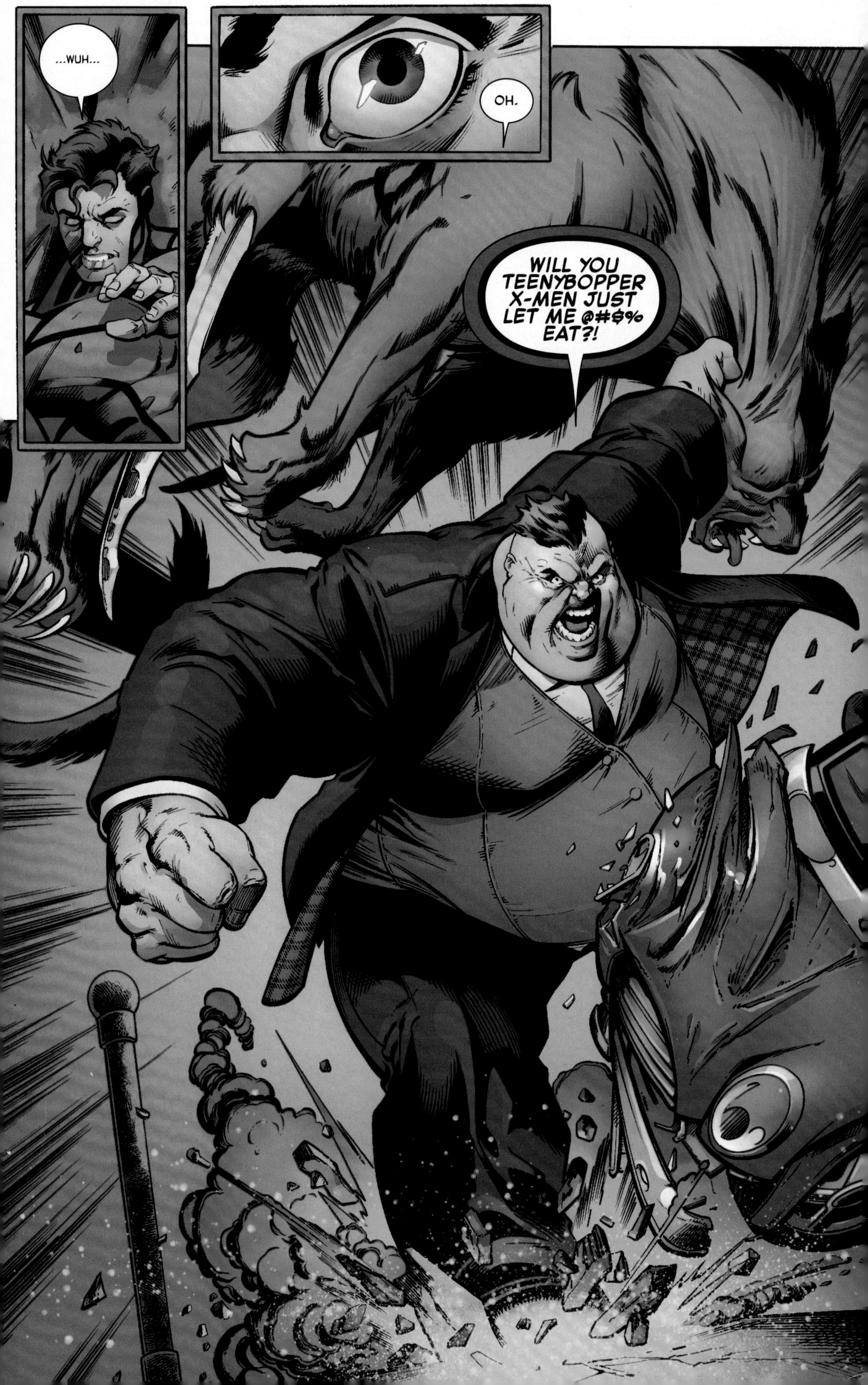
...WUH...
OH.
WILL YOU TEENYBOPPER X-MEN JUST LET ME @#$% EAT?!

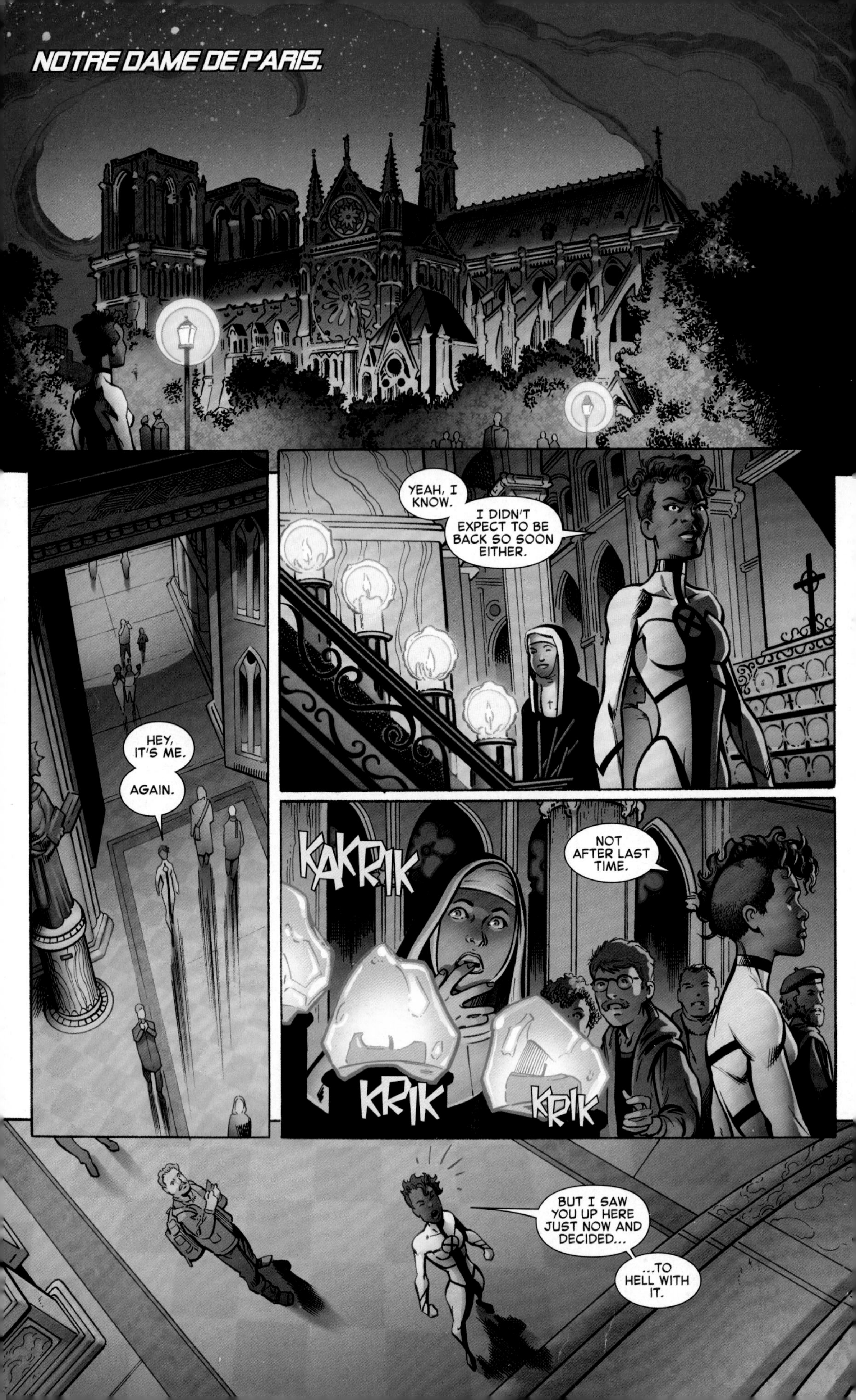
NOTRE DAME DE PARIS.
HEY, IT'S ME.
AGAIN.
YEAH, I KNOW.
I DIDN'T EXPECT TO BE BACK SO SOON EITHER.
KAKRIK
NOT AFTER LAST TIME.
KRIK
KRIK
BUT I SAW YOU UP HERE JUST NOW AND DECIDED...
...TO HELL WITH IT.

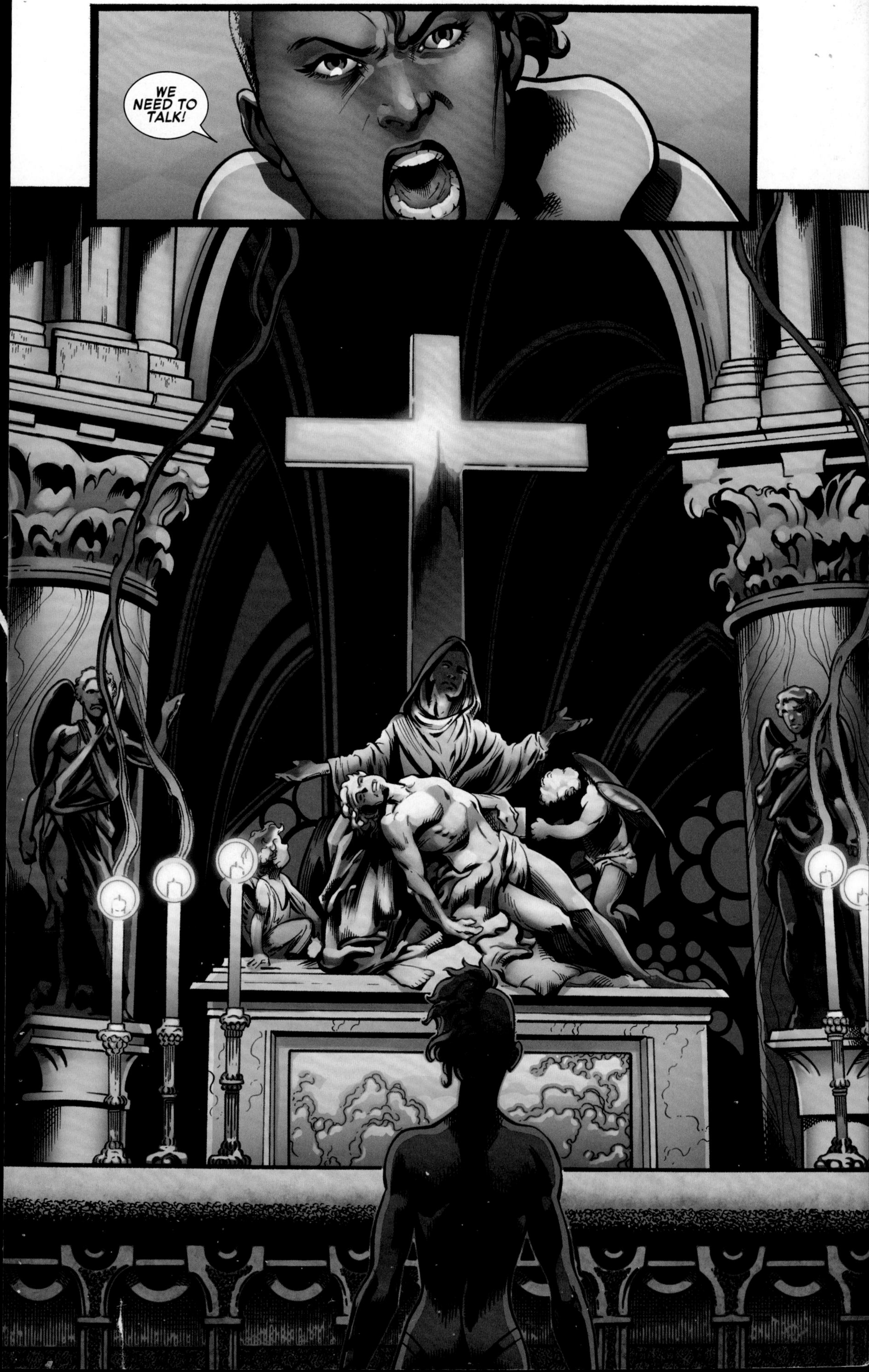
WE NEED TO TALK!

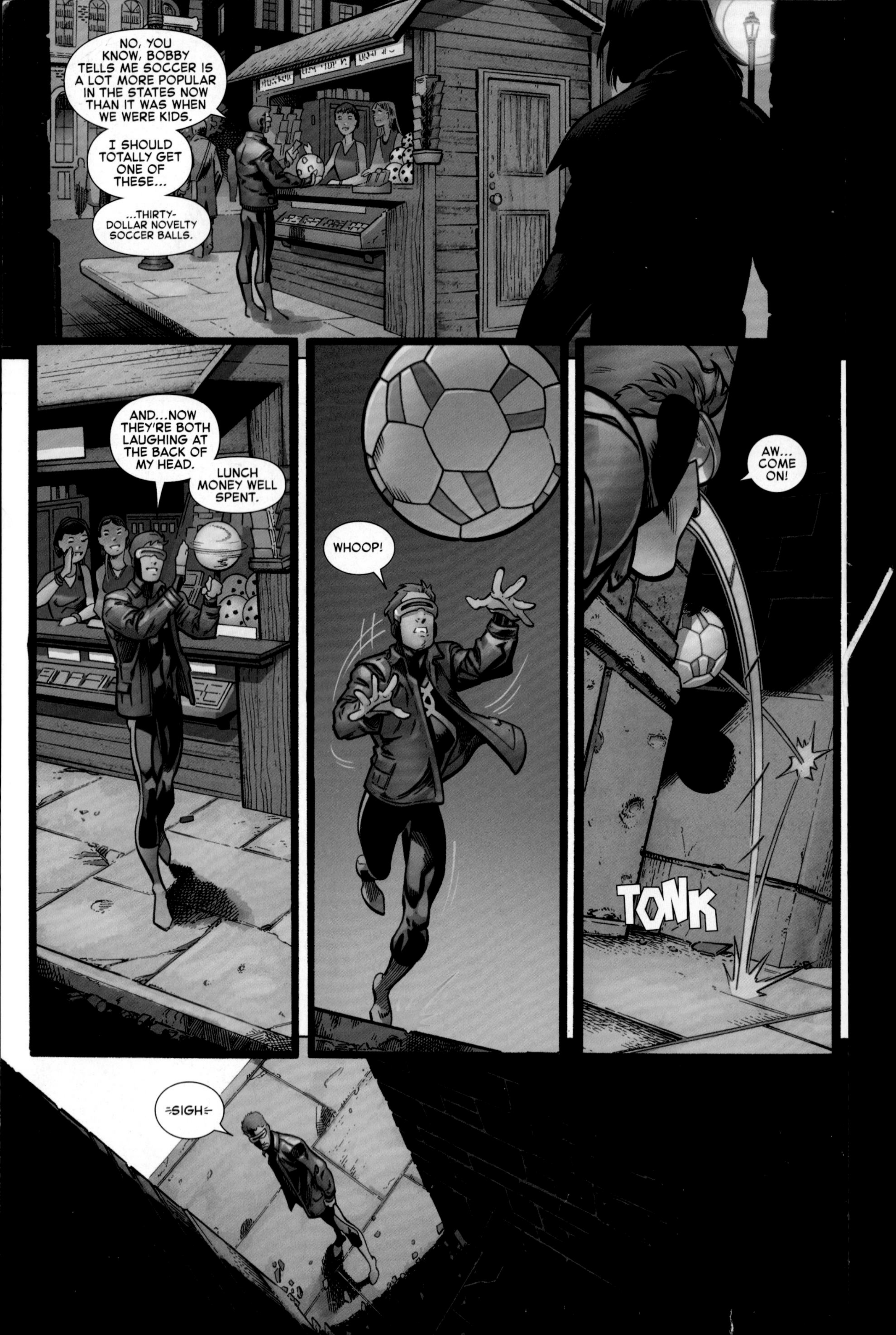

NO, YOU KNOW, BOBBY TELLS ME SOCCER IS A LOT MORE POPULAR IN THE STATES NOW THAN IT WAS WHEN WE WERE KIDS.
I SHOULD TOTALLY GET ONE OF THESE...
...THIRTY-DOLLAR NOVELTY SOCCER BALLS.
AND...NOW THEY'RE BOTH LAUGHING AT THE BACK OF MY HEAD.
LUNCH MONEY WELL SPENT.
WHOOP!
AW... COME ON!
TONK
=SIGH=

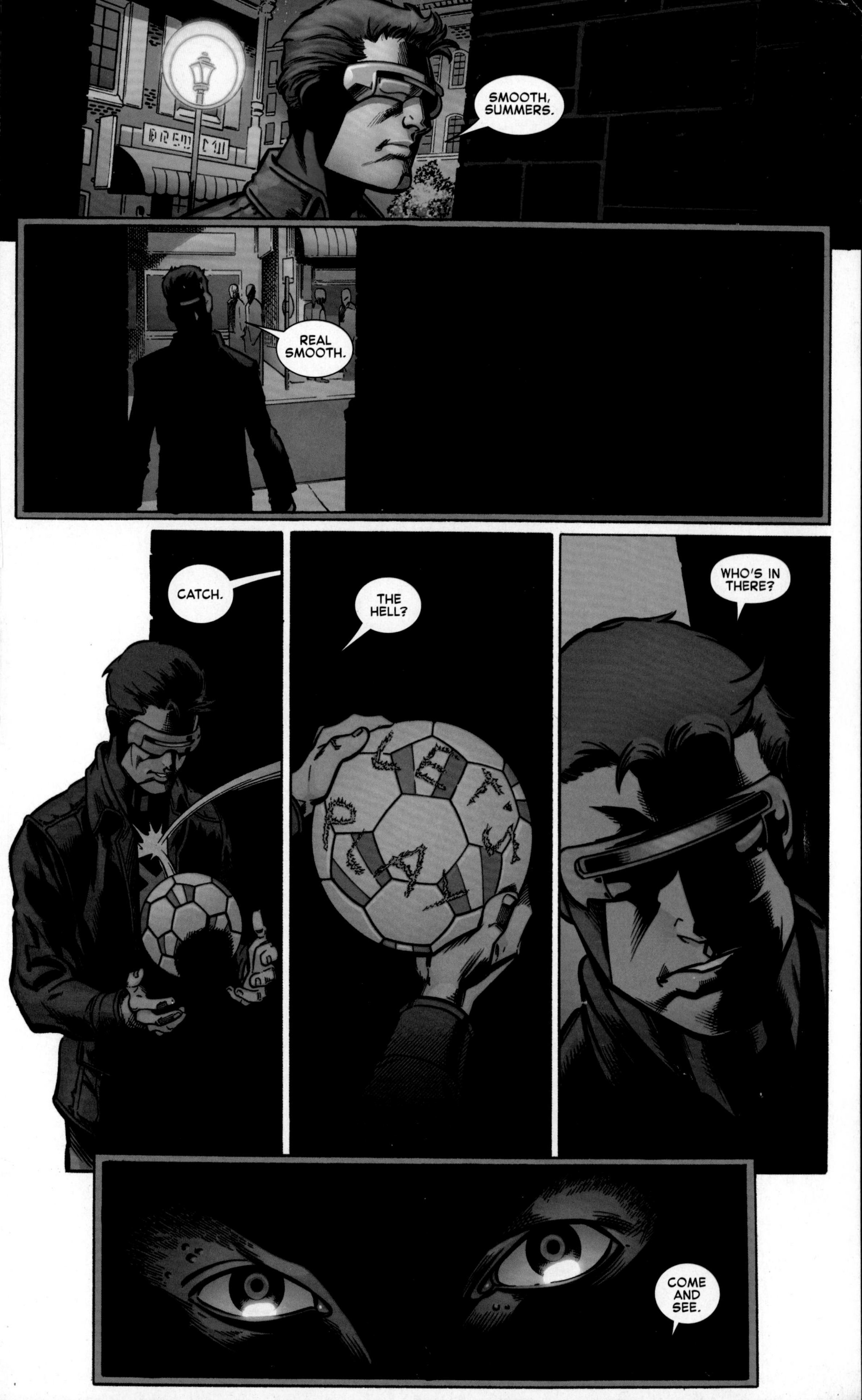
SMOOTH, SUMMERS.
REAL SMOOTH.
CATCH.
THE HELL?
WHO'S IN THERE?
COME AND SEE.

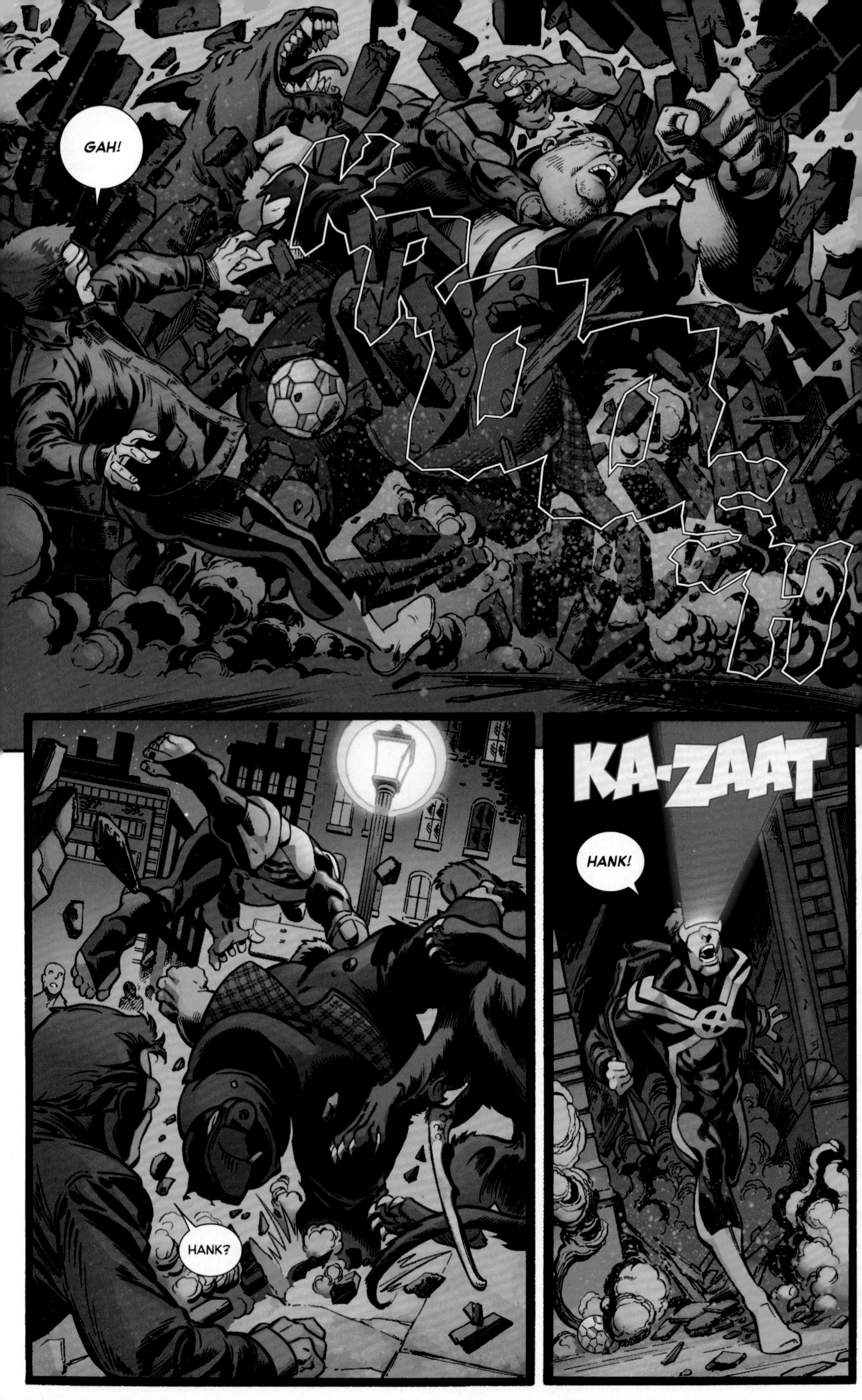
GAH!
HANK?
KA-ZAAT
HANK!

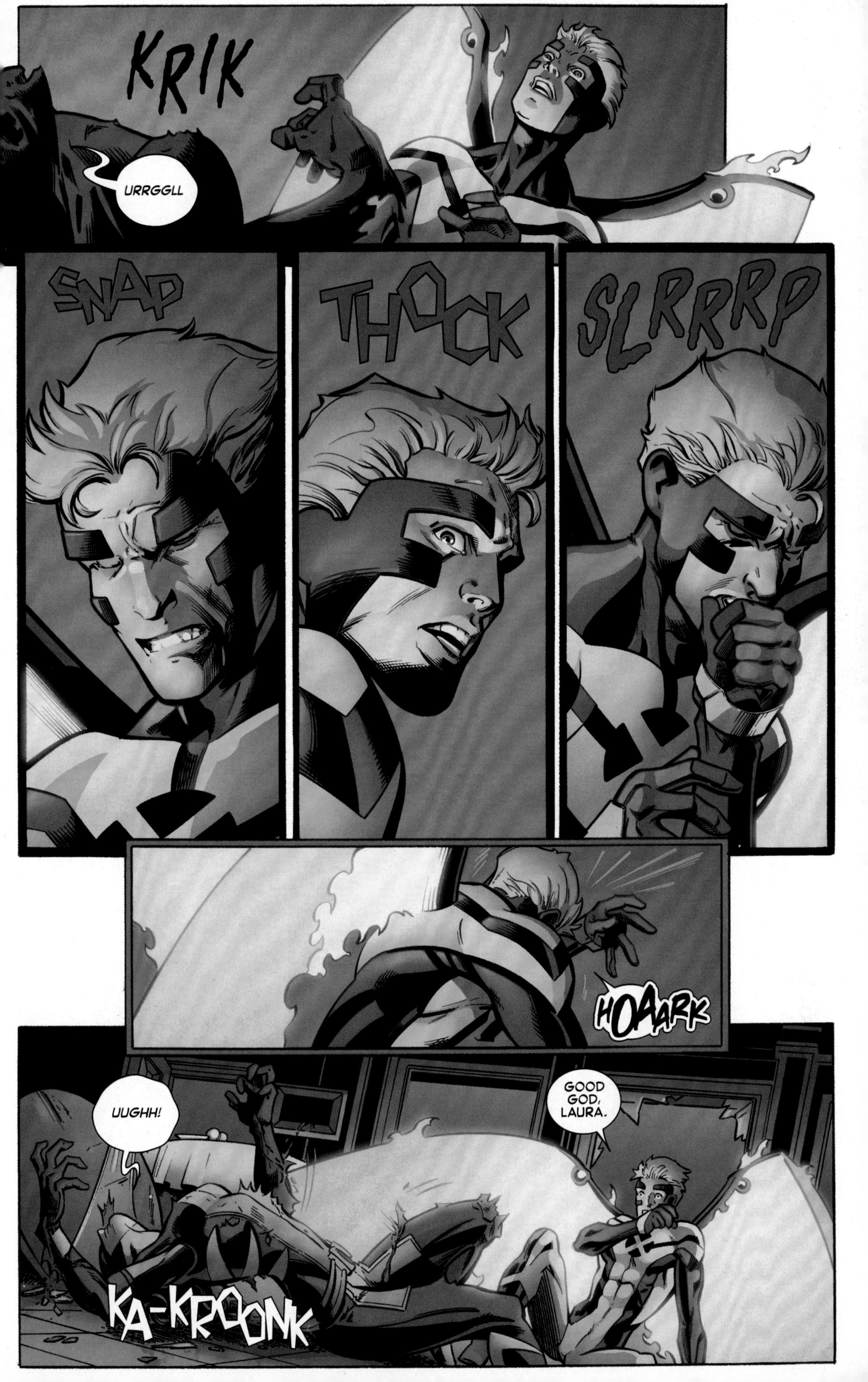
KRIK
URRGGLL
SNAP
THOCK
SLRRRP
HOAARK
UUGHH!
GOOD GOD, LAURA.
KA-KROOONK

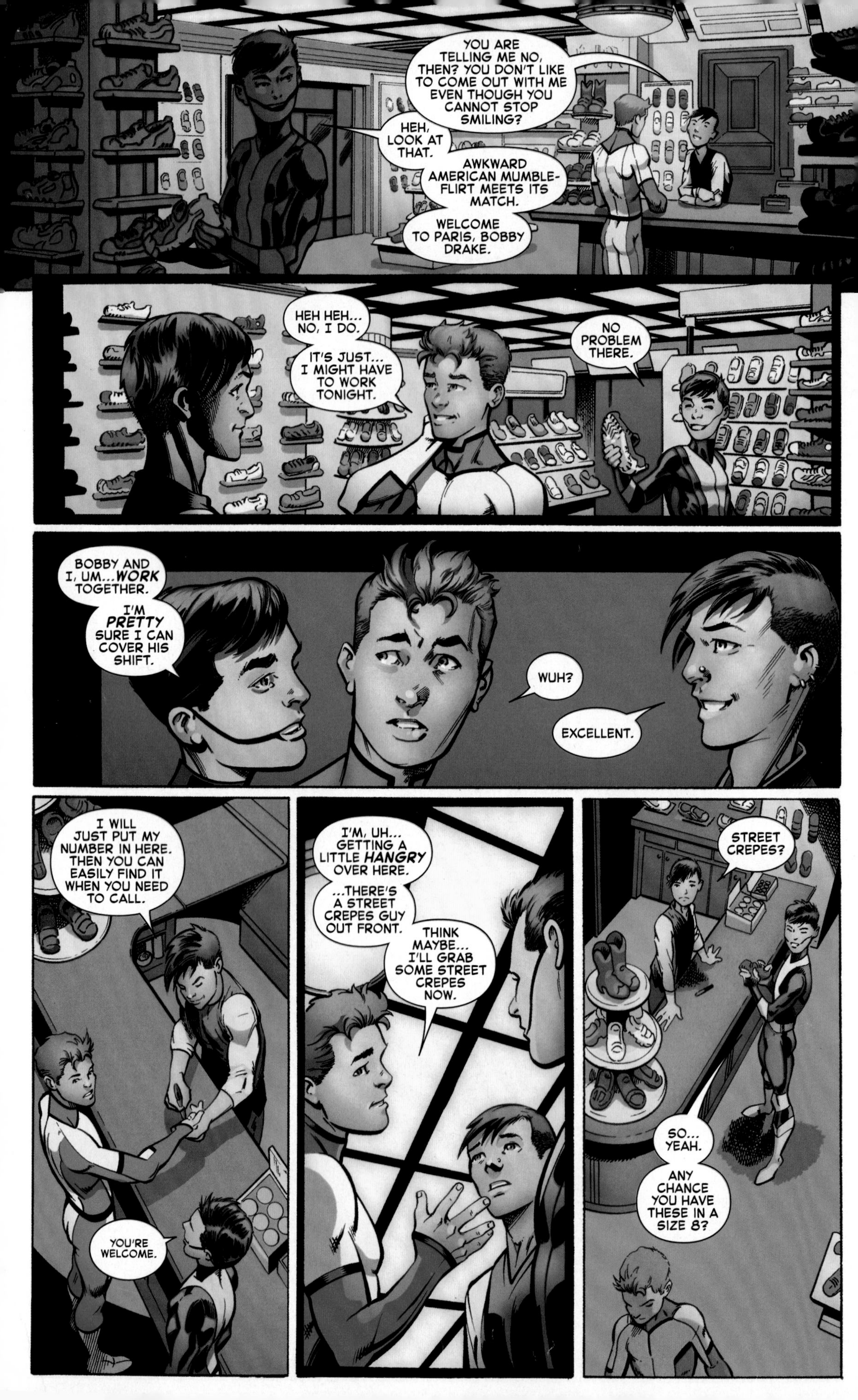
YOU ARE TELLING ME NO, THEN? YOU DON'T LIKE TO COME OUT WITH ME EVEN THOUGH YOU CANNOT STOP SMILING?
HEH, LOOK AT THAT.
AWKWARD AMERICAN MUMBLE-FLIRT MEETS ITS MATCH.
WELCOME TO PARIS, BOBBY DRAKE.
HEH HEH... NO, I DO.
IT'S JUST... I MIGHT HAVE TO WORK TONIGHT.
NO PROBLEM THERE.
BOBBY AND I, UM...WORK TOGETHER.
I'M PRETTY SURE I CAN COVER HIS SHIFT.
WUH?
EXCELLENT.
I WILL JUST PUT MY NUMBER IN HERE. THEN YOU CAN EASILY FIND IT WHEN YOU NEED TO CALL.
YOU'RE WELCOME.
I'M, UH... GETTING A LITTLE HANGRY OVER HERE.
...THERE'S A STREET CREPES GUY OUT FRONT.
THINK MAYBE... I'LL GRAB SOME STREET CREPES NOW.
STREET CREPES?
SO... YEAH.
ANY CHANCE YOU HAVE THESE IN A SIZE 8?

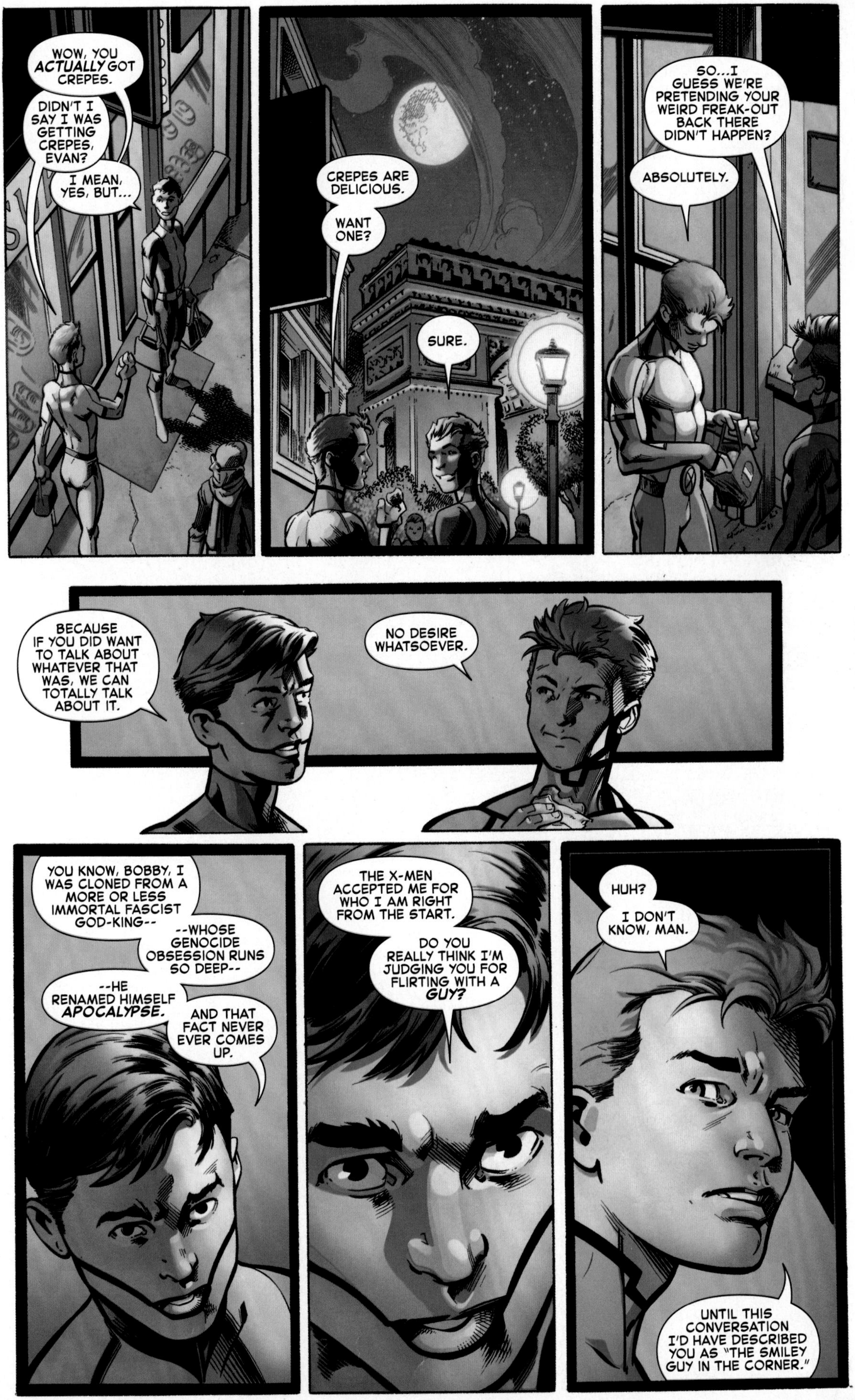
WOW, YOU *ACTUALLY* GOT CREPES.
DIDN'T I SAY I WAS GETTING CREPES, EVAN?
I MEAN, YES, BUT...
CREPES ARE DELICIOUS.
WANT ONE?
SURE.
SO...I GUESS WE'RE PRETENDING YOUR WEIRD FREAK-OUT BACK THERE DIDN'T HAPPEN?
ABSOLUTELY.
BECAUSE IF YOU DID WANT TO TALK ABOUT WHATEVER THAT WAS, WE CAN TOTALLY TALK ABOUT IT.
NO DESIRE WHATSOEVER.
YOU KNOW, BOBBY, I WAS CLONED FROM A MORE OR LESS IMMORTAL FASCIST GOD-KING--
--WHOSE GENOCIDE OBSESSION RUNS SO DEEP--
--HE RENAMED HIMSELF *APOCALYPSE.*
AND THAT FACT NEVER EVER COMES UP.
THE X-MEN ACCEPTED ME FOR WHO I AM RIGHT FROM THE START.
DO YOU REALLY THINK I'M JUDGING YOU FOR FLIRTING WITH A *GUY?*
HUH?
I DON'T KNOW, MAN.
UNTIL THIS CONVERSATION I'D HAVE DESCRIBED YOU AS "THE SMILEY GUY IN THE CORNER."

OKAY, WHAT ABOUT HANK?

IS HANK THE TYPE OF GUY WHO--

I'VE SEEN YOU PUSHING HIM AWAY LATELY.

WHAT? NO!

I'M NOT STUPID.

I KNOW HANK McCOY'S NOT A HOMOPHOBE.

OF COURSE I KNOW THAT.

THEN WHAT'S THE PROBLEM?

HANK'S LIKE MY BIG BROTHER. AND I'M A CRAZY MESS RIGHT NOW.

I'M NOT GONNA PUT THIS ON HIM. I JUST WANT TO BE HANK AND BOBBY. LIKE ALWAYS.

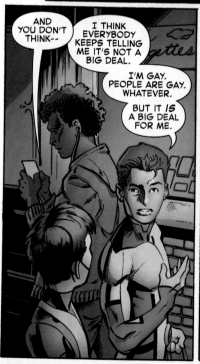

AND YOU DON'T THINK--

I THINK EVERYBODY KEEPS TELLING ME IT'S NOT A BIG DEAL.

I'M GAY. PEOPLE ARE GAY. WHATEVER.

BUT IT IS A BIG DEAL FOR ME.

IT'S A HUGE FRIGGIN' DEAL. OBVIOUSLY. LOOK AT OLD ICEMAN.

THERE'S A GROWN-UP VERSION OF ME WALKING AROUND WHO KEPT THIS SECRET FOR YEARS AND YEARS AND YEARS.

HE NEVER TOLD ANYONE.

THAT'S SCARY. THAT'S SAD.

I DON'T WANT THAT.

BUT, LIKE--

BOBBY, I REALLY HATE TO INTERRUPT, BUT...

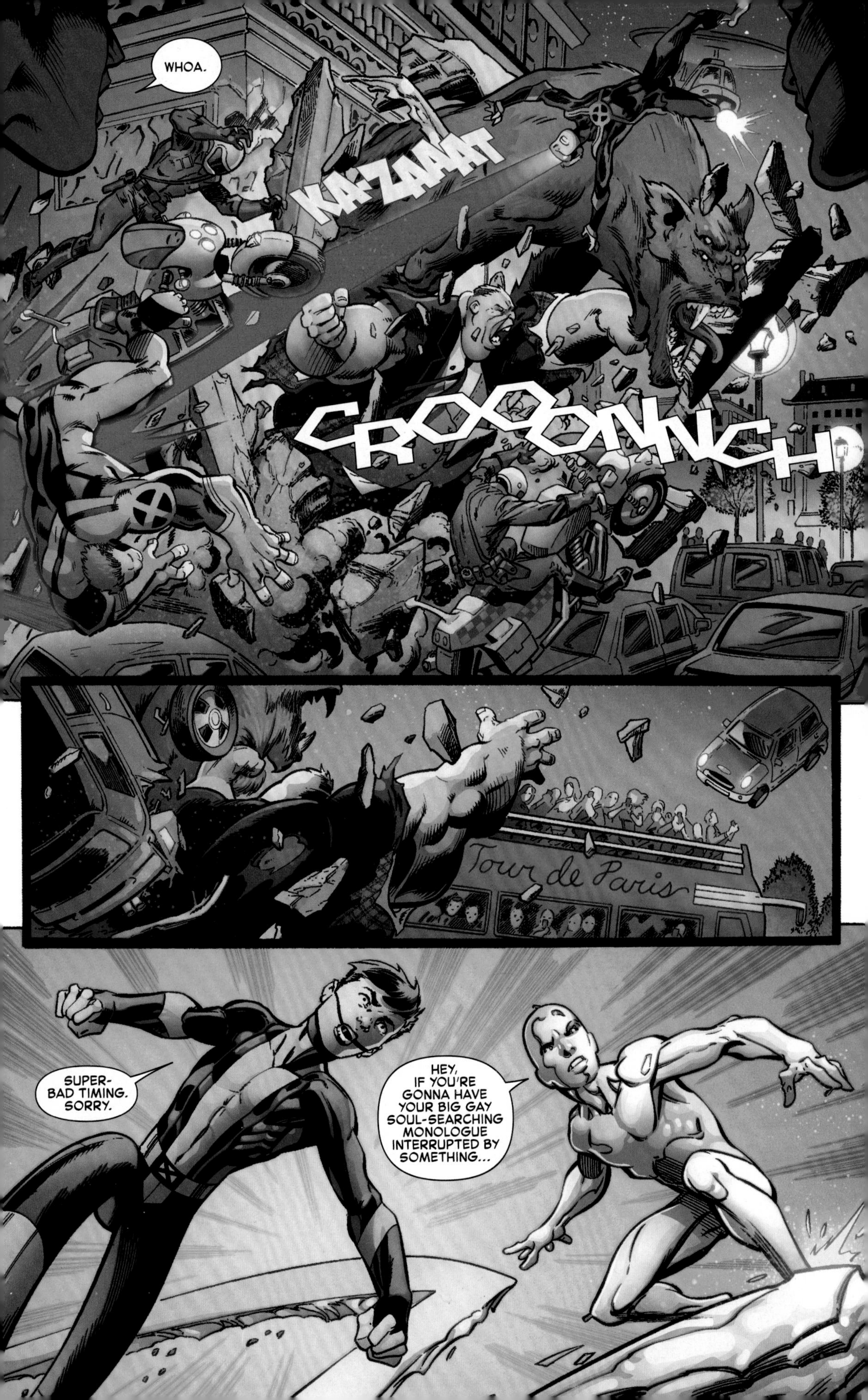
WHOA.
KA-ZAAAT
CROOOONNCH
Tour de Paris
SUPER-BAD TIMING. SORRY.
HEY, IF YOU'RE GONNA HAVE YOUR BIG GAY SOUL-SEARCHING MONOLOGUE INTERRUPTED BY SOMETHING...

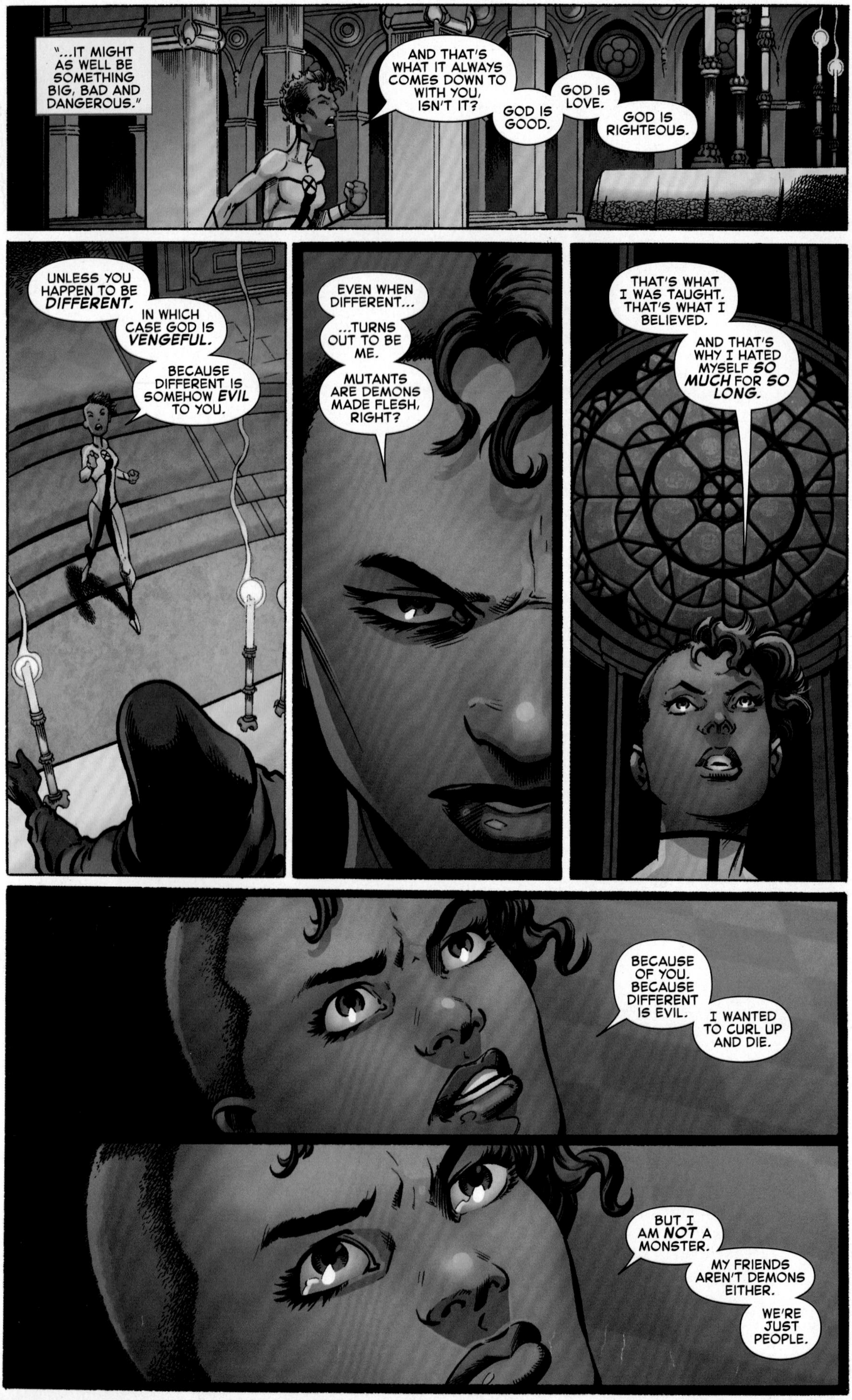
"...IT MIGHT AS WELL BE SOMETHING BIG, BAD AND DANGEROUS."
AND THAT'S WHAT IT ALWAYS COMES DOWN TO WITH YOU, ISN'T IT?
GOD IS GOOD.
GOD IS LOVE.
GOD IS RIGHTEOUS.
UNLESS YOU HAPPEN TO BE DIFFERENT.
IN WHICH CASE GOD IS VENGEFUL.
BECAUSE DIFFERENT IS SOMEHOW EVIL TO YOU.
EVEN WHEN DIFFERENT...
...TURNS OUT TO BE ME.
MUTANTS ARE DEMONS MADE FLESH, RIGHT?
THAT'S WHAT I WAS TAUGHT. THAT'S WHAT I BELIEVED.
AND THAT'S WHY I HATED MYSELF SO MUCH FOR SO LONG.
BECAUSE OF YOU. BECAUSE DIFFERENT IS EVIL.
I WANTED TO CURL UP AND DIE.
BUT I AM NOT A MONSTER.
MY FRIENDS AREN'T DEMONS EITHER.
WE'RE JUST PEOPLE.

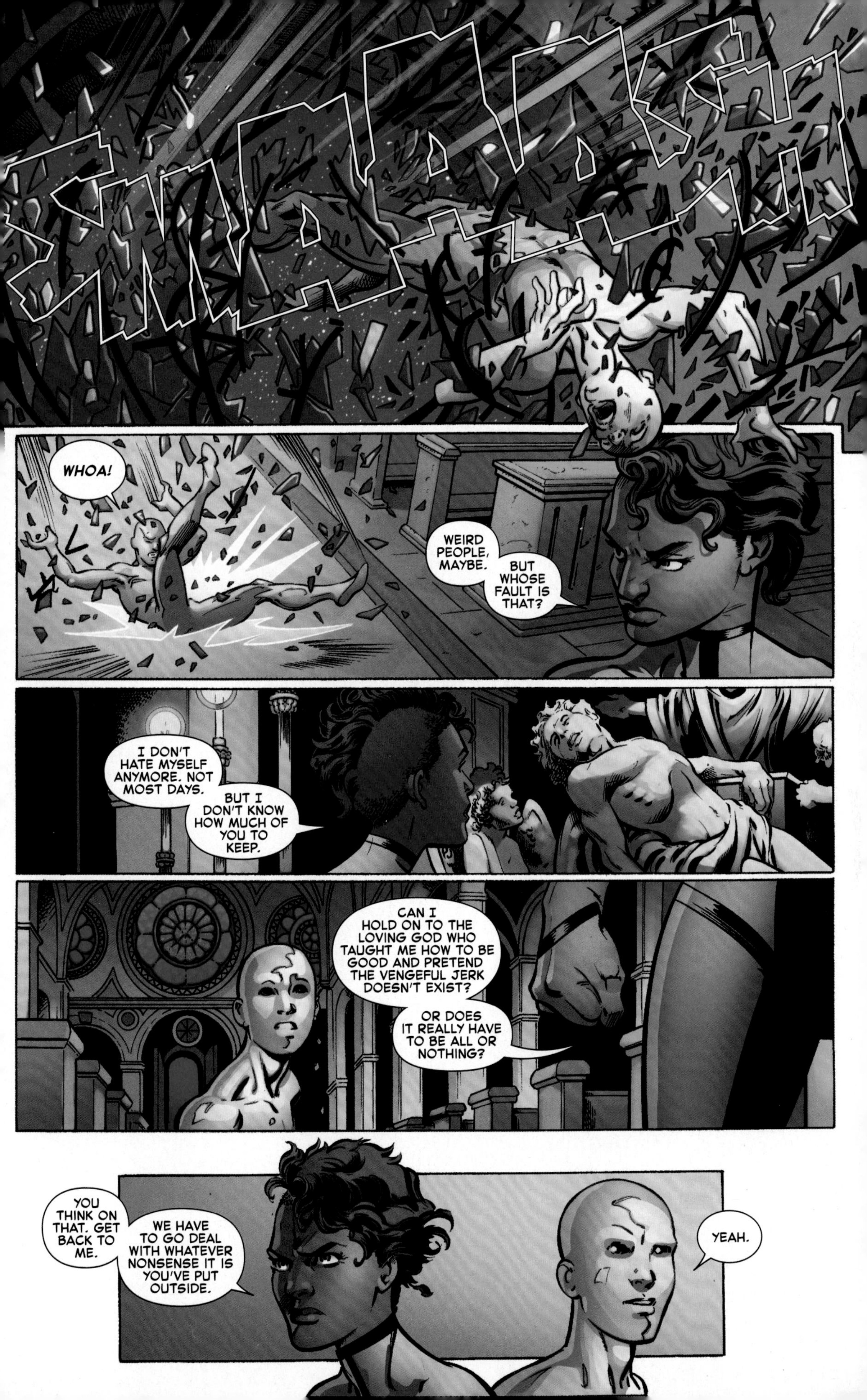
WHOA!
WEIRD PEOPLE, MAYBE.
BUT WHOSE FAULT IS THAT?
I DON'T HATE MYSELF ANYMORE. NOT MOST DAYS.
BUT I DON'T KNOW HOW MUCH OF YOU TO KEEP.
CAN I HOLD ON TO THE LOVING GOD WHO TAUGHT ME HOW TO BE GOOD AND PRETEND THE VENGEFUL JERK DOESN'T EXIST?
OR DOES IT REALLY HAVE TO BE ALL OR NOTHING?
YOU THINK ON THAT. GET BACK TO ME.
WE HAVE TO GO DEAL WITH WHATEVER NONSENSE IT IS YOU'VE PUT OUTSIDE.
YEAH.

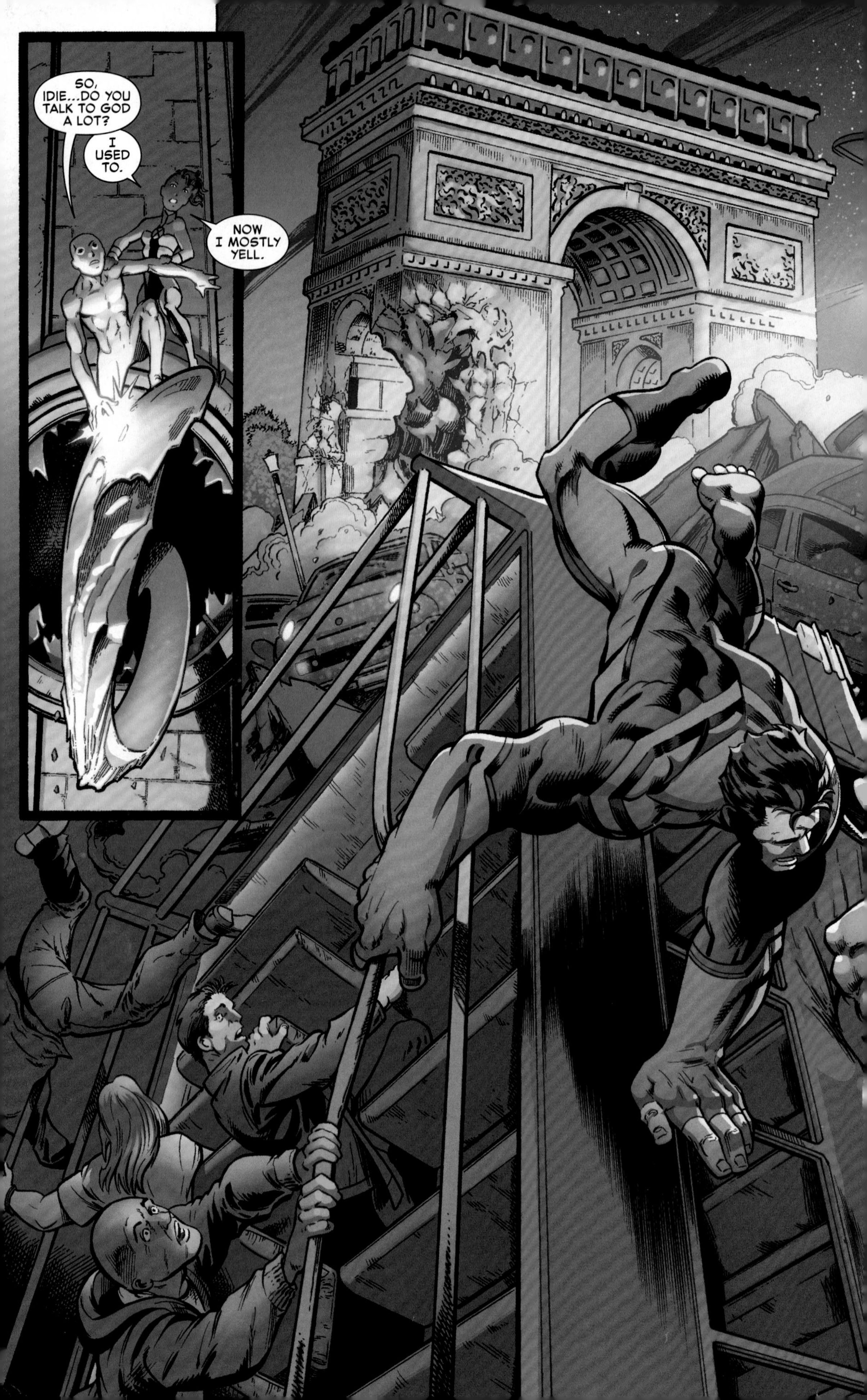
SO, IDIE...DO YOU TALK TO GOD A LOT?
I USED TO.
NOW I MOSTLY YELL.

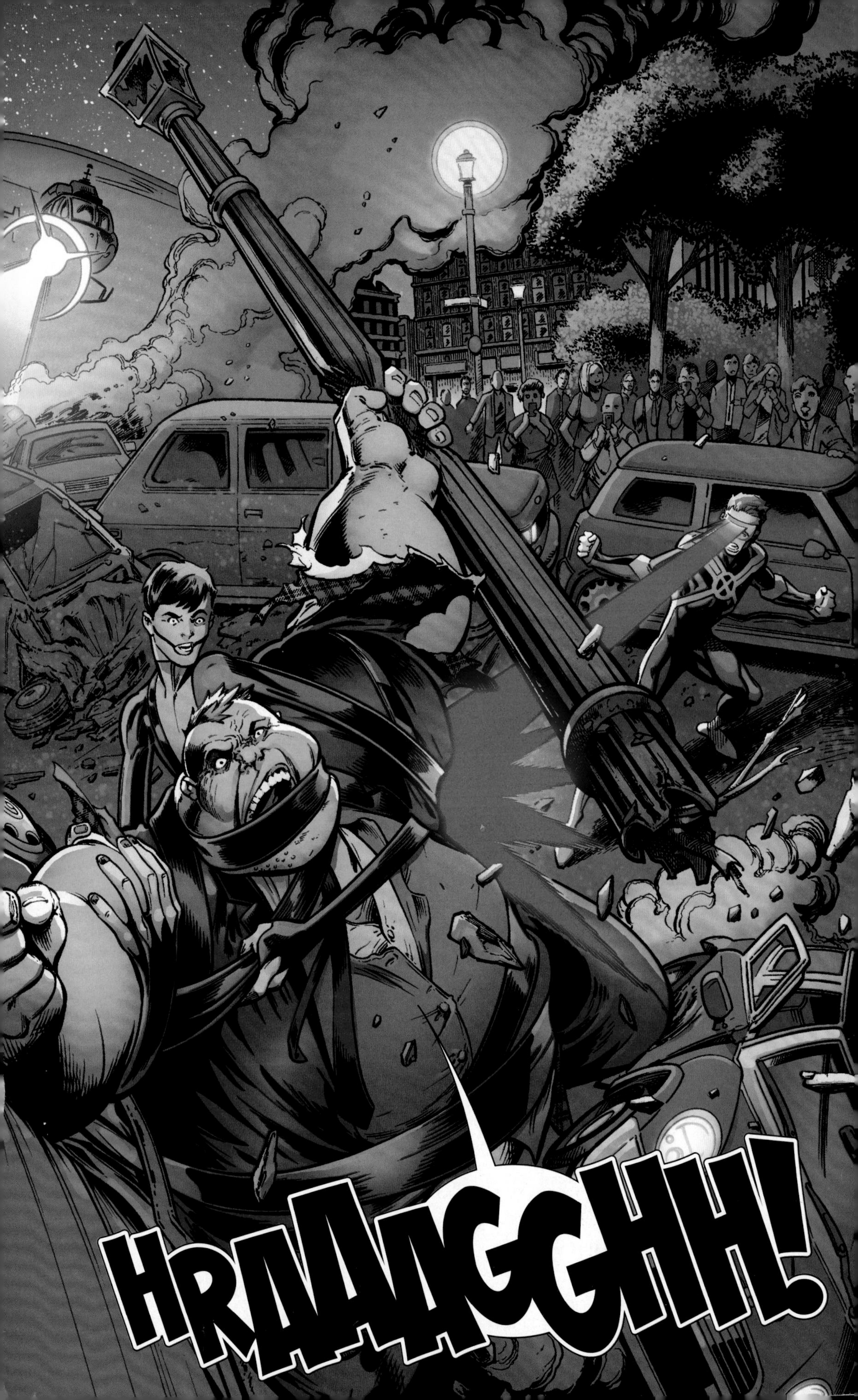
HRAAAGGHH!

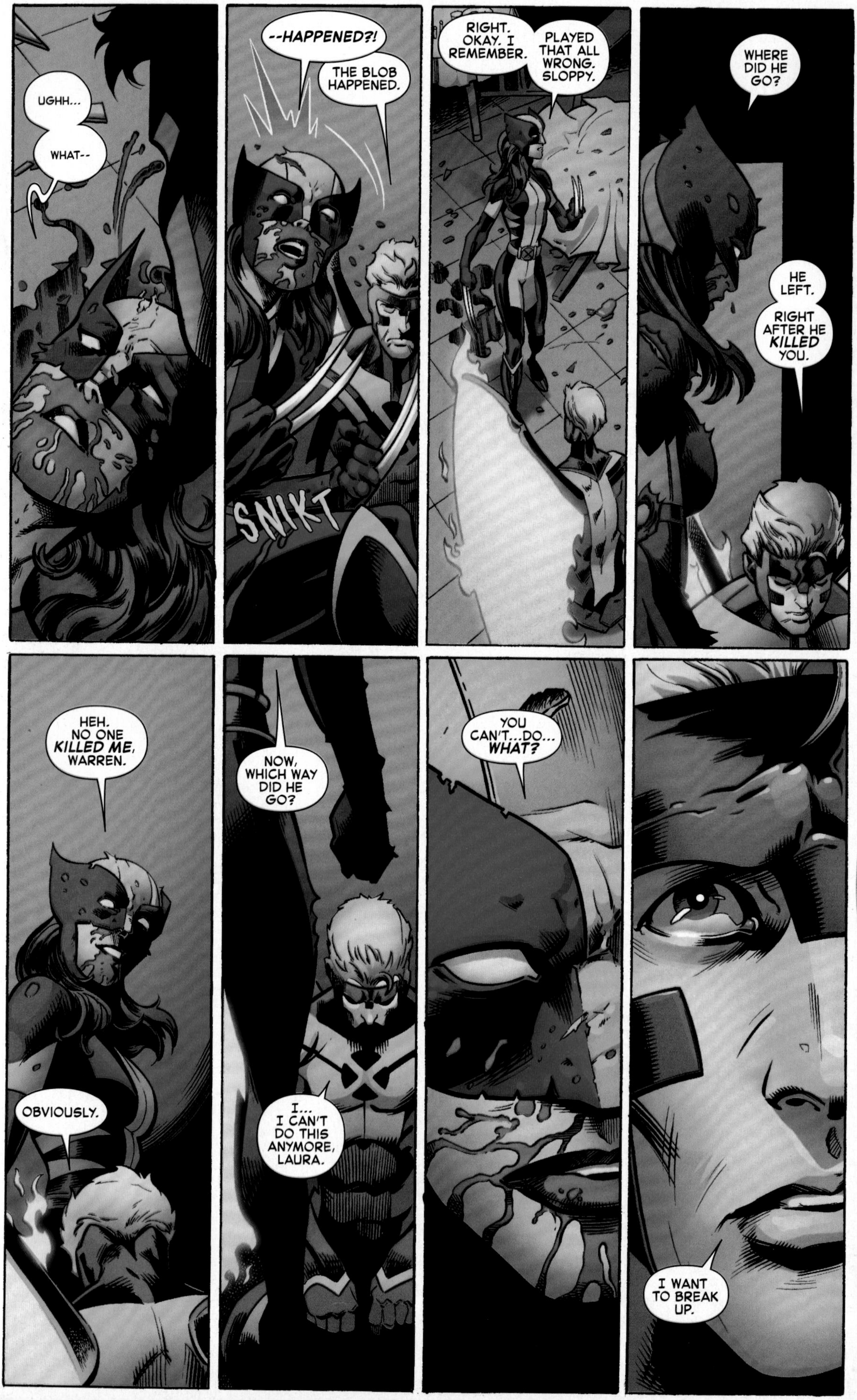
UGHH...
WHAT--
--HAPPENED?!
THE BLOB HAPPENED.
SNIKT
RIGHT. OKAY. I REMEMBER.
PLAYED THAT ALL WRONG. SLOPPY.
WHERE DID HE GO?
HE LEFT.
RIGHT AFTER HE *KILLED* YOU.
HEH. NO ONE *KILLED ME*, WARREN.
OBVIOUSLY.
NOW, WHICH WAY DID HE GO?
I... I CAN'T DO THIS ANYMORE, LAURA.
YOU CAN'T...DO... *WHAT?*
I WANT TO BREAK UP.

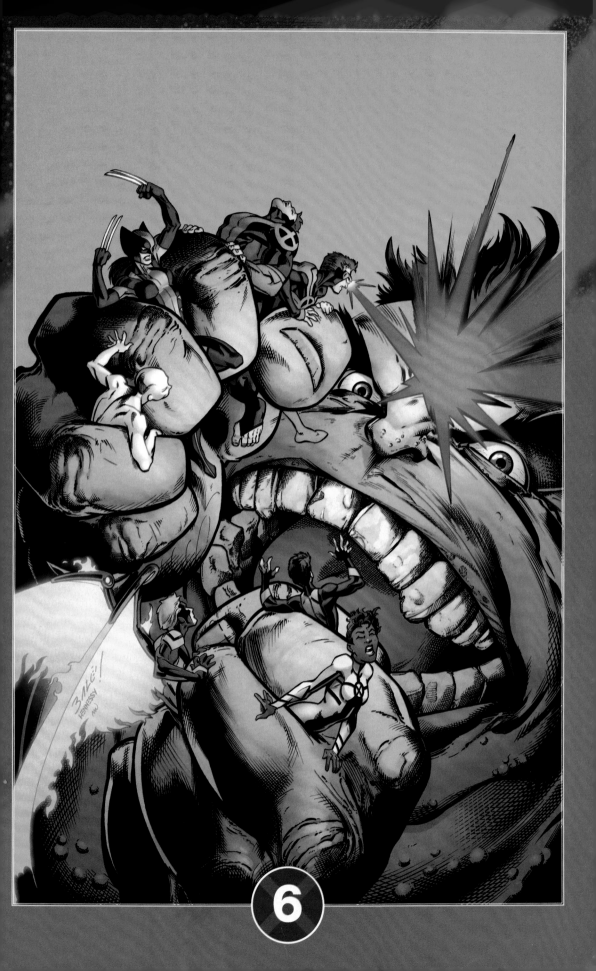

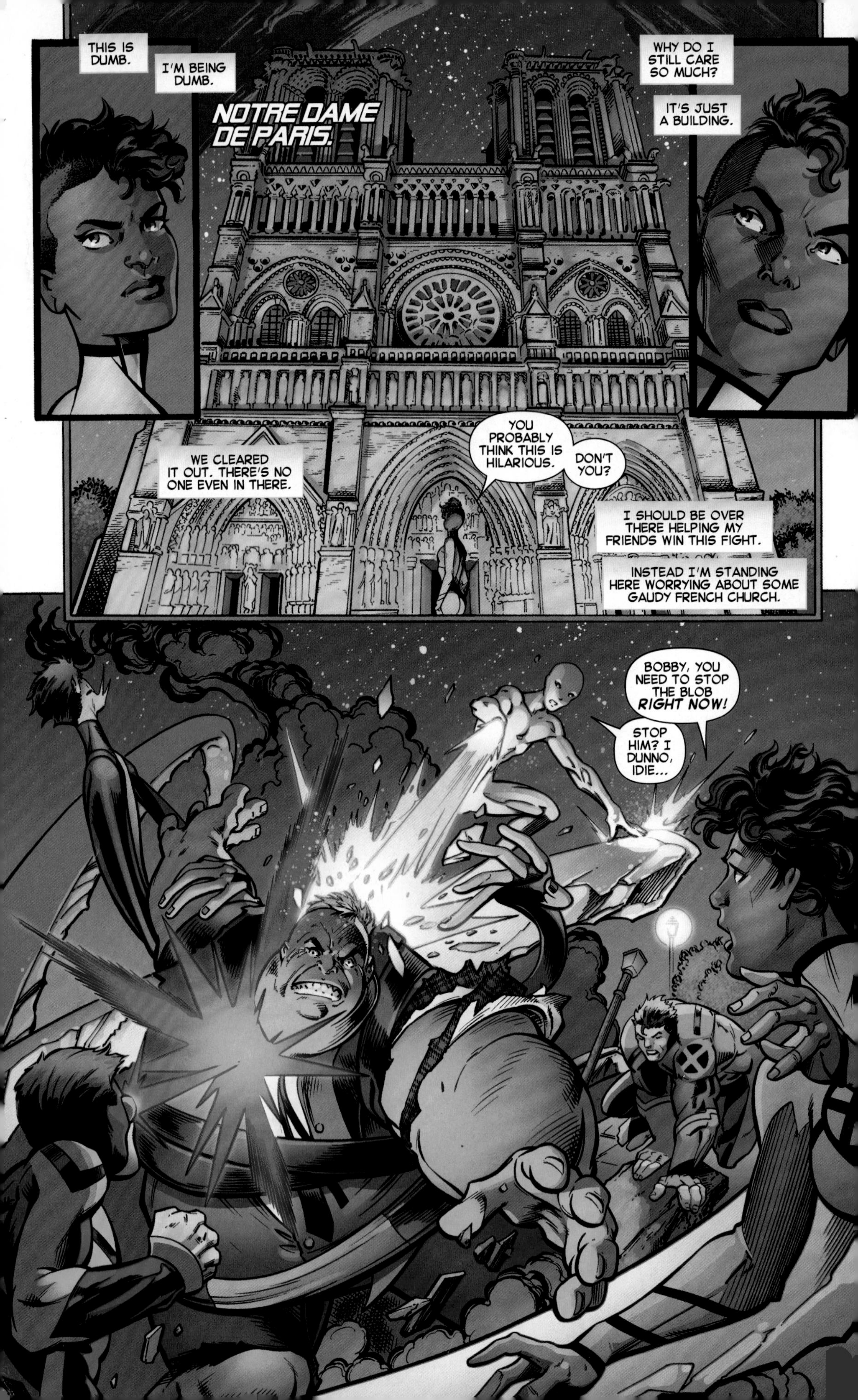
THIS IS DUMB.
I'M BEING DUMB.
NOTRE DAME DE PARIS.
WHY DO I STILL CARE SO MUCH?
IT'S JUST A BUILDING.
WE CLEARED IT OUT. THERE'S NO ONE EVEN IN THERE.
YOU PROBABLY THINK THIS IS HILARIOUS.
DON'T YOU?
I SHOULD BE OVER THERE HELPING MY FRIENDS WIN THIS FIGHT.
INSTEAD I'M STANDING HERE WORRYING ABOUT SOME GAUDY FRENCH CHURCH.
BOBBY, YOU NEED TO STOP THE BLOB RIGHT NOW!
STOP HIM? I DUNNO, IDIE...

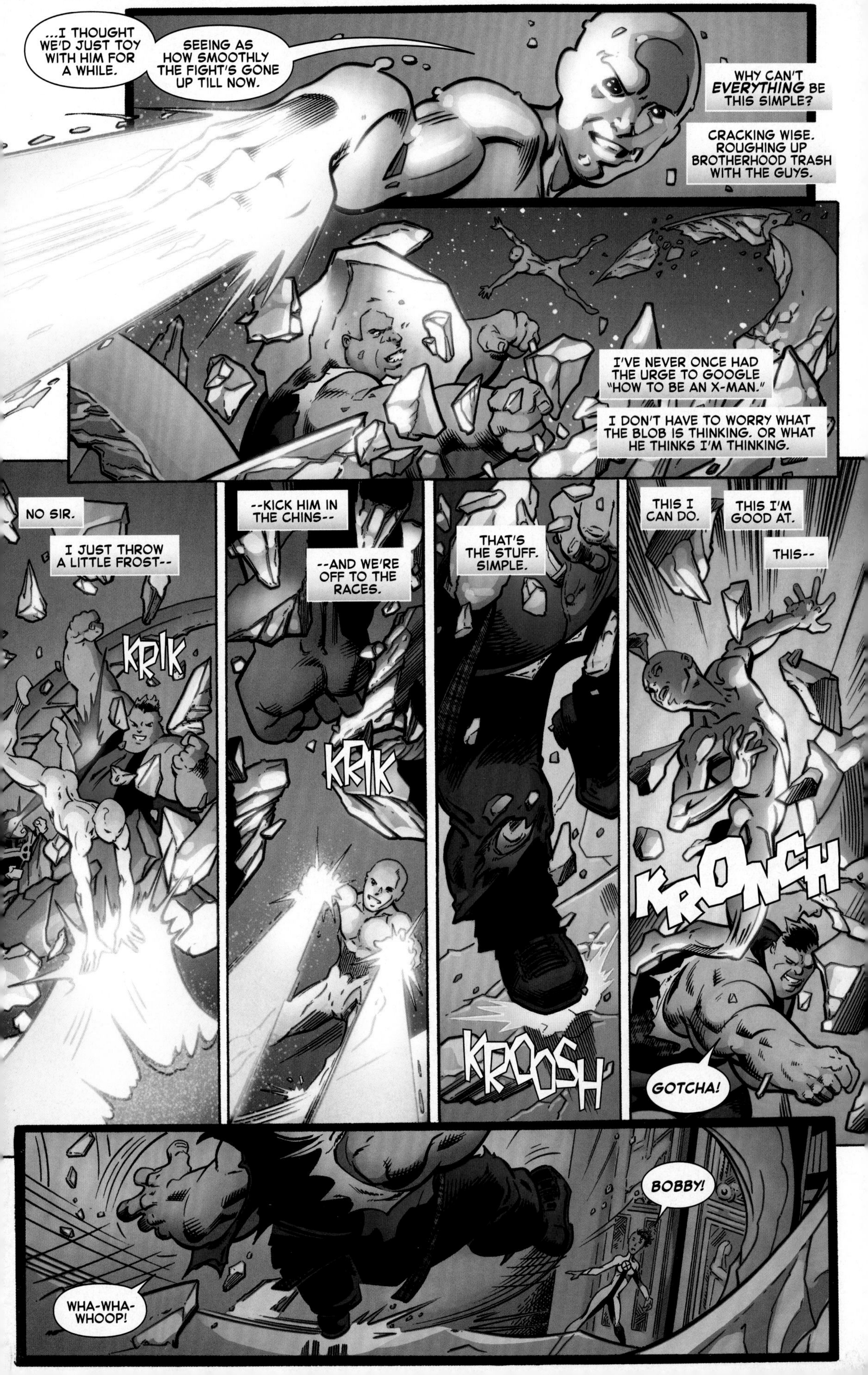

...I THOUGHT WE'D JUST TOY WITH HIM FOR A WHILE.
SEEING AS HOW SMOOTHLY THE FIGHT'S GONE UP TILL NOW.
WHY CAN'T EVERYTHING BE THIS SIMPLE?
CRACKING WISE. ROUGHING UP BROTHERHOOD TRASH WITH THE GUYS.
I'VE NEVER ONCE HAD THE URGE TO GOOGLE "HOW TO BE AN X-MAN."
I DON'T HAVE TO WORRY WHAT THE BLOB IS THINKING. OR WHAT HE THINKS I'M THINKING.
NO SIR.
I JUST THROW A LITTLE FROST--
KRIK
--KICK HIM IN THE CHINS--
--AND WE'RE OFF TO THE RACES.
KRIK
THAT'S THE STUFF. SIMPLE.
KROOSH
THIS I CAN DO.
THIS I'M GOOD AT.
THIS--
KRONCH
GOTCHA!
BOBBY!
WHA-WHA-WHOOP!

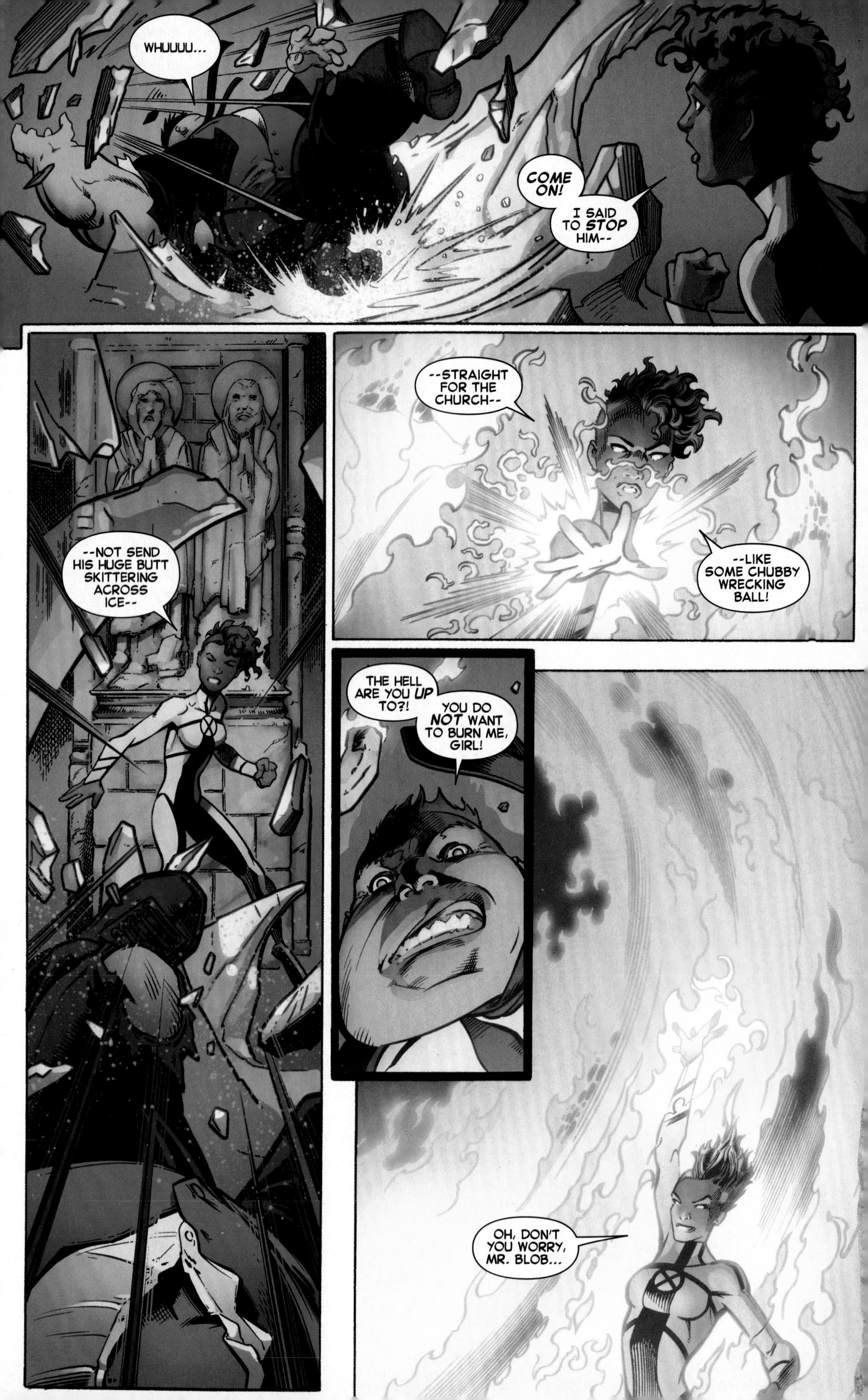
WHUUUU...
COME ON!
I SAID TO STOP HIM--
--NOT SEND HIS HUGE BUTT SKITTERING ACROSS ICE--
--STRAIGHT FOR THE CHURCH--
--LIKE SOME CHUBBY WRECKING BALL!
THE HELL ARE YOU UP TO?!
YOU DO NOT WANT TO BURN ME, GIRL!
OH, DON'T YOU WORRY, MR. BLOB...

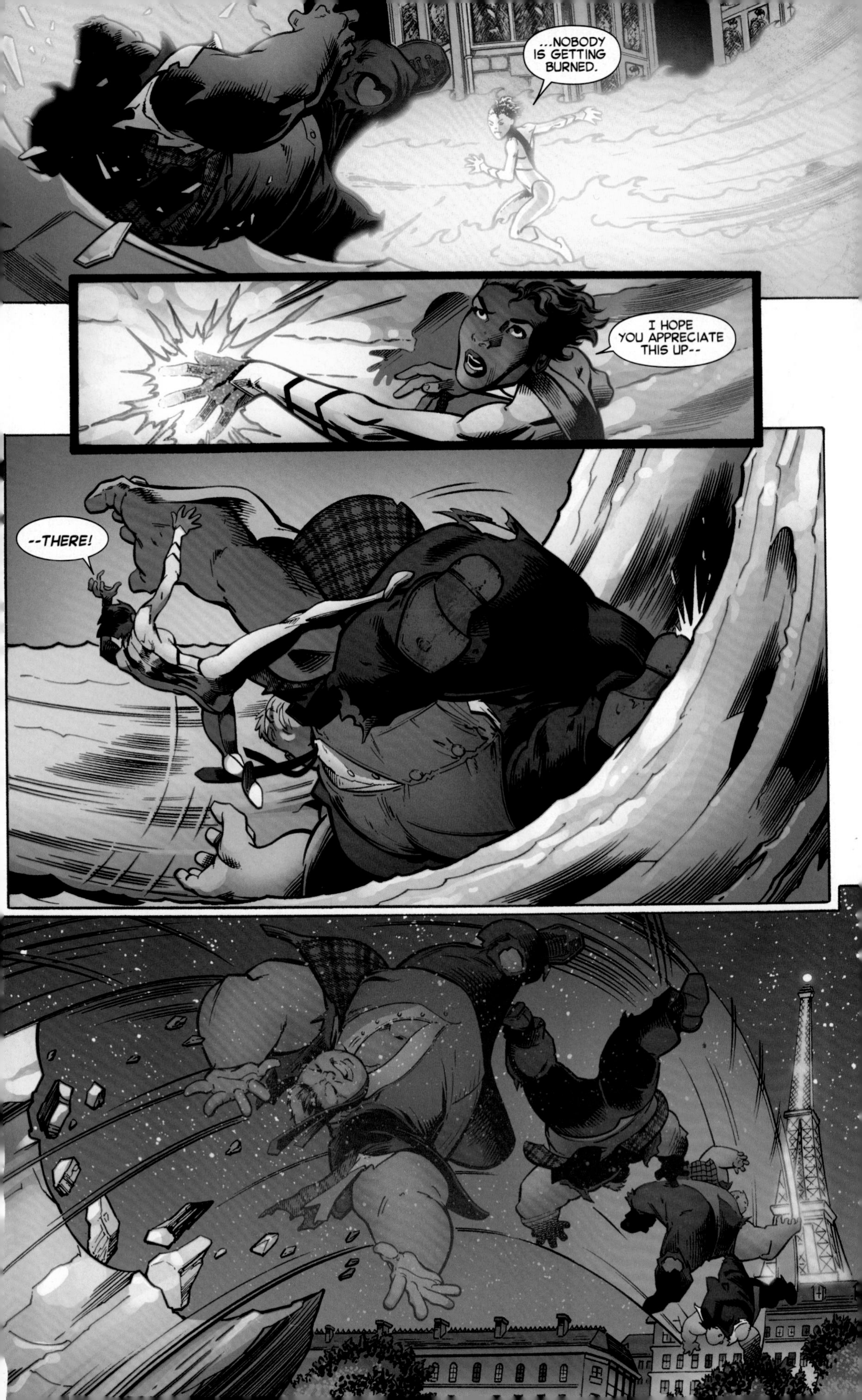
...NOBODY IS GETTING BURNED.
I HOPE YOU APPRECIATE THIS UP--
--THERE!

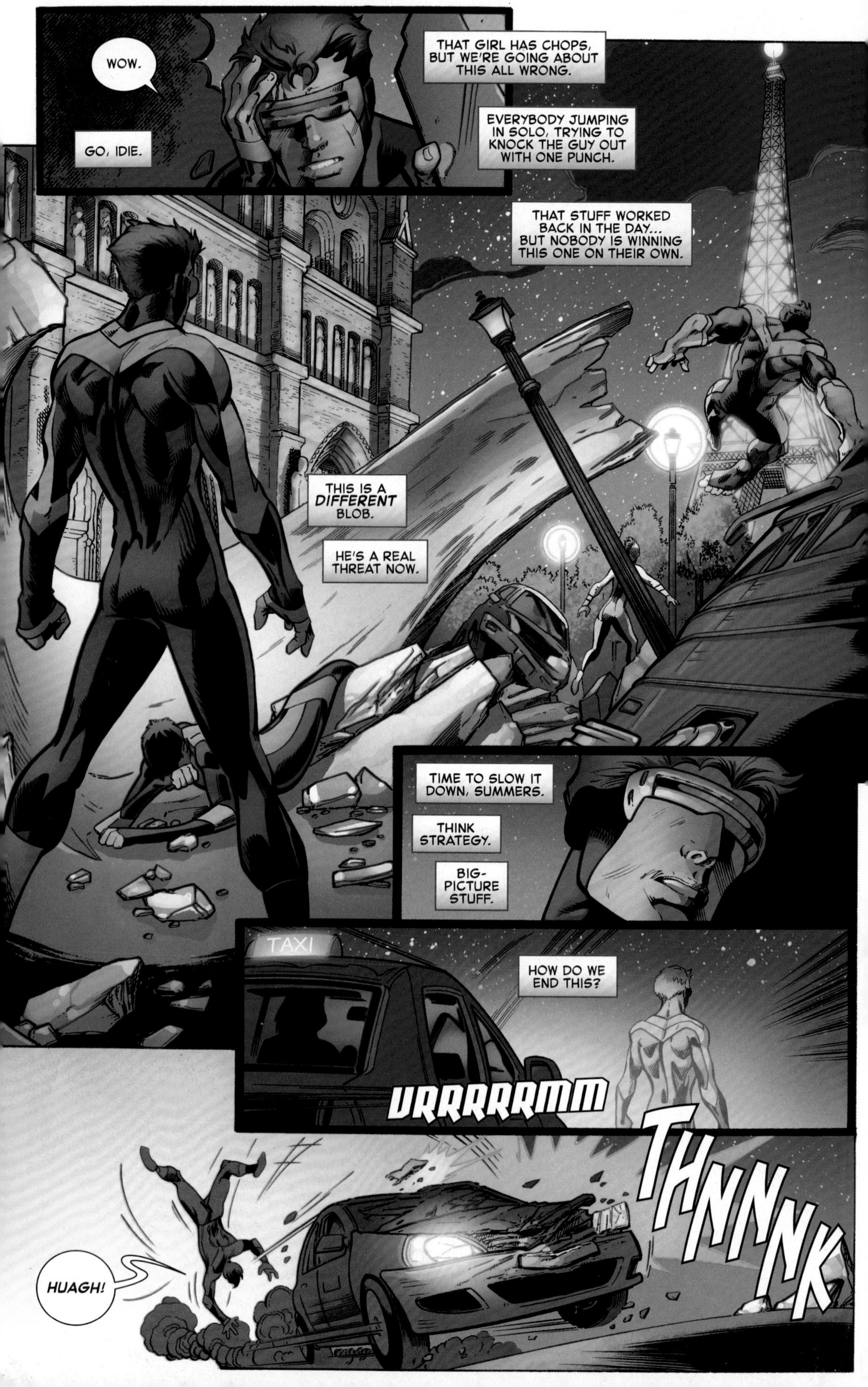
WOW.
THAT GIRL HAS CHOPS, BUT WE'RE GOING ABOUT THIS ALL WRONG.
GO, IDIE.
EVERYBODY JUMPING IN SOLO, TRYING TO KNOCK THE GUY OUT WITH ONE PUNCH.
THAT STUFF WORKED BACK IN THE DAY... BUT NOBODY IS WINNING THIS ONE ON THEIR OWN.
THIS IS A *DIFFERENT* BLOB.
HE'S A REAL THREAT NOW.
TIME TO SLOW IT DOWN, SUMMERS.
THINK STRATEGY.
BIG-PICTURE STUFF.
TAXI
HOW DO WE END THIS?
VRRRRRMM
THNNNK
HUAGH!

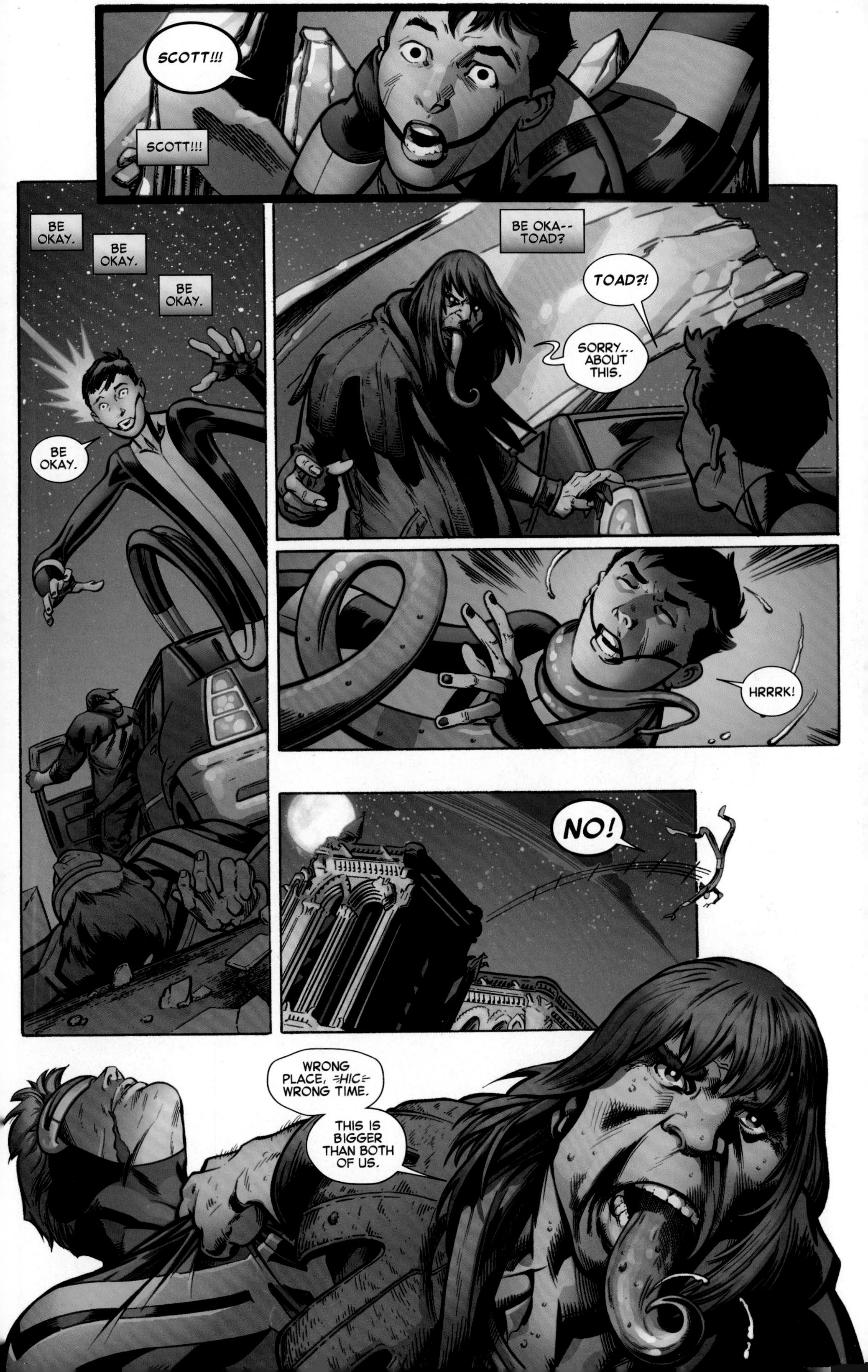
SCOTT!!!
SCOTT!!!
BE OKAY.
BE OKAY.
BE OKAY.
BE OKAY.
BE OKA-- TOAD?
TOAD?!
SORRY... ABOUT THIS.
HRRRK!
NO!
WRONG PLACE, HIC WRONG TIME.
THIS IS BIGGER THAN BOTH OF US.

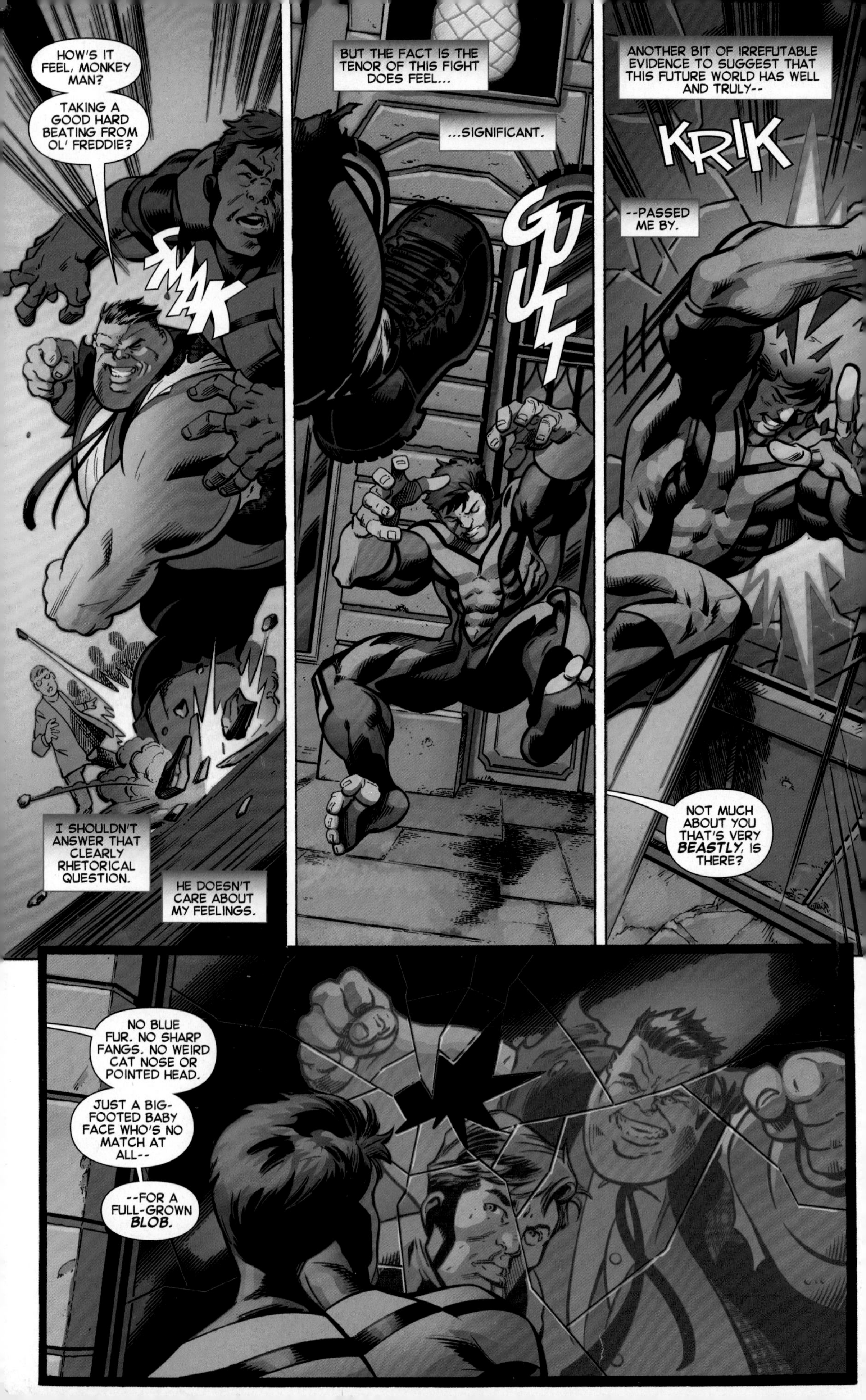
HOW'S IT FEEL, MONKEY MAN?
TAKING A GOOD HARD BEATING FROM OL' FREDDIE?
SMAK
I SHOULDN'T ANSWER THAT CLEARLY RHETORICAL QUESTION.
HE DOESN'T CARE ABOUT MY FEELINGS.
BUT THE FACT IS THE TENOR OF THIS FIGHT DOES FEEL...
...SIGNIFICANT.
GUUUT
ANOTHER BIT OF IRREFUTABLE EVIDENCE TO SUGGEST THAT THIS FUTURE WORLD HAS WELL AND TRULY--
KRIK
--PASSED ME BY.
NOT MUCH ABOUT YOU THAT'S VERY *BEASTLY*, IS THERE?
NO BLUE FUR. NO SHARP FANGS. NO WEIRD CAT NOSE OR POINTED HEAD.
JUST A BIG-FOOTED BABY FACE WHO'S NO MATCH AT ALL--
--FOR A FULL-GROWN **BLOB.**

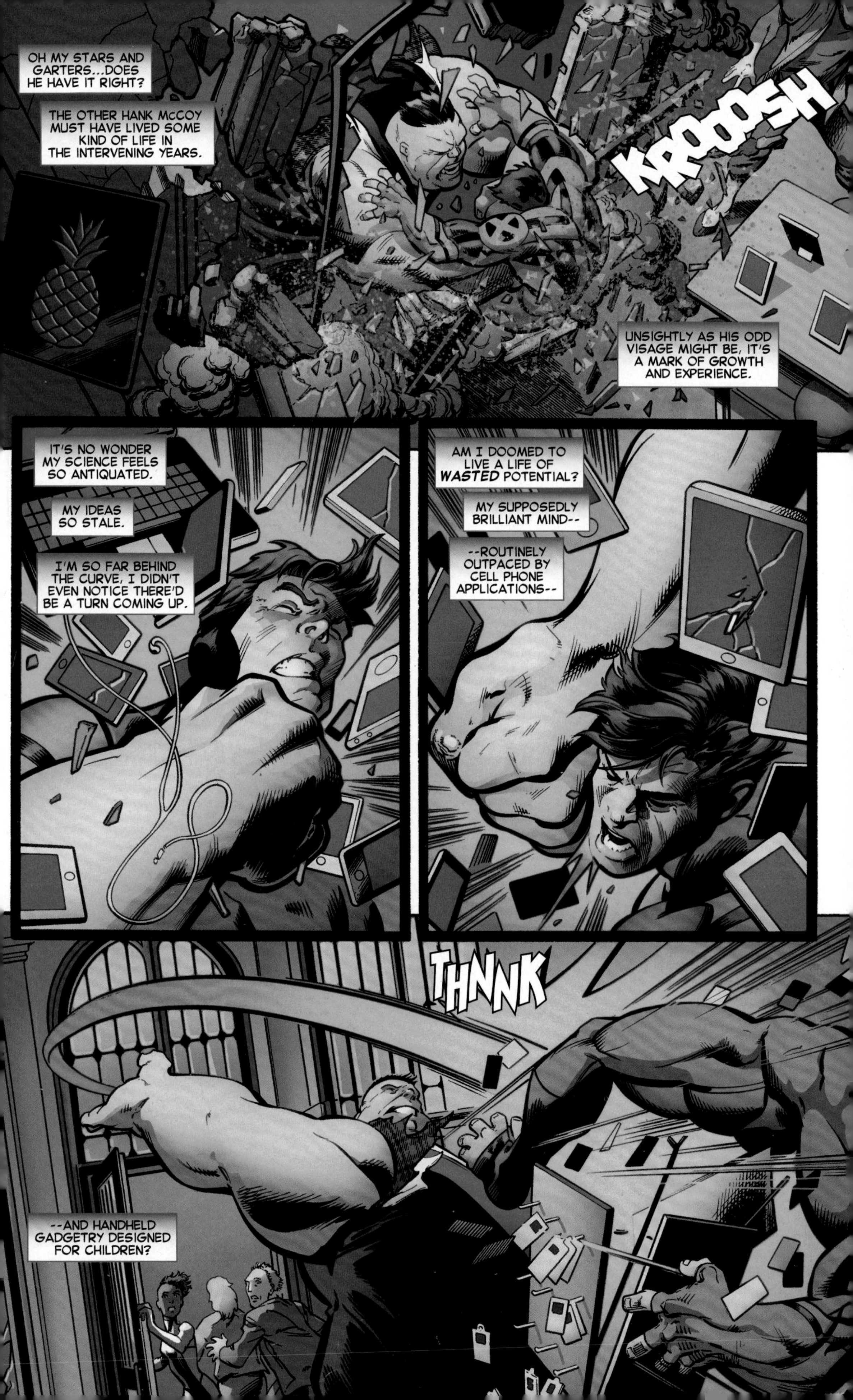
OH MY STARS AND GARTERS...DOES HE HAVE IT RIGHT?
THE OTHER HANK McCOY MUST HAVE LIVED SOME KIND OF LIFE IN THE INTERVENING YEARS.
KROOOSH
UNSIGHTLY AS HIS ODD VISAGE MIGHT BE, IT'S A MARK OF GROWTH AND EXPERIENCE.
IT'S NO WONDER MY SCIENCE FEELS SO ANTIQUATED.
MY IDEAS SO STALE.
I'M SO FAR BEHIND THE CURVE, I DIDN'T EVEN NOTICE THERE'D BE A TURN COMING UP.
AM I DOOMED TO LIVE A LIFE OF *WASTED* POTENTIAL?
MY SUPPOSEDLY BRILLIANT MIND--
--ROUTINELY OUTPACED BY CELL PHONE APPLICATIONS--
THNNK
--AND HANDHELD GADGETRY DESIGNED FOR CHILDREN?

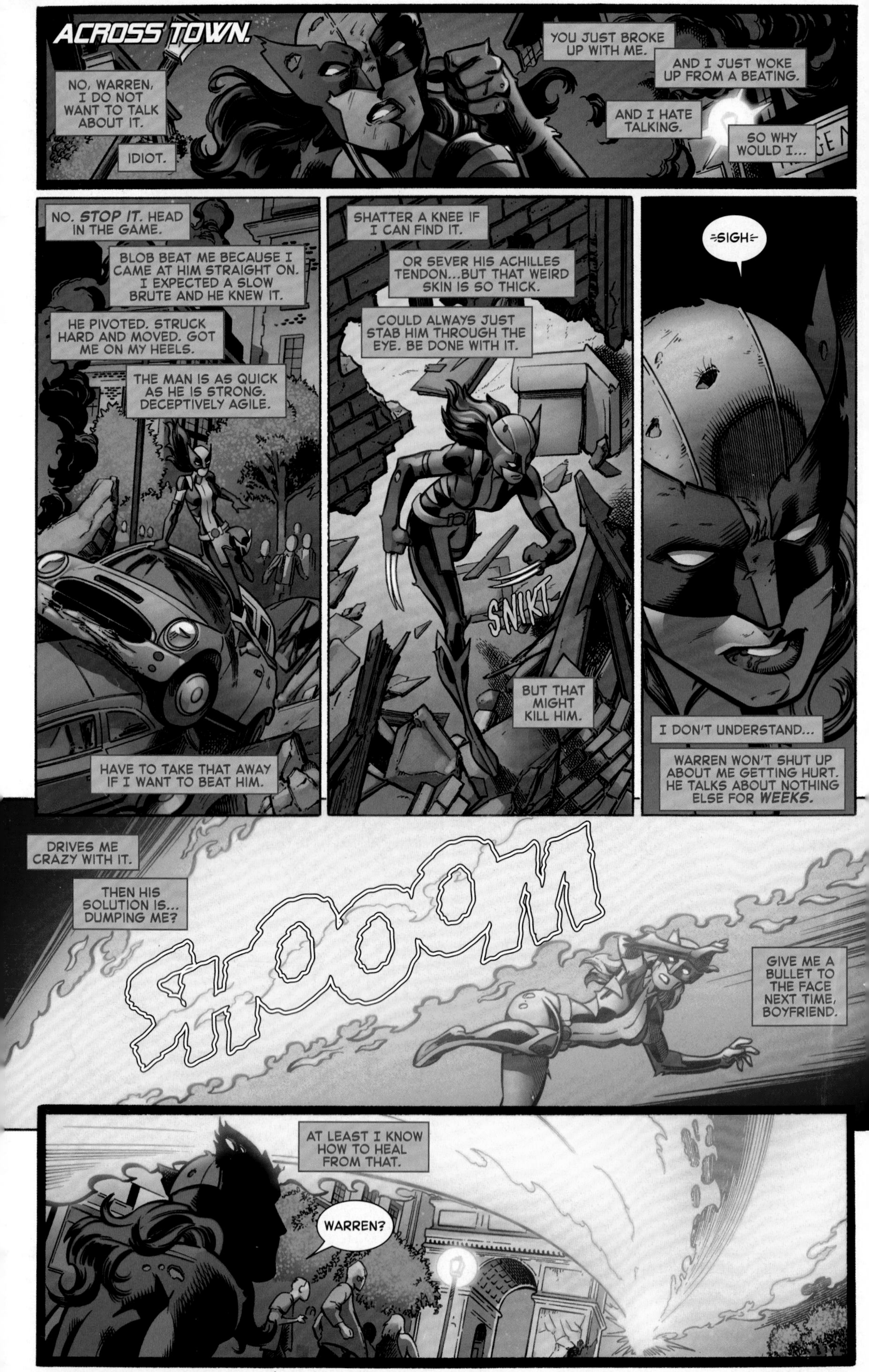
ACROSS TOWN.
NO, WARREN, I DO NOT WANT TO TALK ABOUT IT.
IDIOT.
YOU JUST BROKE UP WITH ME.
AND I JUST WOKE UP FROM A BEATING.
AND I HATE TALKING.
SO WHY WOULD I...
NO. STOP IT. HEAD IN THE GAME.
BLOB BEAT ME BECAUSE I CAME AT HIM STRAIGHT ON. I EXPECTED A SLOW BRUTE AND HE KNEW IT.
HE PIVOTED. STRUCK HARD AND MOVED. GOT ME ON MY HEELS.
THE MAN IS AS QUICK AS HE IS STRONG. DECEPTIVELY AGILE.
HAVE TO TAKE THAT AWAY IF I WANT TO BEAT HIM.
SHATTER A KNEE IF I CAN FIND IT.
OR SEVER HIS ACHILLES TENDON...BUT THAT WEIRD SKIN IS SO THICK.
COULD ALWAYS JUST STAB HIM THROUGH THE EYE. BE DONE WITH IT.
SNIKT
BUT THAT MIGHT KILL HIM.
SIGH
I DON'T UNDERSTAND...
WARREN WON'T SHUT UP ABOUT ME GETTING HURT. HE TALKS ABOUT NOTHING ELSE FOR WEEKS.
DRIVES ME CRAZY WITH IT.
THEN HIS SOLUTION IS... DUMPING ME?
SHOOOM
GIVE ME A BULLET TO THE FACE NEXT TIME, BOYFRIEND.
AT LEAST I KNOW HOW TO HEAL FROM THAT.
WARREN?

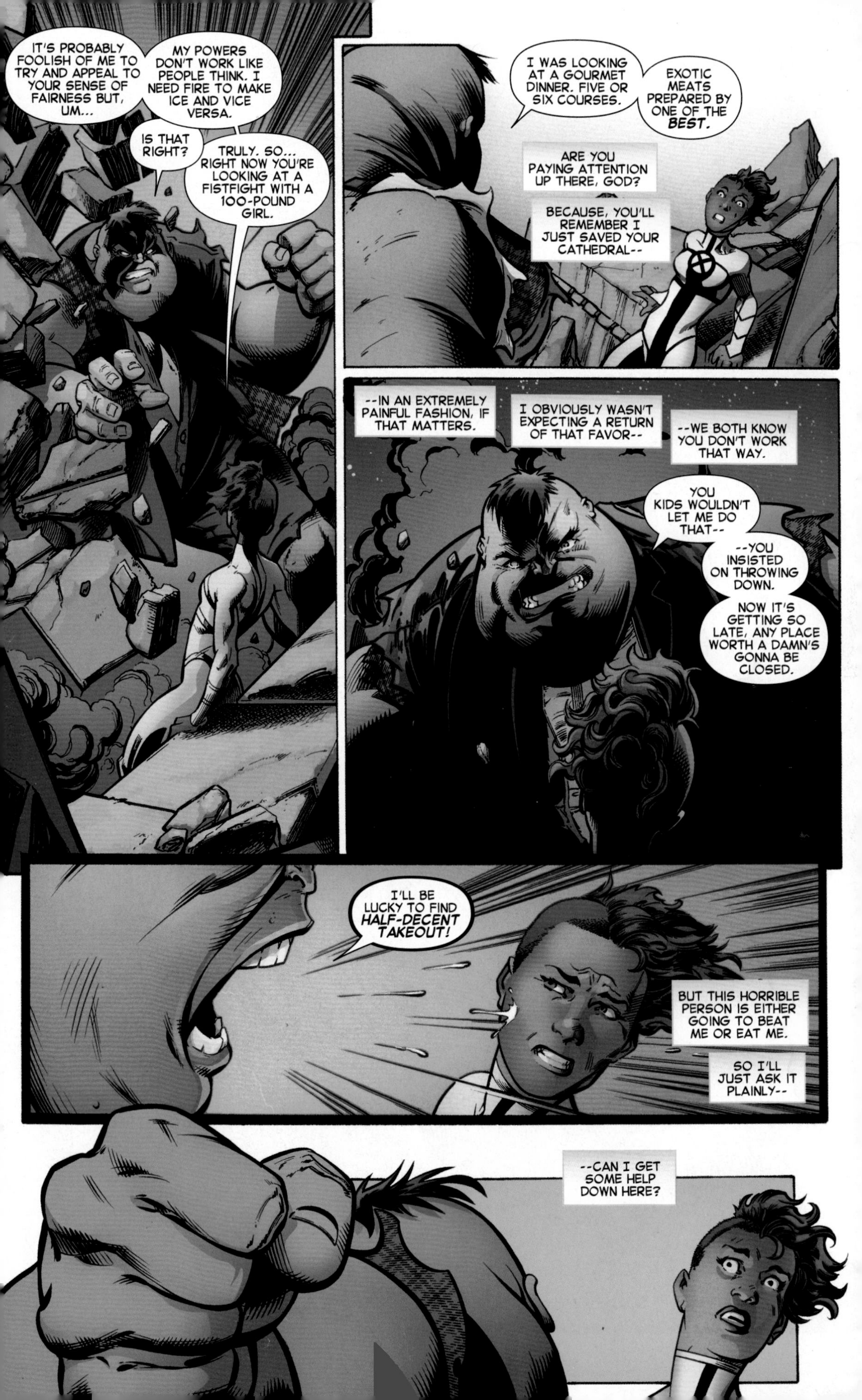
IT'S PROBABLY FOOLISH OF ME TO TRY AND APPEAL TO YOUR SENSE OF FAIRNESS BUT, UM...
MY POWERS DON'T WORK LIKE PEOPLE THINK. I NEED FIRE TO MAKE ICE AND VICE VERSA.
IS THAT RIGHT?
TRULY. SO... RIGHT NOW YOU'RE LOOKING AT A FISTFIGHT WITH A 100-POUND GIRL.
I WAS LOOKING AT A GOURMET DINNER. FIVE OR SIX COURSES.
EXOTIC MEATS PREPARED BY ONE OF THE *BEST.*
ARE YOU PAYING ATTENTION UP THERE, GOD?
BECAUSE, YOU'LL REMEMBER I JUST SAVED YOUR CATHEDRAL--
--IN AN EXTREMELY PAINFUL FASHION, IF THAT MATTERS.
I OBVIOUSLY WASN'T EXPECTING A RETURN OF THAT FAVOR--
--WE BOTH KNOW YOU DON'T WORK THAT WAY.
YOU KIDS WOULDN'T LET ME DO THAT--
--YOU INSISTED ON THROWING DOWN.
NOW IT'S GETTING SO LATE, ANY PLACE WORTH A DAMN'S GONNA BE CLOSED.
I'LL BE LUCKY TO FIND ***HALF-DECENT TAKEOUT!***
BUT THIS HORRIBLE PERSON IS EITHER GOING TO BEAT ME OR EAT ME.
SO I'LL JUST ASK IT PLAINLY--
--CAN I GET SOME HELP DOWN HERE?

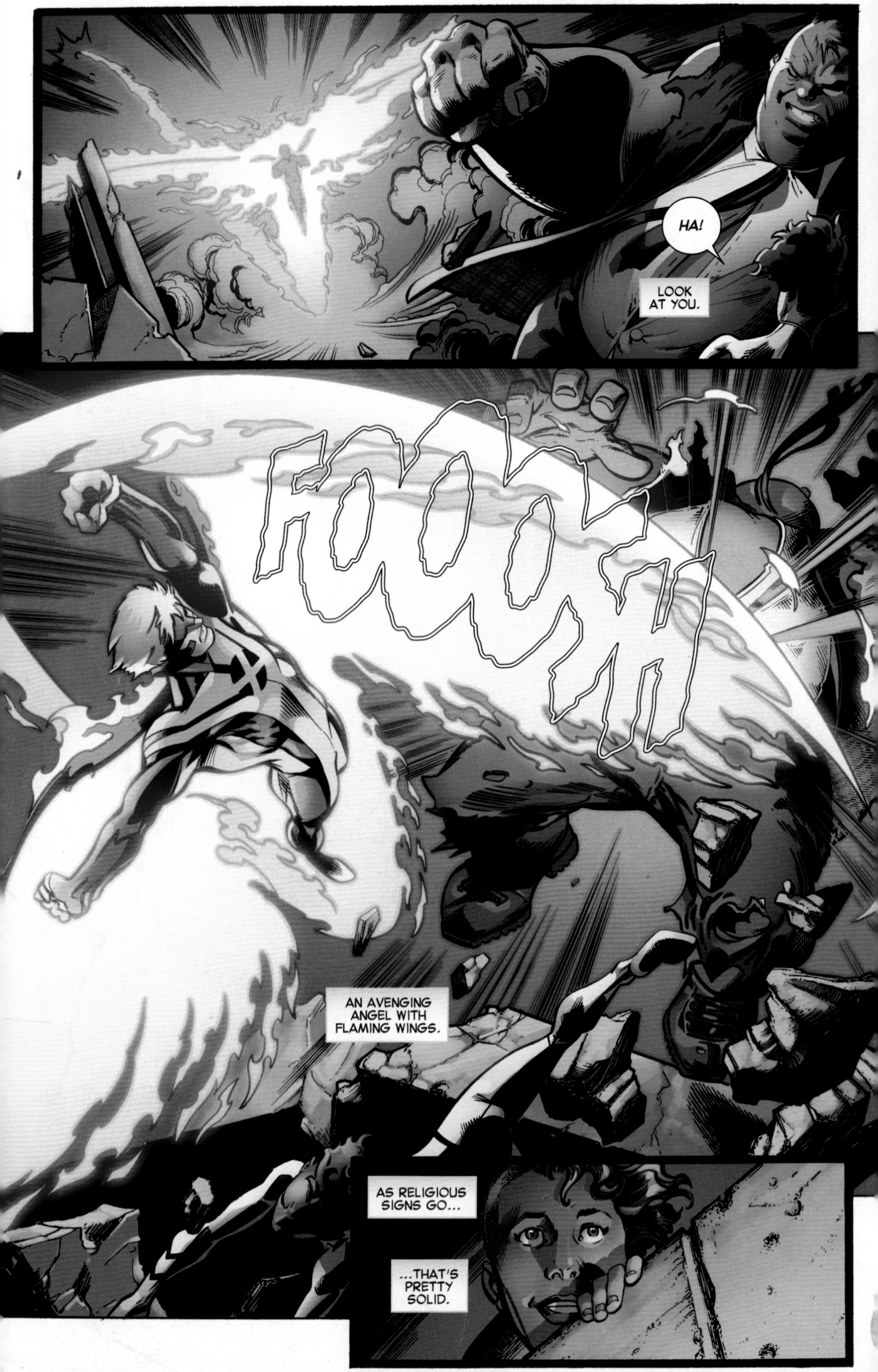
HA!
LOOK AT YOU.
FOOOM
AN AVENGING ANGEL WITH FLAMING WINGS.
AS RELIGIOUS SIGNS GO...
...THAT'S PRETTY SOLID.

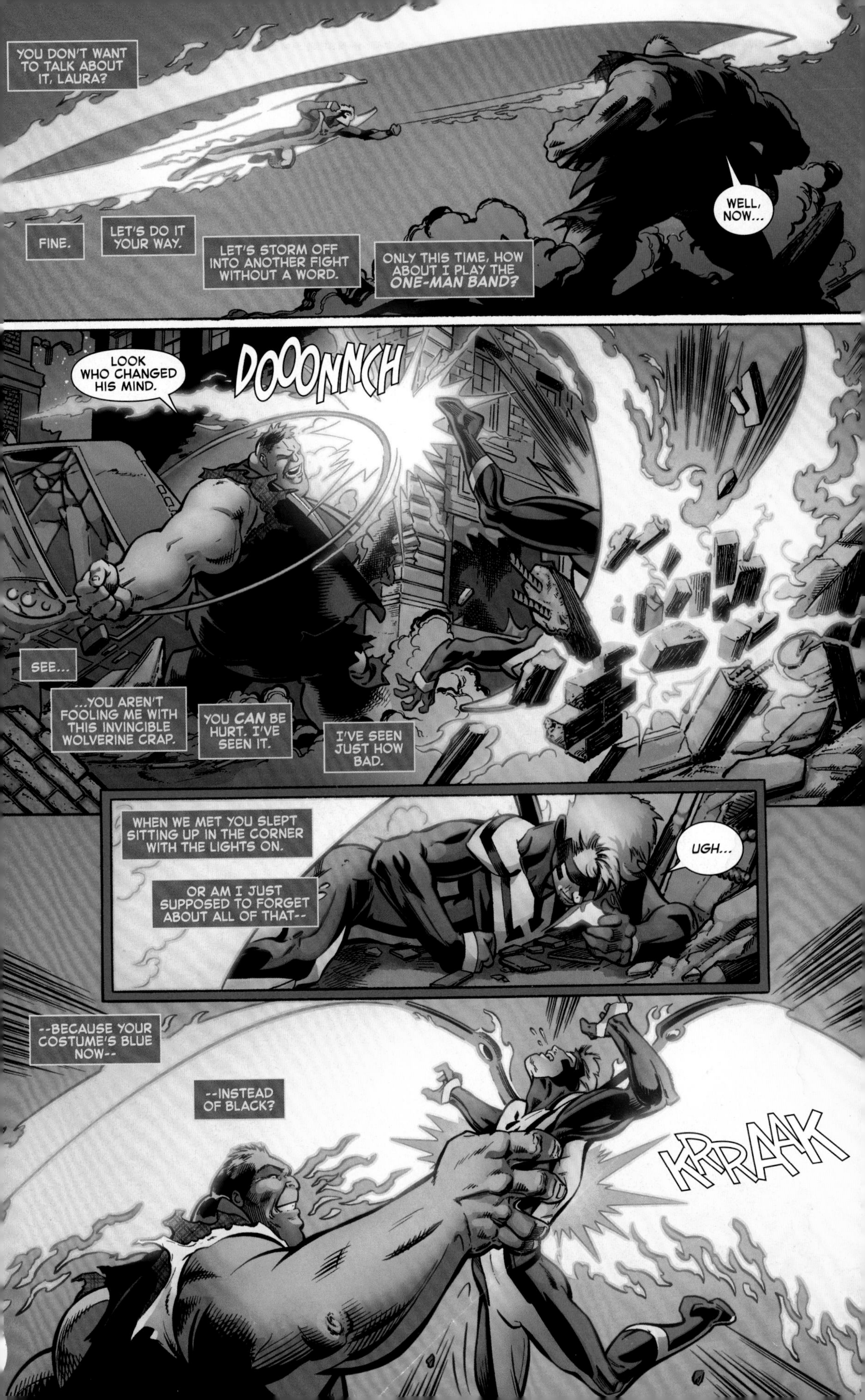
YOU DON'T WANT TO TALK ABOUT IT, LAURA?
WELL, NOW...
FINE.
LET'S DO IT YOUR WAY.
LET'S STORM OFF INTO ANOTHER FIGHT WITHOUT A WORD.
ONLY THIS TIME, HOW ABOUT I PLAY THE ONE-MAN BAND?
LOOK WHO CHANGED HIS MIND.
DOOONNCH
SEE...
...YOU AREN'T FOOLING ME WITH THIS INVINCIBLE WOLVERINE CRAP.
YOU CAN BE HURT. I'VE SEEN IT.
I'VE SEEN JUST HOW BAD.
WHEN WE MET YOU SLEPT SITTING UP IN THE CORNER WITH THE LIGHTS ON.
UGH...
OR AM I JUST SUPPOSED TO FORGET ABOUT ALL OF THAT--
--BECAUSE YOUR COSTUME'S BLUE NOW--
--INSTEAD OF BLACK?
KRRAAK

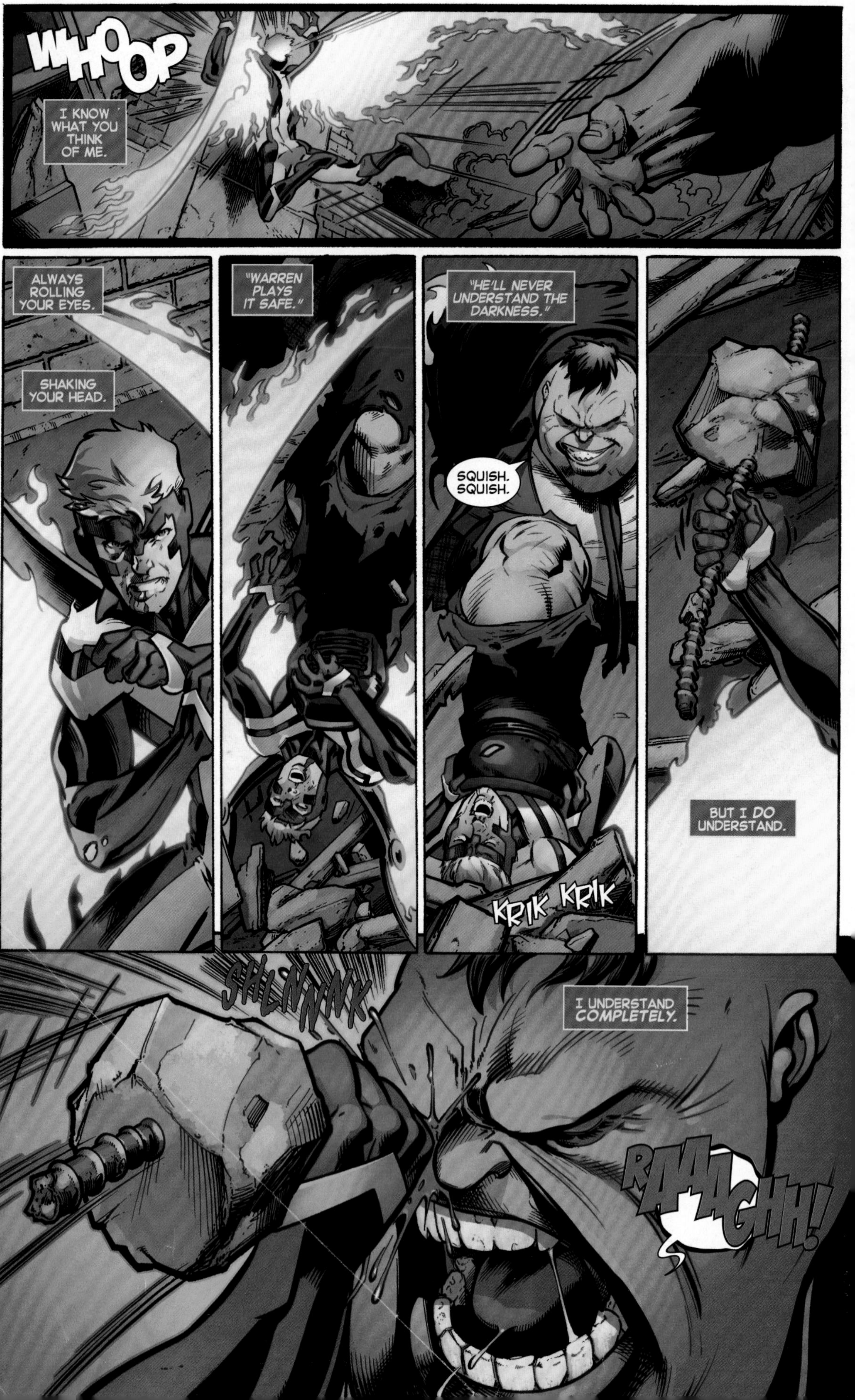
WHOOP
I KNOW WHAT YOU THINK OF ME.
ALWAYS ROLLING YOUR EYES.
SHAKING YOUR HEAD.
"WARREN PLAYS IT SAFE."
"HE'LL NEVER UNDERSTAND THE DARKNESS."
SQUISH. SQUISH.
KRIK KRIK
BUT I DO UNDERSTAND.
SHLNNNK
I UNDERSTAND COMPLETELY.
RAAAAGHH!

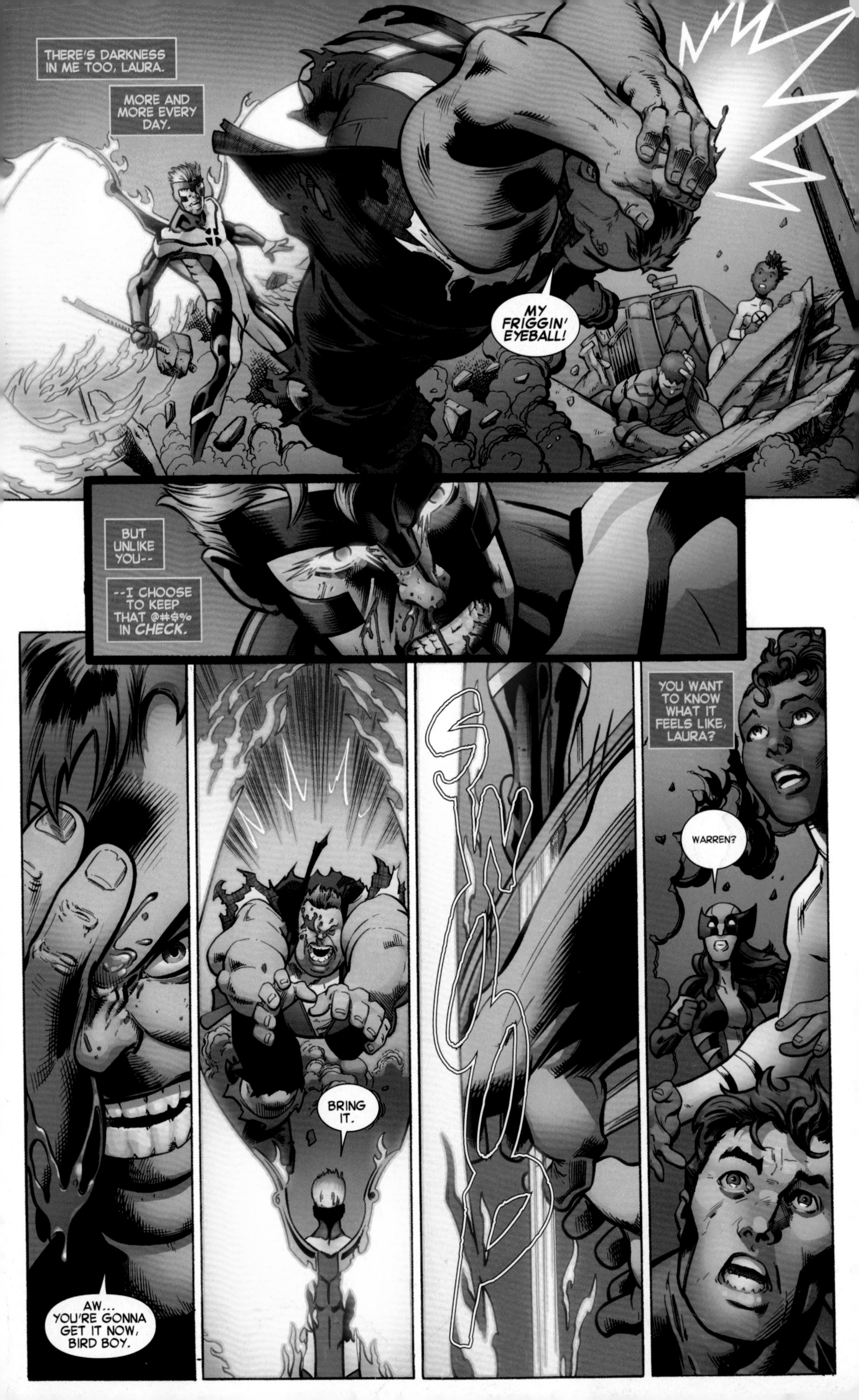

THERE'S DARKNESS IN ME TOO, LAURA.
MORE AND MORE EVERY DAY.
MY FRIGGIN' EYEBALL!
BUT UNLIKE YOU--
--I CHOOSE TO KEEP THAT @#$% IN CHECK.
AW... YOU'RE GONNA GET IT NOW, BIRD BOY.
BRING IT.
YOU WANT TO KNOW WHAT IT FEELS LIKE, LAURA?
WARREN?

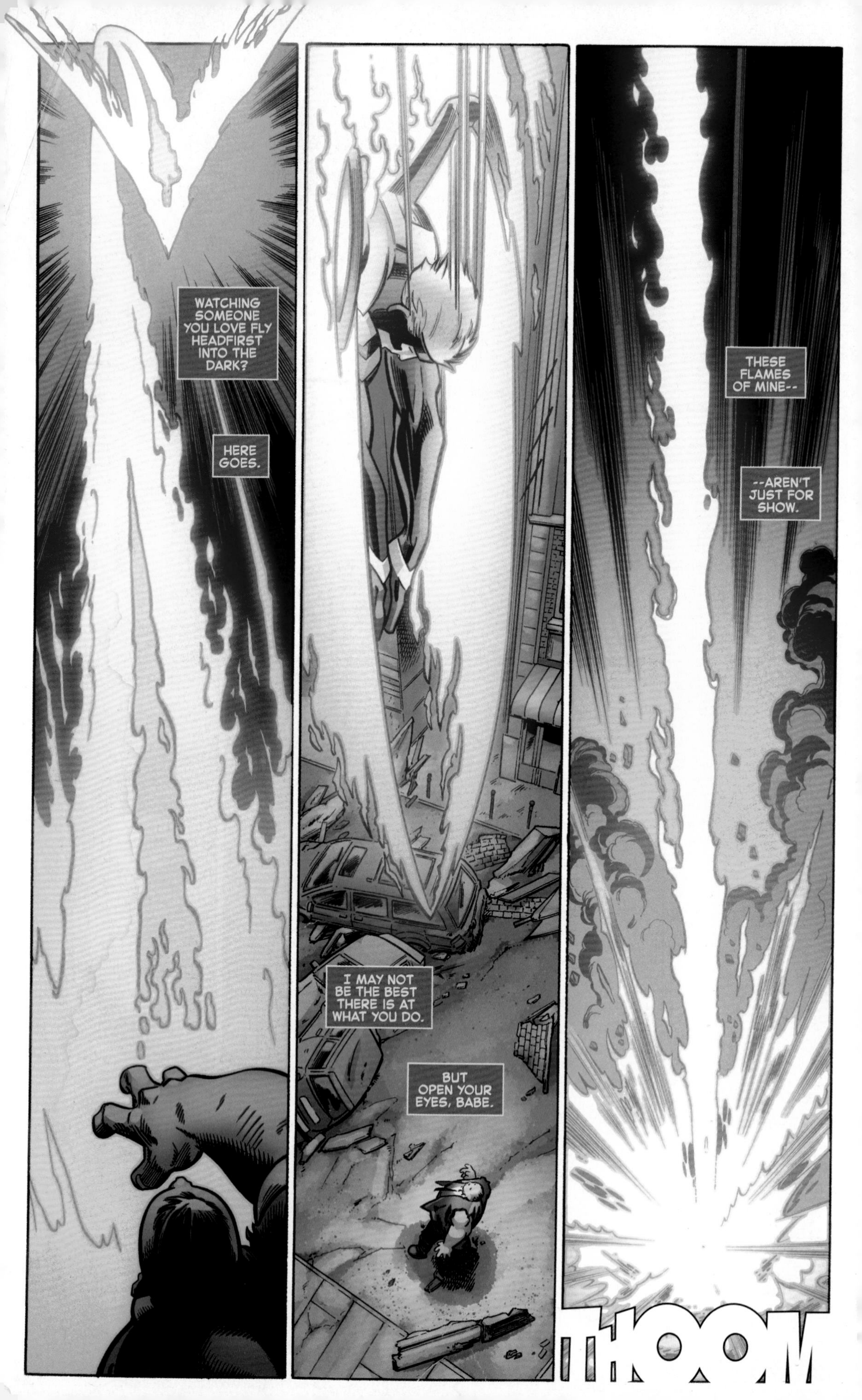
WATCHING SOMEONE YOU LOVE FLY HEADFIRST INTO THE DARK?
HERE GOES.
I MAY NOT BE THE BEST THERE IS AT WHAT YOU DO.
BUT OPEN YOUR EYES, BABE.
THESE FLAMES OF MINE--
--AREN'T JUST FOR SHOW.
THOOM

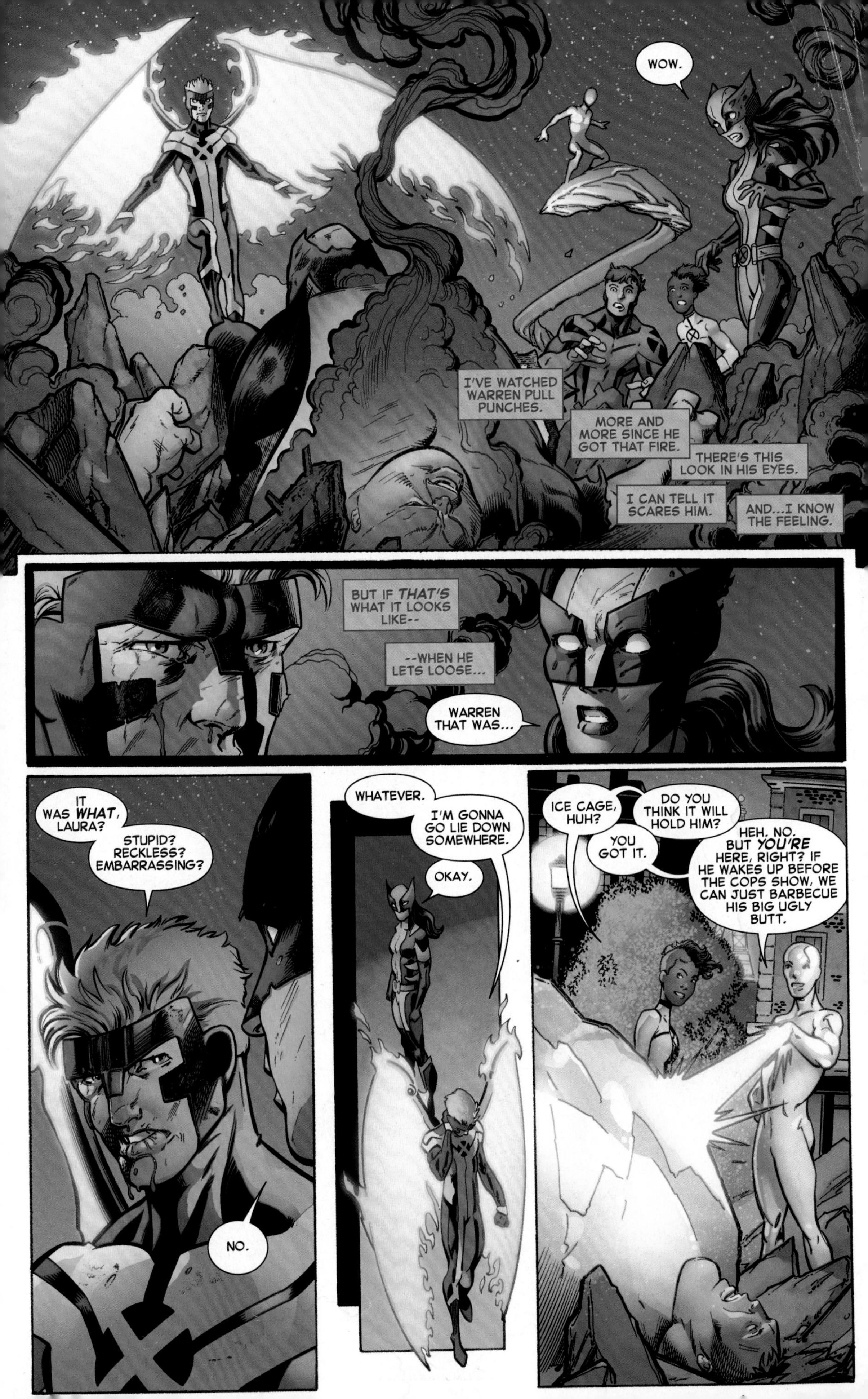
WOW.
I'VE WATCHED WARREN PULL PUNCHES.
MORE AND MORE SINCE HE GOT THAT FIRE.
THERE'S THIS LOOK IN HIS EYES.
I CAN TELL IT SCARES HIM.
AND...I KNOW THE FEELING.
BUT IF THAT'S WHAT IT LOOKS LIKE--
--WHEN HE LETS LOOSE...
WARREN THAT WAS...
IT WAS WHAT, LAURA?
STUPID? RECKLESS? EMBARRASSING?
NO.
WHATEVER.
I'M GONNA GO LIE DOWN SOMEWHERE.
OKAY.
ICE CAGE, HUH?
YOU GOT IT.
DO YOU THINK IT WILL HOLD HIM?
HEH. NO. BUT YOU'RE HERE, RIGHT? IF HE WAKES UP BEFORE THE COPS SHOW, WE CAN JUST BARBECUE HIS BIG UGLY BUTT.

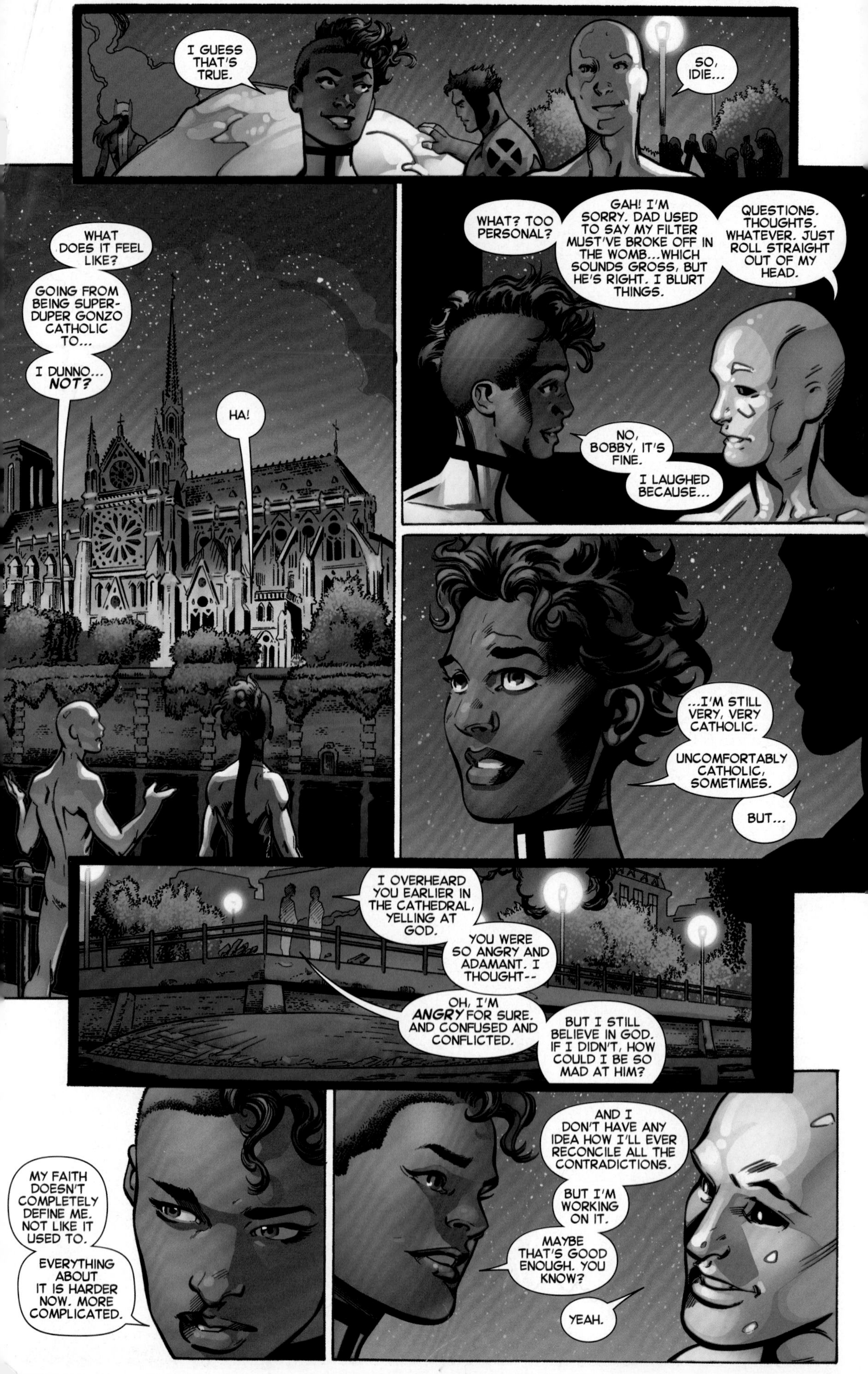
I GUESS THAT'S TRUE.
SO, IDIE...
WHAT DOES IT FEEL LIKE?
GOING FROM BEING SUPER-DUPER GONZO CATHOLIC TO...
I DUNNO... *NOT?*
HA!
WHAT? TOO PERSONAL?
GAH! I'M SORRY. DAD USED TO SAY MY FILTER MUST'VE BROKE OFF IN THE WOMB...WHICH SOUNDS GROSS, BUT HE'S RIGHT. I BLURT THINGS.
QUESTIONS. THOUGHTS. WHATEVER. JUST ROLL STRAIGHT OUT OF MY HEAD.
NO, BOBBY, IT'S FINE.
I LAUGHED BECAUSE...
...I'M STILL VERY, VERY CATHOLIC.
UNCOMFORTABLY CATHOLIC, SOMETIMES.
BUT...
I OVERHEARD YOU EARLIER IN THE CATHEDRAL, YELLING AT GOD.
YOU WERE SO ANGRY AND ADAMANT. I THOUGHT--
OH, I'M *ANGRY* FOR SURE. AND CONFUSED AND CONFLICTED.
BUT I STILL BELIEVE IN GOD. IF I DIDN'T, HOW COULD I BE SO MAD AT HIM?
MY FAITH DOESN'T COMPLETELY DEFINE ME. NOT LIKE IT USED TO.
EVERYTHING ABOUT IT IS HARDER NOW. MORE COMPLICATED.
AND I DON'T HAVE ANY IDEA HOW I'LL EVER RECONCILE ALL THE CONTRADICTIONS.
BUT I'M WORKING ON IT.
MAYBE THAT'S GOOD ENOUGH. YOU KNOW?
YEAH.

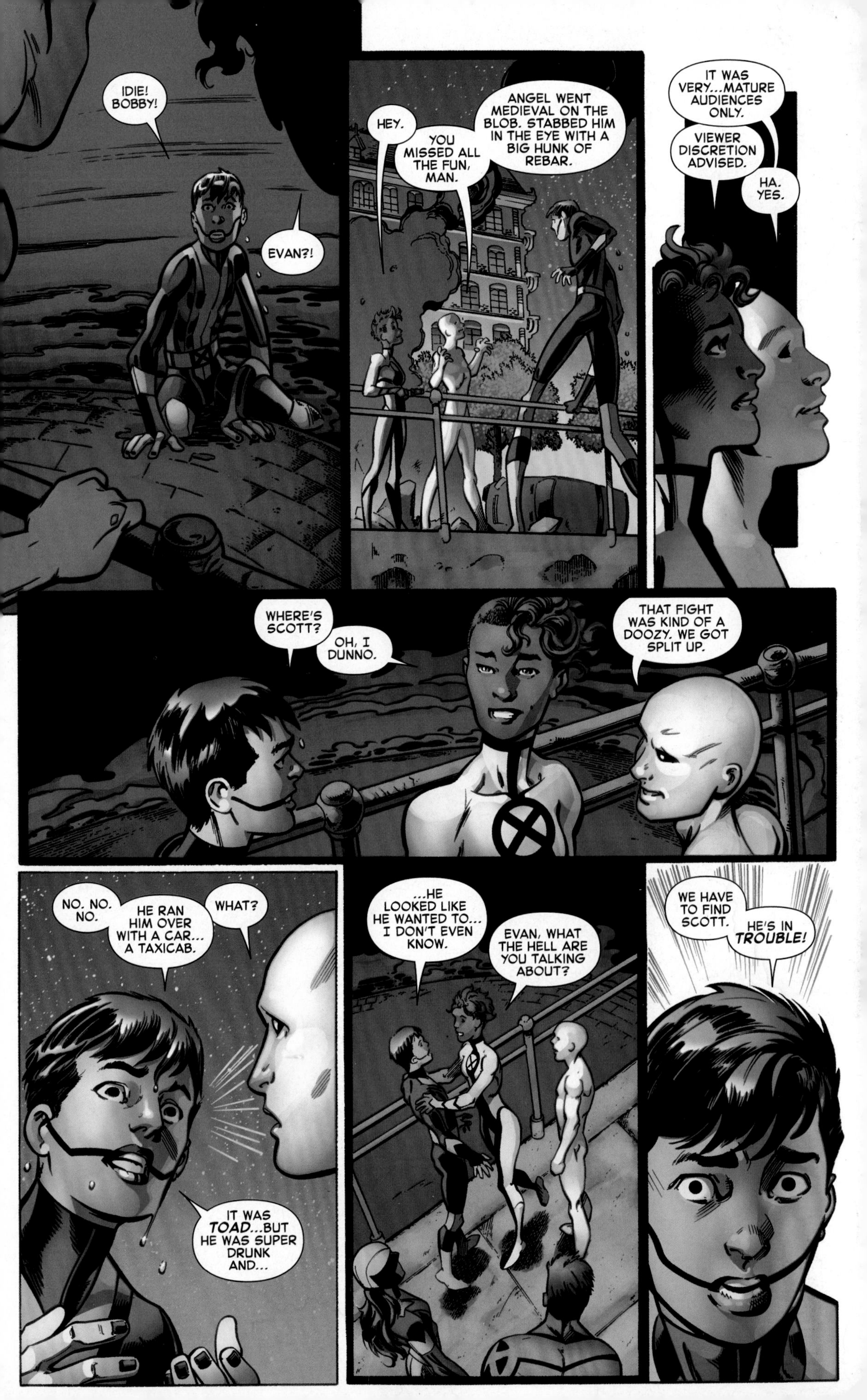
IDIE! BOBBY!
EVAN?!
HEY.
YOU MISSED ALL THE FUN, MAN.
ANGEL WENT MEDIEVAL ON THE BLOB. STABBED HIM IN THE EYE WITH A BIG HUNK OF REBAR.
IT WAS VERY...MATURE AUDIENCES ONLY.
VIEWER DISCRETION ADVISED.
HA. YES.
WHERE'S SCOTT?
OH, I DUNNO.
THAT FIGHT WAS KIND OF A DOOZY. WE GOT SPLIT UP.
NO. NO. NO.
HE RAN HIM OVER WITH A CAR... A TAXICAB.
WHAT?
IT WAS TOAD...BUT HE WAS SUPER DRUNK AND...
...HE LOOKED LIKE HE WANTED TO... I DON'T EVEN KNOW.
EVAN, WHAT THE HELL ARE YOU TALKING ABOUT?
WE HAVE TO FIND SCOTT.
HE'S IN TROUBLE!

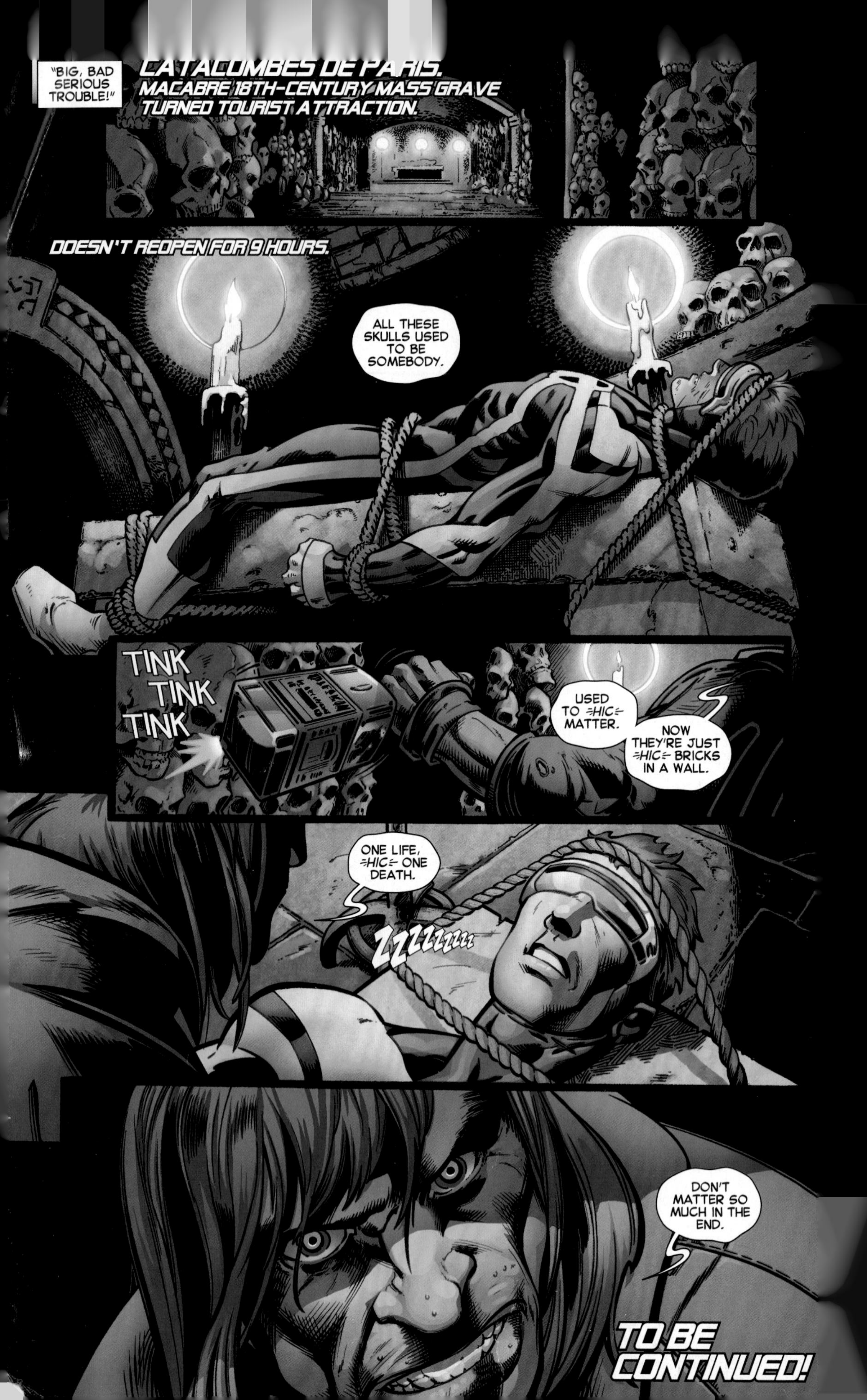
"BIG, BAD SERIOUS TROUBLE!"
CATACOMBES DE PARIS.
MACABRE 18TH-CENTURY MASS GRAVE TURNED TOURIST ATTRACTION.
DOESN'T REOPEN FOR 9 HOURS.
ALL THESE SKULLS USED TO BE SOMEBODY.
TINK
TINK
TINK
USED TO =HIC= MATTER.
NOW THEY'RE JUST =HIC= BRICKS IN A WALL.
ONE LIFE, =HIC= ONE DEATH.
ZZZZzzzzz
DON'T MATTER SO MUCH IN THE END.
TO BE CONTINUED!

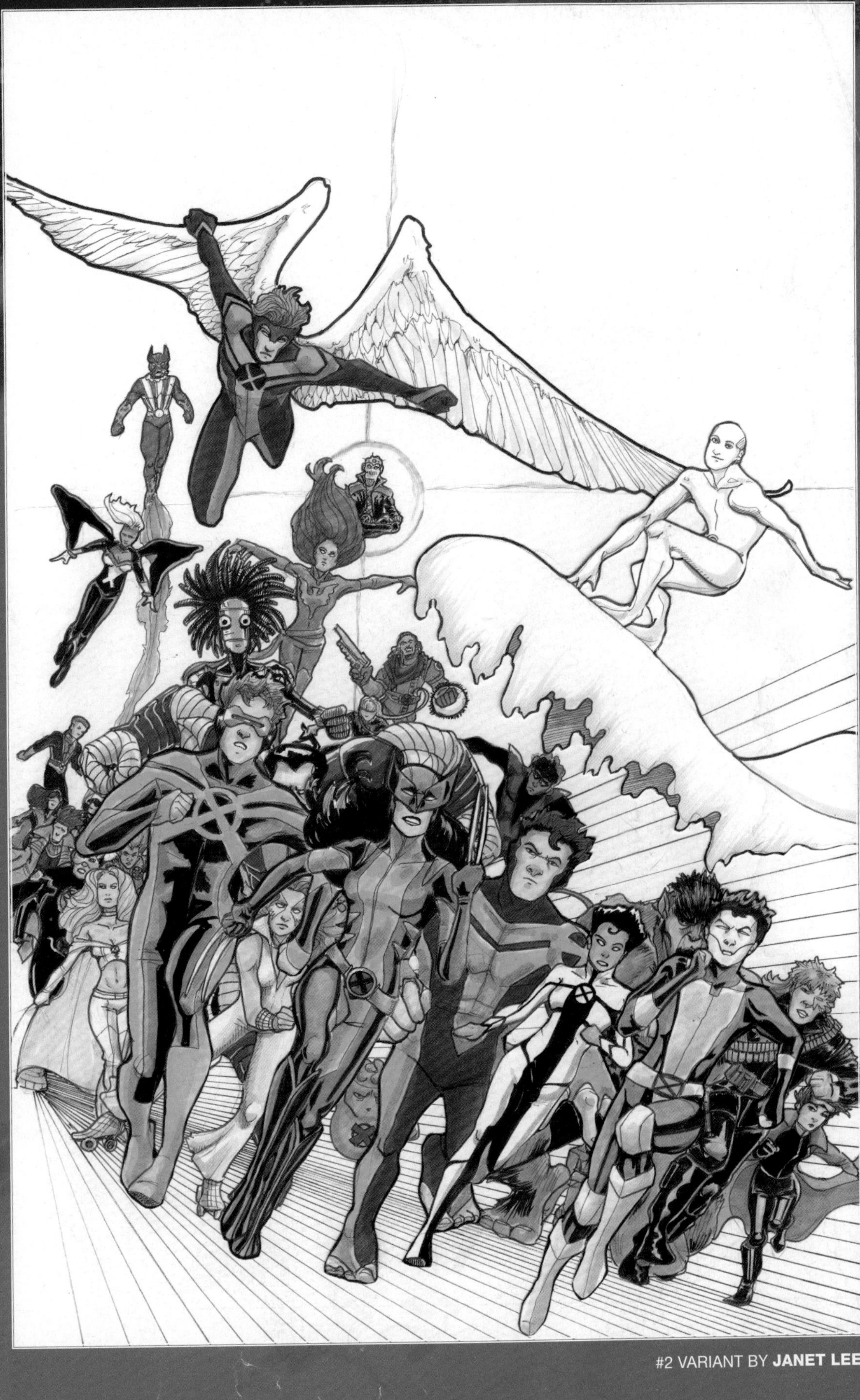

#2 VARIANT BY **JANET LEE**

#3 VARIANT
BY **PASQUAL FERRY** & **JASON KEITH**

#3 MARVEL '92 VARIANT
BY **ROB LIEFELD** & **ROMULO FAJARDO JR.**